POLICY IMPLICATIONS OF TRADE AND CURRENCY ZONES

A Symposium Sponsored By
The Federal Reserve Bank of Kansas City

Jackson Hole, Wyoming
August 22-24, 1991

Contents

GLOBAL IMPLICATIONS OF TRADE AND CURRENCY ZONES

OVERVIEW PANELISTS

Foreword

Long-standing institutional arrangements governing international trade and foreign exchange practices are currently undergoing rapid change. Notable examples include Europe 1992, the U.S.-Canada Free Trade Agreement, and recent initiatives to include Mexico and Latin America in a Western Hemisphere free trade zone.

These dramatic developments have led to the belief that the world trading system is now moving toward a number of geographic free trade zones. Moreover, if free trade zones are accompanied by currency zones, the move toward free trade zones may usher in major changes in the international monetary system. Clearly, such changes could have significant implications for national monetary, financial, exchange rate, and fiscal policies.

To discuss the implications of the current movement toward trade and currency zones, the Federal Reserve Bank of Kansas City brought together distinguished central bankers, academics, and industry representatives for a two-day symposium on "Policy Implications of Trade and Currency Zones" at Jackson Hole, Wyoming, on August 22-24, 1991.

We appreciate the contributions of all those who took part in the symposium and made it a notable success. Special thanks go to Craig Hakkio and Bryon Higgins, both in the Bank's Research Division, who helped develop the program.

   We hope these proceedings will add to better public understanding
of the issues involved and inspire further study and exploration into
the important effects of the movement toward trade and currency
zones.

THOMAS E. DAVIS

Thomas E. Davis

Senior Vice President
and Director of Research
Federal Reserve Bank of Kansas City

The Contributors

Pedro Aspe, *Finance Minister, Mexico*

Mr. Aspe became secretary of finance and public credit for the Government of Mexico in 1988. He had previously served as undersecretary for planning and budgetary control and secretary for programming and budget. A native of Mexico City, he is a graduate of the Instituto Technológico Autónomo de México and Massachusetts Institute of Technology, where he earned the Ph.D. in economics.

C. Fred Bergsten, *Director, Institute for International Economics*

Mr. Bergsten has been director of the Institute for International Economics since its creation in 1981. He was assistant secretary of the U.S. Treasury for international affairs from 1977 to 1981, and undersecretary for monetary affairs in 1980-81. Earlier, he was a senior fellow at the Brookings Institution and a member of the senior staff of the National Security Council where he was an assistant for international economic affairs. A widely published author, he testifies frequently before Congressional committees. In addition to several other posts, Mr. Bergsten serves on the Competitiveness Policy Council created by the Omnibus Trade and Competitiveness Act of 1988.

Charles R. Carlisle, *Deputy Director-General, The GATT*

Mr. Carlisle was named to his present position with the General Agreement on Tariffs and Trade (GATT) in Geneva in January 1987. At the time of this appointment, he was chief textile negotiator with the U.S. Trade Representative in Washington, with the rank of ambassador. Earlier in his career, he was a career foreign service officer, a vice president of St. Joe Minerals Corporation in New York, and president of the American Fiber Manufacturers Association.

Andrew D. Crockett, *Executive Director, Bank of England*

Mr. Crockett first joined the Bank of England in 1966, serving in the Economic Intelligence and Cashiers Departments. He was named personal assistant to the managing director of the International Monetary Fund in 1972 and later became chief of the Fund's Special Studies Division, assistant director of the Middle East Department, and deputy director of the Research Department with primary responsibility for the World Economic Outlook project. Mr. Crockett rejoined the Bank of England in March 1989 as executive director for Overseas Affairs.

John W. Crow, *Governor, Bank of Canada*

Mr. Crow was appointed governor of the Bank of Canada in 1987. He joined the Research Department of the bank in 1973 and subsequently served as adviser to the governor, deputy governor, and senior deputy governor. Before going to the Bank of Canada, he worked at the International Monetary Fund from 1961 to 1973. Mr. Crow is a member of the board of directors of the Federal Business Development Bank and the Canada Deposit Insurance Corporation.

Jacques de Larosière, *Governor, Bank of France*

Mr. de Larosière became governor of the Bank of France in 1987, following 11 years as managing director of the International Monetary Fund. Earlier, he had a long career with the French Treasury Department, serving successively as assistant director, deputy director, and undersecretary. He is currently chairman of the Committee of Governors of the Group of Ten.

Michael R. Emerson, *Ambassador to the USSR from the European Community*

Mr. Emerson has held several positions with the Commission of the European Communities prior to being named Ambassador and head of the delegation to the USSR this year. He was economic adviser to the president, director of macroeconomic forecasting and policies, and director of economic evaluation of community policies. Before joining the EC staff, he worked for the Organization for Economic Cooperation and Development.

Martin Feldstein, *President, National Bureau
of Economic Research*

Mr. Feldstein is professor of economics at Harvard University as
well as president of the National Bureau of Economic Research.
Since joining the Harvard faculty in 1967, his research and teaching
have focused on problems of the U.S. economy and the economics
of the public sector. From 1982 through 1984, he was chairman of
President Reagan's Council of Economic Advisers. He is a fellow
of the Econometric Society and the National Association of Business
Economists and a member of the Trilateral Commission, the Council
on Foreign Relations, and the American Academy of Arts and
Sciences.

Jacob A. Frenkel, *Governor, Bank of Israel*

Mr. Frenkel was named to his present position in mid-1991. He
had been economic counselor and director of research at the Inter-
national Monetary Fund since January 1987. Earlier, he was the
David Rockefeller Professor of International Economics at the
University of Chicago. He is a research associate of the National
Bureau of Economic Research, a fellow of the Econometric Society,
and a member of the Group of Thirty, the advisory committee of the
Institute for International Economics, the executive committee of the
Centre for Economic Policy Research in London, and the G-7
Council.

Leonhard Gleske, *Former Member of the Directorate,
Deutsche Bundesbank*

Mr. Gleske was a member of the Directorate of the Deutsche
Bundesbank from 1976 to 1989. During that period, he was involved
with international monetary issues and served on the Central Bank
Council. He is presently serving a second term as a director of the
Bank for International Settlements. Earlier in his career, Mr. Gleske
spent 12 years as president of the Land Central Bank in Bremen and
served on the Commission of the European Economic Community.

Morris Goldstein, *Deputy Director, Research Department,
International Monetary Fund*

Mr. Goldstein was named deputy director of the IMF's Research
Department in 1987. He first joined the Fund in 1970 and filled

several senior staff positions before accepting his present assign-
ment. He has also been a research fellow at the Brookings Institution,
a senior technical adviser at the U.S. Treasury Department, and a
visiting research associate at the London School of Economics. Mr.
Goldstein is also a former member of the editorial board of IMF *Staff
Papers.*

Alan Greenspan, *Chairman, Board of Governors of the
Federal Reserve System*
Mr. Greenspan was appointed in 1991 to a second four-year term
as chairman of the Federal Reserve Board. He began his first term
in August 1987. Previously, he was chairman and president of the
New York economic consulting firm of Townsend-Greenspan &
Co., Inc., chairman of President Ford's Council of Economic Advis-
ers, chairman of the National Commission on Social Security
Reform, and a member of President Reagan's Economic Policy
Advisory Board. He was also senior adviser to the Brookings
Institution's Panel on Economic Activity, consultant to the Congres-
sional Budget Office, and president of the National Association of
Business Economists.

John G. Heimann, *Chairman, Global Financial Institutions
Group, Merrill Lynch & Co., Inc.*
Mr. Heimann was named to his present position in 1991 after
having served as vice chairman for Merrill Lynch Capital Markets
since 1984. He also chaired the executive committee for Merrill
Lynch Europe/Middle East between 1988 and 1990. Earlier in his
career he worked with Becker Paribas, Inc., banking and housing
agencies in New York State, E.M. Warburg Pincus & Co., and
Smith Barney. He was U.S. Comptroller of the Currency from 1977
to 1981. He is a member of the board and treasurer of the Group of
Thirty and serves on a number of advisory councils for government,
professional, citizens, and university groups.

Paul Krugman, *Professor of Economics, Massachusetts Institute
of Technology*
Mr. Krugman was named to the M.I.T. faculty in 1980, after
earlier serving on the faculty at Yale University. He is a research
associate of the National Bureau of Economic Research and a fellow

of the Econometric Society. He has been a consultant to the Bank of Portugal and the U.S. State Department and is presently on the Board of Advisers of the Institute for International Economics and the Overseas Development Council. In 1982-83, he served on the Council of Economic Advisers as an international policy economist.

David E.W. Laidler, *Professor, University of Western Ontario*
Mr. Laidler has been professor of economics at the University of Western Ontario in London, Ontario since 1975. Earlier, he served on the faculty of the University of Manchester and lectured at the University of Essex. He has degrees from the London School of Economics, Syracuse University, the University of Chicago, and the University of Manchester.

Miguel Mancera, *Director General, Bank of Mexico*
Mr. Mancera became director general of the Bank of Mexico in 1982 after a long career with Mexico's central bank. He joined the staff as an economist in 1958 and later served as administrator of the Export Finance and Export Credit Guarantee Fund (FOMEX), manager of international affairs, deputy director and deputy director general of the institution. He has taught courses in economic theory, international trade, and political economy at several Mexican institutions and is a member of the board of governors of the Instituto Technológico Autónomo de México.

Allan H. Meltzer, *Professor of Political Economy and Public Policy, Carnegie-Mellon University*
Mr. Meltzer has been at Carnegie-Mellon University since 1964. His work in the field of money and capital markets has brought frequent consulting assignments with Congressional committees, the U.S. Treasury Department, the Board of Governors of the Federal Reserve System, foreign governments, and central banks. He is currently serving as a member of President Bush's Economic Policy Advisory Board as well as honorary adviser to the Institute for Monetary and Economic Studies at the Bank of Japan. Mr. Meltzer is a founder and co-chairman of the Shadow Open Market Committee and a fellow of the National Association of Business Economists.

Michael Mussa, *Professor, University of Chicago*
Mr. Mussa has returned to his post as William H. Abbott Professor of International Business at the University of Chicago after two years as a member of President Reagan's Council of Economic Advisers (1986-88). A fellow of the Econometric Society and a research fellow of the National Bureau of Economic Research, he has also taught at the University of Rochester, the Graduate Center of the City University of New York, the London School of Economics, and the Graduate Institute of International Studies in Geneva.

Tommaso Padoa-Schioppa, *Deputy Director General,*
Bank of Italy
Mr. Padoa-Schioppa joined the Bank of Italy in 1970 and was an economist in the Research Department for nine years. From 1979-1983, he was director general for Economic and Financial Affairs at the Commission of the European Communities in Brussels. In 1983, he returned to the Bank of Italy as central director for economic research. A member of the Banking Advisory Committee of the European Community and of the Working Party 3 of the Economic Policy Committee of the Organization for Economic Cooperation and Development, Mr. Padoa-Schioppa also served as secretary to the Committee for the Study of European Economic and Monetary Union (the Delors Committee).

Kumiharu Shigehara, *Director of the Institute for Monetary and*
Economic Studies, Bank of Japan
Mr. Shigehara, appointed to his present position in December 1989, first joined the Bank of Japan in 1962. He undertook a number of assignments for the Organization for Economic Cooperation and Development (OECD) during 1970-74, 1980-82, and 1987-89, serving last as director of the Policy Studies Branch. Between OECD assignments, Mr. Shigehara returned to the Bank of Japan and assumed various posts including associate adviser on international finance and domestic policy planning, representative to the Committee of Bank Supervisors at the Bank for International Settlements, and deputy director of the Institute for Monetary and Economic Studies.

Lawrence H. Summers, *Vice President and Chief Economist, The World Bank*

Mr. Summers joined the World Bank in 1991. He is on leave from his position as Nathaniel Ropes Professor of Political Economy at Harvard University. In 1987, he was the first social scientist to receive the National Science Foundation's Alan T. Waterman Award. A fellow of the American Academy of Arts and Sciences and a research associate of the National Bureau of Economic Research, Mr. Summers was domestic policy economist at the President's Council of Economic Advisers in 1982-83 and has served as a consultant to the U.S. Treasury and the Department of Labor as well as to the governments of Jamaica, Indonesia, and Mexico and a number of major American corporations. He is also a member of the Brookings Panel on Economic Activity and a former editor of *The Quarterly Journal of Economics.*

Paul Volcker, *Chairman, James D. Wolfensohn, Inc.*

Mr. Volcker is chairman of James D. Wolfensohn, Inc. and professor of international economic policy at Princeton University. He was first named chairman of the Board of Governors of the Federal Reserve System in 1979 and was reappointed to a second four-year term in 1983. He was president of the Federal Reserve Bank of New York from 1975 to 1979 and undersecretary for monetary affairs in the U.S. Treasury Department from 1969 to 1974. During a 30-year career in government service, Mr. Volcker served under five presidents. He now chairs the North American Committee of the Trilateral Commission and serves on the boards of a number of international councils and institutes.

Salvatore Zecchini, *Assistant Secretary-General, OECD*

Mr. Zecchini was named to his present post in 1990. He also serves as director for the Center for Cooperation with the European Economies in Transition. From 1984-1989, he was executive director of the International Monetary Fund. Earlier, he worked twelve years in the economic research department of the Bank of Italy, the last three as director. Besides his Master's degree from Columbia University and doctoral study in economics at the Wharton School of Finance at the University of Pennsylvania, he has a law degree from the University of Palermo.

Symposium Summary

George A. Kahn

The world trading system may be coalescing into a set of geographic free trade zones. Europe 1992, the U.S.-Canada Free Trade Agreement, and the initiatives to include Mexico and Latin America in a Western Hemisphere free trade zone provide recent examples of efforts to remove tariff and nontariff barriers to trade among countries in geographic regions. If accompanied by currency zones—the adoption within regions of fixed exchange rates or a common currency—this move toward trade zones could bring major changes in the international monetary system and in domestic economic policies.

The move toward trade and currency zones comes at a time of great change in the world economy. International financial markets have become increasingly deregulated. International trade in goods and services has increased. The world economy has moved closer to a tripolar monetary system with the U.S. dollar, German deutsche mark, and Japanese yen serving as principal currencies. And multilateral negotiations to promote free trade, such as the General Agreement on Tariffs and Trade (GATT), have stalled.

To explore possible ramifications of trade and currency zones, the Federal Reserve Bank of Kansas City invited distinguished central bankers, academics, and industry representatives to a symposium entitled "Policy Implications of Trade and Currency Zones." The symposium was held August 22-24, 1991, in Jackson Hole, Wyoming.

xvii

In opening comments, Federal Reserve Chairman Alan Greenspan underscored the importance of the topic and surveyed the issues to be addressed. Acknowledging our limited experience with trade and currency zones, he argued that answers would have to come both "from the abstract world of economic models and from the ongoing experience gained in the cases of European economic and monetary union and the North American Free Trade Area that are already being planned." He also stated that "insights into the economic implications we can expect from trade and currency zones should guide us in choosing appropriate macroeconomic policies now and in the future—whether we are 'inside' or 'outside' a zone."

This article summarizes the symposium papers and the discussions they stimulated. In general, most of the program participants supported the move to a trade and currency zone in Europe, although some expressed doubt about the benefits of trade and currency zones in other parts of the world. The first section of the article discusses whether the move toward trade and currency zones will promote trade among countries. The second section describes financial market and macroeconomic policy implications of trade and currency zones. The third section explores global implications.

Will trade and currency zones promote world trade?

Two areas of heated debate at the symposium were whether the move toward free trade zones will promote world trade and whether currency zones will be necessary to achieve the full benefits of free trade zones. Participants agreed that if the move to free trade zones is accompanied by further progress on the GATT, free trade zones will help foster world trade. But participants disagreed sharply about the effects of free trade zones in the absence of further progress in reducing trade barriers on a multilateral basis. Participants also disagreed about whether currency zones will be necessary to realize the full benefits of trade zones.

Effects of free trade zones on world trade

Conference participants disagreed about the effects of free trade zones on world trade. Paul Krugman argued that free trade zones will foster trade regardless of whether further progress is made at the global level. C. Fred Bergsten countered that free trade zones will impede world trade unless they are accompanied by further progress toward global trade liberalization.

Bad in theory, good in practice. Krugman acknowledged the solid theoretical arguments against free trade zones but still argued that such areas will probably help rather than hurt the world economy. Moreover, problems with the GATT negotiations are so deep-seated that further progress is unlikely. As a result, regional free trade zones are a promising alternative to multilateral negotiations for promoting free trade.

Krugman's central point was that free trade zones are bad in theory but good in practice. He indicated free trade zones are bad in theory because they potentially divert trade from low-cost to high-cost suppliers. Trade diversion occurs when a member of a free trade zone imports a good or service from a country inside its zone rather than from a lower cost, nonmember country. He also indicated free trade zones can harm nonmember countries, not only by reducing the demand for their exports, but also by reducing the relative prices of their exported products. The decline in prices in nonmember countries relative to prices in member countries—a "beggar-thy-neighbor" effect—reduces nonmember country welfare. Additionally, he held that trade zones potentially impede trade by promoting trade warfare.

Krugman nonetheless argued that, in practice, free trade zones are likely to help more than they hurt the world economy, mainly because they increase the size of markets. Larger markets lead to greater productive efficiency and competitiveness. Thus, trade zones are likely to create more trade than they divert.

Moreover, he stated that trade zones seem to be forming along "natural" geographic boundaries. Countries naturally tend to trade more with their neighbors than with distant countries because transporting goods and services and communicating over long distances is costly. As a result, free trade zones among neighboring countries may, in practice, be good for the world. The gains from freeing trade within regional zones will be larger and the costs of reducing trade across zones smaller than implied by moving to zones that are not based on natural geographic boundaries.

Finally, Krugman argued that moving toward global trade liberalization through the GATT process is hopelessly stalled, making free trade zones the only viable alternative. Among the reasons Krugman cited for the demise of the GATT are the decline of the United States as the principal world economic power, the increasing importance of such nontariff barriers as domestic regulatory and investment policies, and the growth of new players in the world economy, such as the Japanese, who arguably play by a different set of rules.

Bad in theory, bad in practice. In sharp contrast to Krugman, C. Fred Bergsten claimed that moving toward free trade zones was bad in both theory and practice. Moreover, Bergsten argued that free trade zones are particularly bad when viewed as an alternative to further progress toward global free trade. Finally, Bergsten maintained that free trade zones need not be viewed as an alternative to globalism, because the GATT negotiations are still viable.

Bergsten cited a number of reasons to support his view that free trade zones are bad in practice. First, he argued that geography is not nearly as important as in the past as a determinant of "natural" trade regions. With technological advance, transportation and communications costs are no longer central to trading patterns. Second, while Europe and possibly North America may be "natural trading areas," no other such areas exist. Third, trade diversion may not be simply a consequence of trade zones but, in some cases, a goal. And finally, a Western Hemisphere free trade zone is likely to divert trade from lower-cost producers in Europe, Asia, Australia, and New Zealand to higher-cost producers in the Western Hemisphere.

Assuming that the movement toward free trade areas is likely to continue, Bergsten argued that the movement should occur in the context of an effective and credible global trade system. One way to ensure the movement toward free trade zones supplements rather than replaces globalism is to enforce and expand the GATT. The

GATT process can still work, according to Bergsten. Trade patterns in the Americas and in Asia remain "quintessentially multilateral." The markets of the three economic superpowers—Europe, Japan, and the United States—remain deeply intertwined. The superpowers have worked closely together on economic issues in the past and should be able to cooperate in the future. And although recent GATT negotiations have stalled, the GATT process has always been a messy one, filled with false starts and stops.

Are currency zones necessary?

In addition to differing on the net benefits of trade zones, conference participants expressed a range of views on currency zones. Although participants agreed that moving to currency zones will make it harder to conduct independent national monetary policies, they disagreed about whether this cost of currency zones exceeded the benefits. Martin Feldstein argued that currency zones are unnecessary and potentially harmful. Miguel Mancera argued that while the benefits of currency zones might be "impressive," floating exchange rates are more desirable. Other participants, including David Laidler, Michael Emerson, and Salvatore Zecchini, argued that currency zones might be beneficial to some, such as the Europeans, but not to others.

According to Feldstein, the cost of currency zones is high relative to their benefits. The primary economic benefit of currency zones is the boost to trade from eliminating uncertainty about exchange rate fluctuations. Exchange rate fluctuations inhibit businesses from importing inputs because unanticipated exchange rate movements in the wrong direction can potentially eliminate profits. Thus, eliminating exchange rate fluctuations would reduce uncertainty about the value of international transactions and, thereby, promote international trade. Feldstein argues, however, that these benefits are likely to be small. Econometric studies have failed to detect an adverse effect of exchange rate volatility on international trade. Moreover, businesses can hedge exchange rate risk through futures markets for foreign exchange.

In contrast, the costs of currency zones are possibly quite large.

The primary economic cost of currency zones is the loss of independent national monetary policies. Under fixed exchange rates, central banks use the tools of monetary policy to keep exchange rates constant. As a result, these tools are unavailable for pursuing other national economic objectives. Under a single currency, countries surrender policy autonomy to a supranational monetary authority.

For example, with a freely floating currency, national monetary policymakers can counter a decline in the demand for a country's products by stimulating monetary growth and reducing interest rates. This response to a decline in demand is not possible if there are no national currencies or if exchange rates are irrevocably fixed. And without such a response, the output and employment costs of adverse demand shocks could be high.

Why then has Europe moved toward a currency zone? Feldstein argued that the reasons are more political than economic. Proponents of a currency zone believe a single European monetary authority could limit the ability of national governments to pursue inflationary monetary policies. More important, however, a single European currency would accelerate the political unification of Europe which, in turn, would result in greater centralization of fiscal policies.

Miguel Mancera took a more eclectic view of currency zones. Mancera recognized significant benefits from currency zones, including reduced investment risks, the equalization of interest rates across countries, and lower international transactions costs. Nevertheless, because inflation rates vary widely within and among countries, Mancera questioned the advisability of currency zones. Under floating exchange rates, a country can potentially insulate itself from inflationary shocks affecting other countries. In a currency zone, these shocks might spread to all countries. Mancera indicated that for this and other reasons, Mexico could not possibly participate in a currency zone, although it probably will participate in a trade zone.

Other conference participants viewed currency zones somewhat more favorably, especially in the case of Europe. Salvatore Zecchini argued that a move to currency zones could be beneficial because without them, businesses might face significant exchange rate risk. In contrast to Feldstein, Zecchini argued that futures markets in foreign exchange were too thin and underdeveloped to sufficiently reduce exchange rate risk. In addition, political institutions must be in place to ensure that smaller countries retain some influence over the policies of the trade or currency zone. This influence over policy should be viewed as compensation for the loss of political autonomy. While Zecchini felt that these conditions did not apply in North America, he felt they did apply in some of the countries of the European Community.

David Laidler viewed the formation of a currency zone as possibly good for Europe but definitely bad for North America. Like Feldstein, Laidler viewed the move toward currency zones as a political as well as an economic development. The move to either a common currency or irrevocably fixed exchange rates implies a loss of national sovereignty. Any move to give up national currencies must be viewed in part as a move toward political unity.

Although countries could maintain national currencies under a system of irrevocably fixed exchange rates, Laidler suggested that this form of currency zone also reduces political autonomy. The choice of an inflation rate is a political as well as an economic decision. Moving to fixed exchange rates—or to a common currency— takes the issue of inflation out of the national political arena. It also removes from political accountability any national authority that might otherwise be responsible for a country's inflation perfor-mance.

Laidler added that while the move to a trade zone in Europe has been accompanied by closer political ties, no such political move-ment has occurred in North America. European countries have already surrendered considerable authority to European political entities, but no such surrender has occurred or is likely to occur in North America. Therefore, while a currency zone might work in Europe, it would not likely work in North America.

Michael Emerson agreed that while the political and economic prerequisites for a currency zone were probably in place in Western

Europe, they are not well established in other regions of the world. For example, before joining a trade or currency zone, the Eastern European countries must first join the world economy. They must adopt convertible currencies and world price structures. Only as a second stage of development can they consider regional trade and currency agreements. Even then they must work toward economic convergence with the rest of Europe before considering economic integration. Likewise, the USSR must grapple with its own problems of currency convertibility and determine whether its new federalist structure makes a compelling case for a currency zone. Finally, the Pacific region appears to be more interested in open trade on a global basis than in integration along economic, monetary, or political lines.

National policy implications of trade and currency zones

The move toward trade and currency zones has implications not only for world trade in goods and services but also for national financial markets and macroeconomic structure. For example, financial markets within a trade zone may need to be harmonized so that capital, as well as goods and services, flows freely across countries. In addition, as monetary policy becomes more harmonized across countries in a trade zone, monetary policy will increasingly be determined at a supranational level. National fiscal policies could play a more important role in economic fluctuations at the national level and therefore may need to be harmonized to ensure fiscal discipline.

Financial market implications

Andrew Crockett and John Heimann examined four questions relating to the financial market implications of trade and currency zones. Do trade zones lead to increasing financial market integration across countries? Does economic integration lead to changes in financial market structure? What supervision and regulation will be required to ensure the efficiency and safety of financial markets? And, how will financial relationships across major trade zones be managed?

Financial market integration. Crockett argued that realizing the full benefits of trade zones requires liberalizing financial flows. As a result, trade zones create an incentive to liberalize finance. Removing international barriers to trade in banking, insurance, and other financial services results in greater specialization and competition in the supply of these services. As a result, costs of supplying financial services decline. By increasing competitive pressures, financial market liberalization also promotes productivity growth and innovation in the financial services industry. Finally, removing capital controls improves the flow of funds from savers to investors and channels investment funds to their most profitable use.

Liberalizing capital flows, in turn, requires closer harmonization of exchange rate policies. Large capital movements can undermine exchange rate stability. If capital liberalization leads to speculation and wide swings in exchange rates, it may undermine the benefits of trade zones. As a result, Crockett suggested that financial market liberalization may call for closer cooperation on exchange rate policies and, possibly, currency zones.

In discussing Crockett's paper, Heimann agreed that trade zones lead to financial market liberalization, which in turn leads to closer cooperation on exchange rate policies. Heimann also pointed out that these tendencies have been at work at the global level. In particular, as the G-7 countries have become more economically integrated, international capital flows have increased. At the same time, increasing speculation in capital markets has led to exchange rate volatility. This increased volatility of exchange rates underlies the management of exchange rates by the G-7 countries since the Louvre Accord was reached in 1987.

Financial market structure. Crockett argued that financial market structures are likely to evolve slowly in response to freer capital flows. A variety of different structures coexist in the world today and freer financial markets are likely to have only a gradual effect in harmonizing these structures. While least-cost producers of financial services will tend to displace higher-cost producers, it is not clear that market structures will change dramatically.

Most studies of financial markets have shown that structure has little effect on efficiency. For example, economies of scale in financial services are small relative to the size of financial markets. As a result, many small firms can supply these services as efficiently as a few large firms. Thus, despite significant international differences in financial market structure, little movement toward homogenization can be expected in the short run. And, even in the long run, complete homogenization of financial markets is unlikely.

Heimann agreed with Crockett's assessment of the short-run effect of trade zones on financial market structure. Over the longer run, however, Heimann sees the financial system evolving into two tiers—global markets served by global institutions and regional and national markets served by regional and national institutions. This development represents the continuation of events that have been going on for years.

Regulatory and supervisory issues. Financial market regulation and supervision grows more complex as financial firms reach across national boundaries. Crockett gave three guiding principles for regulating and supervising financial markets in trade and currency zones. First, let financial institutions offer financial services throughout the trade zone. Second, issue firms a single license so they may operate freely across national boundaries. The license should be issued by either a supranational regulatory authority or, providing mutual recognition by other countries, by a national regulatory authority. Third, regulators should concern themselves more with harmonizing capital standards for credit institutions than with harmonizing market practices. Given limited information about the optimal structure of securities markets, alternative structures should be allowed to coexist and compete.

Heimann echoed Crockett's views on supervision and regulation. Specifically, Heimann argued for an "international supervisory system of harmonized standards" and urged regulators to closely supervise capital market activities.

Financial relationships between trade zones. With the world trading system moving toward several trade zones, Crockett suggested that negotiations between zones for market access in the financial sector will become increasingly important. Two main approaches are possible. The "mirror image" approach would require "identical conditions of establishment for financial institutions in different markets." In contrast, "national treatment" would require a zone to apply the same rules and regulations to all financial institutions within its borders—but the zone would not have to offer the same privileges and regulations as other zones. Of the two approaches, national treatment holds the greater promise as a basis for financial relationships between countries or trade zones.

In regulating market access, Heimann cited proposals for strengthening the regulatory system using three sets of regulations—home country, host country, and harmonized rule. These regulations underlie the principles of national treatment, mutual recognition, and effective market access.

Macroeconomic implications

Trade and currency zones have important consequences, not only for financial market policy, but also for domestic macroeconomic policies. Jacob Frenkel and Morris Goldstein, focusing on the implications of currency zones, discussed both monetary and fiscal policy. They argued that price stability is the appropriate goal of monetary policy and recommended a two-speed approach to currency union. They also stressed the importance of adopting mechanisms to ensure fiscal discipline. Michael Mussa and Tommaso Padoa-Schioppa, panelists in a session on macroeconomic policy implications, largely agreed with Frenkel and Goldstein on monetary and fiscal policy.

Monetary policy. Frenkel and Goldstein argued that the principal goal of monetary policy in a currency union should be price stability. In Europe and elsewhere a consensus has formed that only by achieving price stability can other goals of macroeconomic policy, such as high employment and economic growth, be achieved over the long run. This view has led to proposals that the monetary authority for the proposed European currency zone have an explicit mandate to pursue price stability as its primary goal. To ensure that the monetary authority carries out this mandate, the authority should have a significant degree of political independence and should be prohibited from issuing credit to the public sector.

Frenkel and Goldstein also addressed the issue of how countries in a trade zone should handle the transition to a currency zone. Frenkel and Goldstein recommended a two-speed approach in which one subgroup of countries takes a fast approach, while another subgroup takes a slow approach. Countries that have achieved low inflation rates and share other economic characteristics might move quickly toward a currency zone. Such a fast track approach would give "maximum credibility to exchange rate stability by eliminating exchange rates within the union," reduce or eliminate instability caused by capital mobility and divergent national monetary policies, and allow fast-track countries to realize all of the efficiency gains from having a single currency.

Countries with disparate economic performance would move more slowly toward membership in the currency zone. The slow approach would allow these countries to remain a part of the move toward monetary union without having to converge at a faster-than-desired pace to the economic performance levels of the fast-track countries. Thus, the two-speed approach would preserve momentum in the move to a currency zone.

While generally agreeing with Frenkel and Goldstein on the monetary policy implications of currency zones, Mussa emphasized the role of politics in determining monetary arrangements. Mussa argued that currency zones have historically been closely associated with areas of political authority. Thus, closer monetary ties and tighter exchange rate agreements come not just from a desire for greater economic unity but also from a desire for greater "political solidarity." The success of the European Community in establishing a currency zone, according to Mussa, depends more on the strength of shared political views than on a tally of economic costs and benefits.

In his discussion of monetary policy implications, Padoa-Schioppa emphasized monetary relationships between currency zones. Padoa-

Schioppa argued that a European currency zone would lead to a "genuine multicurrency reserve system based on a tripolar relationship." Despite the fixity of exchange rates within currency zones, the exchange rate regime governing the three main reserve currencies—the dollar, yen, and European currency unit—should remain one of a mildly managed float.

Fiscal policy. Conference participants agreed that fiscal discipline was critical to the success of a currency union. Frenkel and Goldstein observed that, so far at least, moves toward currency union had not improved fiscal discipline in European countries. If sound fiscal policies are not forthcoming in a currency zone, the very objectives of the currency zone could be threatened.

Given the importance of sound fiscal policies, Frenkel and Goldstein described several mechanisms for ensuring fiscal discipline in a currency zone. One mechanism would be the marketplace itself. Member countries running excessive deficits with no recourse to finance deficits through money creation would face a rising default premium on government debt. The rising cost of government borrowing, along with reduced credit availability, would force governments to improve fiscal policies. Another mechanism would be fiscal policy rules. For example, rules might be enacted that place an upper limit on the size of budget deficits and government debt relative to GNP. Yet another mechanism would be peer-group, multilateral surveillance. Under this mechanism, constraints on national fiscal policies would be more flexibly applied to discourage irresponsible fiscal policies of member countries.

Of these mechanisms, Frenkel and Goldstein prefer a combination of market discipline and peer-group surveillance. Given the right institutional setting, market discipline could be used as the primary mechanism to keep member countries' fiscal policies sound. Peer-group surveillance could be used as a supplement to encourage countries to solve pre-existing fiscal problems, preferably before they enter the currency zone. Peer-group surveillance could also be used to prevent "large fiscal policy excesses" in member countries.

Mussa agreed with this assessment of fiscal policy, but added that the most important mechanism for imposing discipline occurs when member countries get into fiscal crunches. At such times, both creditors and debtors need to know they will bear part of the cost of a financial crisis. Debtors must know they will bear a cost so that they will avoid irresponsible behavior. Creditors must know they will bear a cost so that they will "pull the plug" on excessive borrowing by the government.

Padoa-Schioppa went somewhat further in advocating the need for fiscal policy discipline. He argued that fiscal policy rules were desirable per se to reduce the budgetary discretion of member countries. He also argued that, in the case of the European Community, countries should give up some of their fiscal policy independence to a central fiscal authority. This transfer of responsibility should not take the form of EC control over national budgets, but rather the form of a more flexible use of the EC budget.

Global implications of trade and currency zones

Just as trade and currency zones will alter economic relationships within geographic regions, so will trade and currency zones alter relationships among regions of the world economy. One result of these changing relationships could be a tripolar monetary and trade system. Such a system could either enhance economic cooperation or foster hostile economic relationships among regions. This issue of a tripolar system was taken up by Allan Meltzer, Leonhard Gleske, and Kumiharu Shigehara. Related broad issues were addressed by Lawrence Summers, Jacques de Larosière, Charles Carlisle, Pedro Aspe, Paul Volcker, and John Crow.

The emerging tripolar system

Meltzer argued that the world economy needs a new set of rules to maintain and enhance economic stability. Without new rules, the economic progress of the postwar period will not be sustained. Meltzer emphasized the importance of rules for maintaining trade and monetary stability.

Trade rules. Although the GATT remains in place, its rules are not being enforced. The lack of enforcement mechanisms has led to three responses. One response has been a move to managed, or "fair," trade in which producers form cartels to divide up markets for their products. Other responses include unilateral actions and bilateral and multilateral negotiations. But with the latest round of GATT negotiations stalling, another mechanism has emerged—the move toward trade zones.

Meltzer argued that the development of trade zones is not a viable alternative to multilateral trade agreements, despite the failure of current GATT rules. With the formation of trade zones, trade *within* zones will increase at the expense of trade *among* zones. Grouping countries into three zones—Europe, the Americas, and Asia— Meltzer emphasized the importance of trade among zones. In the Americas and Asia, free trade among zones, or interzone trade, is greater than free trade within zones, or intrazone trade. Hence, developing intrazone trade "as a substitute for open, international trade" would not be in the interests of Japan and the United States. The European Community is the exception to this rule. Unlike the American and Asian zones, the European Community trades more within its zone than with the other two zones combined.

Shigehara shared Meltzer's concerns about the formation of trade zones. He suggested that the resulting industrial reorganization in Europe may be costly to firms outside of Europe. As bigger firms begin to exploit economies of scale, smaller firms will come under competitive pressure. As a result, European governments may attempt to keep high-cost firms in business by using protectionist measures against competing firms outside of Europe.

Monetary stability. Meltzer, Shigehara, and Gleske agreed that most countries will continue to rely on the dollar, deutsche mark, and yen as reserve currencies. Meltzer, however, emphasized that continued use of these currencies as major reserve currencies will require the United States, Germany, and Japan to keep price levels stable. If the United States maintains price stability, Meltzer believed the dollar would provide a store of value for many foreigners, remain the primary reserve currency, and continue to be used as the currency for pricing and purchasing commodities. Gleske agreed that, given domestic price stability, the dollar would likely remain the world's principal reserve currency.

Given price stability in the major world economies, Meltzer argued that a tripolar monetary system would provide international monetary stability. Countries with flexible exchange rates would experience greater stability of prices and exchange rates. Moreover, smaller countries could avoid inflation by fixing their exchange rates to one or more of the major reserve currencies.

Meltzer, Shigehara, and Gleske agreed that, while the European Community will probably form a currency zone, North America and Asia will not. European countries have more in common economically, socially, historically, and politically than do countries in Asia or North America. For example, Shigehara argued that in East Asia, countries were characterized by different stages of economic and financial development and different historical, cultural, and institutional backgrounds. These factors would limit the monetary integration of the Asian economies. Furthermore, Asian governments show little interest in relying on the yen as a reserve currency—the dollar still accounts for over half of the reserves of Asian governments. In addition, Shigehara argued that monetary union is a step toward political union, which is a goal in Europe but not in Asia.

Unlike North America and Asia, Europe is likely to adopt a currency zone. Gleske argued that Europe will benefit from this development. As Europe organizes its currency zone, Europe's real economy will become less susceptible to fluctuations in foreign exchange rates. The share of foreign trade in the GNP of Europe will fall sharply relative to the share of foreign trade in the GNP of many individual European countries. As a result, foreign exchange fluctuations will have less of an adverse effect on the European economy. In fact, the effect has already been reduced by the exchange rate mechanism and gradual stabilization of exchange relationships within the European Monetary System.

Overview remarks

Conference participants making broad overview comments expressed a range of views about the benefits of the move to trade and currency zones. Lawrence Summers and Jacques de Larosière were optimistic about the trend. Charles Carlisle and Pedro Aspe had mixed feelings. And Paul Volcker and John Crow were pessimistic.

The optimistic view. Summers argued that further progress was needed in liberalizing world trade. Toward that end, he supported any move to reduce barriers to trade, whether it be unilateral, bilateral, or multilateral. In particular, Summers said that most prospective trade zones were "likely to involve natural trading barriers and therefore to increase trade by more than they divert trade." And even if trade diversion occurs, it will be more likely to increase welfare rather than to reduce it. Moreover, trade zones will probably improve the domestic policies of member countries. And finally, trade zones could help accelerate the move to global trade liberalization.

De Larosière, providing a European point of view, favored the move to trade and currency zones in Europe. He claimed that the move to a European trade zone has stimulated member countries' economic growth and trade. In the process, trade has increased not only among member countries but also with the rest of the world. As Europe has moved to a trade zone, exchange rates have stabilized, economic performance in member countries has converged, and monetary union now appears likely. Finally, de Larosière argued that Europe's move to trade and currency zones does not imply isolation from the rest of the world. The European Community's economic integration will continue to benefit nonmember countries.

The mixed view. Carlisle argued that trade and currency zones could be either a positive or negative development. First, GATT statistics show that trade is not becoming more regionalized. Second, political realities make it unlikely that the world will coalesce into more than two great trade zones. Third, trade zones are not necessarily inconsistent with multilateral trade liberalization. Fourth, given that trade zones are going to develop, they must supplement, not replace, global trade liberalization. Finally, if trade zones replace global trade liberalization, all countries will be hurt.

Aspe agreed that membership in trade and currency zones could be extremely beneficial, especially to a small economy, so long as progress continues to be made at the global level. To this end, Mexico has joined the GATT and has expressed a willingness to join in various Western Hemisphere trade zones. Aspe argued that countries should be willing to act unilaterally, multilaterally, or as a part of a trade zone to reduce tariff and nontariff barriers to trade.

The pessimistic view. Volcker expressed concern about the trend toward trade zones. Siding with Bergsten, Volcker felt that regional trade zones would erect barriers to trade against the outside world and divert trade from nonmember countries. Moreover, he argued that trade zones could lead to greater interregional volatility in exchange rates. In response to the move to trade zones, Volcker suggested that Article XXIV of the GATT, which restricts trade zones from taking protectionist actions, be more vigorously enforced. Although the article has been violated, particularly by the erection of nontariff barriers, remedial actions have not been taken.

Crow agreed with Volcker. Because of the dangers of trade and currency zones erecting protectionist barriers, Crow argued that further progress should be made on the GATT. Eastern Europe, the Soviet Union, and many developing countries are all striving to join the global trade system, and nothing should be done to prevent these emerging market-oriented economies from joining the GATT. In addition, Crow agreed with Meltzer that maintaining price stability is the best way to ensure the efficiency of world trade and payments.

Conclusions

The world economy may be moving toward trade and currency zones. Conference participants generally agreed that the move would be beneficial if it occurred along with further progress toward global trade liberalization. Participants also agreed that trade and currency zones would have profound effects on domestic financial, monetary, and fiscal policies and on trade and monetary relationships among regions of the world economy.

Conference participants disagreed about whether the move toward trade and currency zones would impede further multilateral trade liberalization or be beneficial without further multilateral progress. Participants also had different views about whether currency zones were necessary to achieve the full advantages of trade zones. From the discussions, though, it was clear that Europe would proceed toward establishing both trade and currency zones. Participants concurred that, of all of the proposed trade and currency zones, Europe is best suited to benefit from both.

George A. Kahn is a senior economist at the Federal Reserve Bank of Kansas City. Carol Manthey, a research associate at the bank, assisted with the preparation of the article.

Opening Remarks

Alan Greenspan

It is a pleasure to be here with you once again. As at past meetings here, the Federal Reserve Bank of Kansas City has arranged a particularly challenging and stimulating program—one that commands our attention despite the attractions and distractions of this magnificent setting. Let me take a moment to add a word of special thanks to Roger Guffey for his part in overseeing the whole series of symposia here at Jackson Hole that many of us have found so informative and valuable over the years. This will be his last meeting here as official "host," as his tenure as president of the Federal Reserve Bank of Kansas City is coming to an end. We thank you, Roger, for this meeting and those of past years and wish you well in your post-Federal Reserve endeavors.

With movements toward trade zones proceeding in many parts of the world—the single market program and economic and monetary union in the European Community (EC) and the Enterprise for the Americas Initiative and the proposed North America free trade area here in this hemisphere—it is both timely and appropriate that we consider the economic factors behind these efforts and their implications for global markets and for policy formulation. The outcome of the Uruguay Round of multilateral negotiations unfortunately is still undetermined. Against this background, we need to learn why the impetus has shifted to regional agreements; what precisely are the benefits those agreements offer; and how to ensure that the benefits of the regional trade agreement do not translate into global losses as a result of trade diversion and resource misallocation.

The dividends offered by free trade zones are primarily microeconomic in nature—greater economics of scale in production, more competitive industrial structures, improved labor and capital mobility, and more efficient allocation of investment throughout the region. These gains come about as barriers to the flow of goods and services are lowered and as restrictions such as those on foreign ownership of domestic firms and on repatriation of earnings are removed. Inevitably, during the process of adjustment some workers and owners of capital in place will regard themselves as "losers" in the move to a free trade area. On balance, we expect the microeconomic gains to translate into a healthier macroeconomic performance as well, with an improved outlook for long-term growth.

How do we estimate ahead of time the net gain in welfare for each of the members of a proposed free trade area? What policies are appropriate for ensuring that in response to lower trade barriers capital and labor successfully move from industries where they are no longer competitive to those where they can be efficiently and profitably employed? At what stage of economic development is a country ready for participation in a free trade area? Can countries of different size or at different stages of development all benefit from forming a free trade area with each other? What should be the policy of participating countries in their trade with countries not in the free trade area?

These are all important questions that we might usefully take up during our two days of discussion. They are questions that the member states of the European Community have dealt with over the life of the Common Market and are grappling with again as the now-larger EC proceeds to shape the terms of the single market by the end of 1992. Indeed, they are questions that those responsible for negotiating the North America Free Trade Agreement will need to answer in concrete terms for Mexico, Canada, and the United States.

Our agenda extends beyond free trade areas to a consideration of currency zones as well. The relationship between the two is a topic that is still much debated. Since the United States is both a free trade area and a single currency zone, I cannot dismiss the proposition that a single currency is an important ingredient in a successful free trade zone. A single currency makes it possible for producers and consumers to eliminate the risk, uncertainty, and expense associated with transacting in several currencies and with protecting against potential exchange rate variability. A single currency simplifies somewhat the problem of planning by enterprises and of making investment decisions. It reduces even further the significance of national borders to firms producing within a free trade area and thus helps to promote the integration of all the regions of the area into a single, efficient economic system.

At the present time, the member countries of the European Community are in the process of negotiating economic and monetary union. Achievement of a single European internal market and a single European currency offers the benefits I have just described, but entails some costs as well. It will require significant institutional changes and political compromises as well as some loss of economic flexibility as whatever scope remains for adjustment of member countries' nominal exchange rates is eliminated. The transition from the present system to full monetary union is likely to be difficult, and the decision of when to lock in existing exchange rates may be crucial. Implementation of European economic and monetary union may add to the complexity of expanding EC membership in the future.

The proposed changes associated with European economic and monetary union are far-reaching. While their effects will be felt primarily within Europe, no doubt there will be impacts on all exchange rates and international financial markets in general. Similarly, the achievement of a free trade area in goods and services, including financial services, within North America can be expected to have some impact on financial markets elsewhere.

The past decade has witnessed significant changes in global financial markets as deregulation in many countries and technological advances in information processing and communication have made it possible for financial markets throughout the world to become more closely integrated. The lowering of barriers to competition within proposed trade and currency zones should accelerate that process for the countries within the zones and may well influence the course of developments outside these zones. The balance of competition between banks and other financial institutions and markets, the range of financial services and products available to consumers, the nature of the risks borne by financial intermediaries, the pace of innovation, and the efficiency with which financial intermediation in general is done may all be affected by the increased competition in financial markets that is expected to result from the formation of a free trade area.

The emergence of trade and currency zones poses additional challenges for the ways in which we regulate financial markets. Small regulatory differences between countries within the zone might well tip the balance of competition in favor of one country's firms relative to those of the other. Regulatory inconsistencies across the members of the zone might well be exploited by firms and result in undesired outcomes in terms of the nature and the distribution of risk borne by financial institutions. It would appear that the move toward trade and currency zones needs to be complemented by efforts to achieve greater coordination of supervision and regulation of national financial markets.

In what ways do trade and currency zones have an influence on macroeconomic policies? Their fundamental contribution is to counter any tendency that might be present for policy choices— whether trade policy, exchange rate policy, or monetary and fiscal policy—to be made at the expense of one's neighbor by making neighboring economies so interdependent that such a policy would be self-defeating. At the same time, however, the trade and/or currency zones define a new border—and thus a new "neighbor." It is essential that those responsible for policy choices do not allow the emergence of trade and currency zones to foster a climate of policy choices for the benefit of "insiders" at the expense of "outsiders." ·

Trade and currency zones raise issues of policy implementation as well. Clearly the scope for independent monetary policy is lost, but to what extent do other macroeconomic policy instruments within the region need to be coordinated? Is some degree of tax harmonization needed to assure a "level playing field" for all economic entities in the zone? Does currency union require limits on national budget policy choices? Is the effectiveness of fiscal policy on the part of one government altered by increased "spillovers" to the partner economies within the zone? Should monetary policy in the low-inflation member of the zone function as an anchor for monetary policy in the other members? Will changes in the structure of financial intermediation affect the transmission of monetary policy, and, if so, how? Our experience with trade and currency zones is still limited. As a consequence, experience will not be a sufficient guide to answer these questions unambiguously.

The range of issues before us is quite broad. We seek answers from the abstract world of economic models and from the ongoing experience gained in the cases of European economic and monetary union and the North American free trade area that are already being planned. We need to address these questions from the perspective of industrial countries and from that of countries still in the process of industrializing. Insights into the economic implications we can expect from trade and currency zones should guide us in choosing appropriate macroeconomic policies now and in the future—whether we are "inside" or "outside" a zone. I recognize that we are not likely to reach complete insight or agreement on these issues in our discussions during the next two days, but I expect the exchange of views, both within the formal sessions and outside of them, to be both stimulating and informative.

The Move Toward Free Trade Zones

Paul Krugman

From World War II until about 1980, regional free trade agreements and global trade negotiations under the General Agreement on Tariffs and Trade (GATT) could reasonably be seen as complements rather than substitutes—as two aspects of a broad march toward increasingly open international markets. Since then, however, the two have moved in opposite directions. The 1980s were marked by stunning and unexpected success for regional trading blocs. In Europe, the European Community (EC) not only enlarged itself to include the new democracies of Southern Europe, but made a lunge for an even higher degree of economic unity with the cluster of market-integrating measures referred to as "1992." In North America, Canada ended a century of ambivalence about regional integration by signing a free trade agreement (which is also to an important extent an investment agreement) with the United States; even more startlingly, the reformist Salinas government in Mexico has sought, and appears likely to get, the same thing. And in East Asia, while formal moves toward regional free trade are absent, there was after 1985 a noticeable increase in Japanese investment in and imports from the region's new manufacturing exporters.

Meanwhile, however, the multilateral process that oversaw the great postwar growth in world trade seems to have run aground. The major multilateral trade negotiation of the decade, the Uruguay Round, was supposed to be concluded in late 1990. Instead, no agreement has yet been reached. And while some kind of face-saving document will probably be produced, in reality the Uruguay Round has clearly failed either to significantly liberalize trade or to generate good will that would help sustain further rounds of negotiation.

The contrast between the successes of regional free trade agreements and the failure of efforts to liberalize trade at the global level has raised disparate reactions. Official pronouncements, of course, call for renewed progress on all fronts. In practice, however, choices of emphasis must be made. Some politicians and economists despair of the multilateral process under the GATT, and would like to see further effort focused on regional or bilateral negotiations that seem more likely to get somewhere. Others, seeing the multilateral process as ultimately more important, fear that regional deals may undermine multilateralism. It is possible to find respected and influential voices taking fairly extreme positions on either side. For example, MIT's Rudiger Dornbusch has not only been a strong partisan of a U.S.-Mexico free trade pact, but has called for a U.S. turn to bilateral deals even with countries far from North America, such as South Korea. On the other side, Columbia's Jagdish Bhagwati, now a special adviser to the GATT, not only advocates remaining with the traditional process but has actually condemned the prospective U.S.-Mexico deal.

How can reasonable and well-informed people disagree so strongly? The answer lies, in part, in the inherent ambiguity of the welfare economics of preferential trading arrangements; it lies even more in the peculiarly contorted political economy of international trade negotiations.

Even in terms of straightforward welfare economics, the welfare effects of the creation of free trade areas are uncertain; indeed, it was precisely in the study of customs unions that the principle of the "second best," which says that half a loaf may be worse than none, was first formulated. A customs union, even if it only reduces trade barriers, may worsen trade distortions; moreover, consolidation of nations into trading blocs may lead even intelligent governments with the welfare of their citizens at heart to adopt more protectionist policies toward the outside world, potentially outweighing the gains from freer trade with their neighbors.

Worse yet, however, the motives of governments as they engage in trade negotiations are by no means adequately described by the idea that they maximize national welfare. In general, trade policy (like any microeconomic policy) is very much influenced by pressure from organized interest groups; the traditional framework of trade negotiation under the GATT channels these political pressures in a way that has generally led toward freer trade, but from an economist's point of view, this framework has led to the right results for the wrong reasons. Given this, it is very difficult to decide whether a shift in the domain of negotiations will be a good or a bad thing.

Should the move toward free trade areas be applauded or condemned? The purpose of this paper is to help clarify the issues in a fundamentally murky debate. It is primarily a discussion of conceptual issues rather than a survey of actual recent moves toward free trade areas, although since the key questions about that move are inherently empirical, some appeal to facts and cases is necessary.

The paper is in three parts. The first part reviews the relatively straightforward economics of preferential trading arrangements. The second part is an attempt to describe and analyze the political economy of trade negotiations, and the reasons why changes in this political economy have recently pushed the world in the direction of regional free trade areas. The third part tries to pull the economics and politics together, for a general discussion of the problem of free trade areas versus multilateralism.

The economics of trading blocs

In spite of the major rethinking of the theory of international trade that has taken place over the past dozen years, few economists would disagree with the proposition that a world with free trade will be better off than under any other plausible set of trade policies. Yet preaching the virtues of global free trade somehow does not seem to get us there, and it often seems easier to negotiate free trade or at least trade liberalization on a more local basis. Indeed, in spite of the growing ease of international communication, the 1980s saw a shift of emphasis away from global trade negotiations toward regional deals.

The apparent conflict between what economists say should be in everyone's interest and what actually seems to happen politically should be a warning flag—it suggests that whatever is going on in international trade negotiations, it is not welfare maximization. And as I will argue in the second part of this paper, any assessment of the move toward free trade areas depends critically on understanding what governments actually do as well as what they should do. Still, suppose one takes it as a given that for some reason it is possible to negotiate a degree of trade liberalization among subsets of countries that goes beyond what is possible at a world level. The question is then, should trade liberalization be permitted to proceed at two speeds? Or should one try to ban special deals and insist that countries offer to everyone the same terms they offer to anyone?

A naive view would be that since free trade is a good thing, any move toward freer trade should be welcomed. Unfortunately, the case is not that simple. At least three (not entirely unrelated) objections may be offered to preferential free trade agreements:

(1) *Trade diversion:* Trade liberalization among a subset of countries, even if it is not accompanied by an increase in protectionism against extra-bloc imports, may create perverse incentives that lead to specialization in the wrong direction.

(2) *Beggar-thy-neighbor effects:* The formation of free trade areas may well hurt countries outside those areas, even without any overt increase in protectionism.

(3) *Trade warfare:* Regional trading blocs, being larger than their components, will have more market power in world trade; this may tempt them to engage in more aggressive trade policies, which damage the trade between blocs and may (through a kind of Prisoners' Dilemma) leave everyone worse off.

The analysis of the effects of preferential trading arrangements is the subject of a huge and intricate literature. We can, however, quickly survey some of the main results that seem to be relevant to the current problem of regionalism in world trade.

Trade creation vs. trade diversion

In a classic analysis, Jacob Viner (1950) pointed out that a move to free trade by two nations who continue to maintain tariffs against other countries could leave them worse rather than better off. Viner's insight remains fundamental to all analysis of preferential trading arrangements, and is worth restating.

The essential idea can be seen from a numerical example (Table 1).[1] Imagine that one country—which, not entirely innocently, we call Spain—can produce wheat for itself, import it from France, or import it from Canada. We suppose that the cost to Spain of producing a bushel of wheat for itself is 10, that the cost of a bushel of wheat bought from France is 8, and that the cost of a bushel bought from Canada is only 5.

Table 1
A Hypothetical Example of A Free Trade Area

	Tariff Rate		
	0	**4**	**6**
Cost of Wheat from:			
Spain	10	10	10
France, before customs union	8	12	14
France, after customs union	8	8	8
Canada	5	9	11

Suppose initially that Spain has a tariff that applies equally to all imported wheat. If it imports wheat in spite of the tariff, it will buy it from the cheapest source, namely Canada. This case is illustrated in the table by the column labeled "Tariff = 4." If the tariff is high enough, however—as in the case where it equals 6—Spain will grow its own wheat.

Now suppose that Spain enters a customs union with France, so that French wheat can enter free of tariff. Is this a good thing or a bad thing?

If the tariff was initially 6, the customs union is a good thing: Spain will replace its expensive domestic production with cheaper imported French wheat, freeing its own resources to do more useful things. If, however, the tariff was initially 4, the customs union will cause Spain to shift from Canadian wheat to more expensive French wheat, shifting from a low-cost to a high-cost source. In that case the customs union may well lower welfare.

As Viner pointed out, in the first, favorable case, the customs union causes Spain to replace high-cost domestic production with imports; it thus leads to an increase in trade. In the unfavorable case, by contrast, Spain shifts from a foreign source outside the free trade area to another source inside. Thus Viner suggested that "trade creating" customs unions, in which increased imports of trading bloc members from one another replace domestic production, are desirable; "trade diverting" customs unions, in which imports are diverted from sources outside the union to sources inside, are not. Loosely speaking, if the extra trade that takes place between members of a trading bloc represents an addition to world trade, the bloc has raised world efficiency; if the trade is not additional, but represents a shift away from trade with countries outside the bloc, world efficiency declines.

This simple criterion is extremely suggestive, and makes it easy to understand how regional trade liberalization can actually reduce rather than increase world efficiency. Perhaps the most obvious real-world example, as the illustration itself suggested, is the effect of EC enlargement on agricultural trade. The Southern European countries are induced, by their entry into the EC, to buy grain and other cold-climate products from costly European sources rather than the low-cost suppliers on the other side of the Atlantic. Meanwhile, the Northern European countries are now induced to buy Mediterranean products like wine and oil (and perhaps also labor-intensive manufactured goods) from Southern Europe rather than potentially cheaper suppliers elsewhere, for example, in North Africa. It is by no means implausible to suggest that because of these trade-diverting effects on agriculture, EC enlargement reduced rather than increased world efficiency.

While the creation/diversion idea captures the essence of the problem, however, its suggestion that customs unions are about as likely to cause harm as good is somewhat too pessimistic. For both theoretical and empirical reasons, one needs to bear in mind that the simple creation/diversion idea misses some potential gains from customs unions, even ones that are mostly trade-diverting.

First and least interesting of these additional gains is the reduction of consumption distortions. Even if Spain's initial tariff does not prevent it from importing Canadian wheat, the tariff will still distort consumer incentives. And shifting to free trade with France will reduce this consumer distortion even while diverting trade.

A second gain from regional free trade, which is very important in practice, comes from the increased size and hence both productive efficiency and competitiveness of oligopolistic markets subject to economies of scale. When the European Common Market was formed in 1958, substantial trade diversion seemed a likely outcome. What turned the arrangement into a strong economic success was the huge intra-industry trade in manufactures, and the associated rationalization of production, that the Treaty of Rome made possible. [2]

Finally, a third gain from formation of a customs union is that regional integration characteristically improves a region's terms of trade at the rest of the world's expense.

This last effect is obviously something less than an unmitigated good thing. It makes a regional trade deal more attractive, but it also suggests that such deals can, in effect, be beggar-thy-neighbor policies.

The beggar-thy-neighbor effect

Imagine a world consisting of three countries, A, B, and C. It is easiest to imagine that each country is specialized in the production of a different set of goods. Also suppose initially that all three countries maintain the same tariff rate against all imported goods. Now suppose that A and B form a customs union, eliminating the tariff on goods shipped to each other, while maintaining their tariffs on goods imported from C. What happens to C?

The presumption is that C is made worse off, through a deterioration of its terms of trade. To see why, consider what would happen as the result of the customs union if the prices of all goods remained the same. Then A and B would each tend to buy more of each others' products, substituting away from consumption both of their own products and from consumption of goods imported from C. The net effect on the demand for A's and B's goods would be ambiguous, because each country would buy less of its own goods but sell more to the other. The demand for C's products, however, would unambiguously fall. Thus to clear markets, the relative price of C's goods will normally have to fall; unless there is too much asymmetry, the prices of both A's and B's products will rise in terms of C's.

This terms of trade loss will increase the benefits of a customs union to A and B. Indeed, a customs union may well be desirable from their point of view even if it leads primarily to trade diversion rather than trade creation—because it is precisely trade diversion, that is, a shift of demand away from imports from the outside world, that leads to the improvement in the terms of trade. The extra gain will, however, come at the rest of the world's expense. The point is that even if formation of a customs union does not involve any increase in external tariffs, it can still, in effect, be a beggar-thy-neighbor policy.

Again, this is not an abstract point. The United States has been concerned that the enlargement of the EC deprives its agricultural exporters, in particular, of traditional markets, and has sought offsetting *reductions* in EC protection against agricultural products. And indeed this is what must happen if a customs union is not to be a de facto beggar-thy-neighbor policy. Formation of the union must be accompanied by a reduction in external tariffs.

A customs union that also reduces tariffs on imports from outside can still be beneficial, through the normal gains from trade and specialization. Indeed, the idea that one could adjust tariffs so as to keep a customs union's trade with the outside world unchanged is the basis of a well-known demonstration that a customs union is always potentially beneficial to its members (Kemp and Wan 1976). But will a group of countries forming a trade area normally lower their external tariff sufficiently to avoid any trade diversion?

This depends on their motivations in forming the customs union in the first place. In practice, trading areas are formed for a variety of reasons, in which a careful assessment of costs and benefits is not usually high on the list. In the messy world of motivations discussed in the second part of this paper, it is possible either that a trading area might offer the rest of the world concessions in order to mollify it, or that the new bloc might have economically irrational autarkic tendencies as a way of emphasizing the political content of integration. For example, in the context of fairly amicable trade relations, one could imagine the EC cutting tariffs and subsidies in order to compensate the United States for any loss of markets due to increased European integration. In another context, one could imagine the emergence of a political context in which Fortress Europe shows a preference for self-sufficiency even beyond the beggar-thy-neighbor point.

Before we turn to political economy, however, let us at least ask what the economically rational action would be. And it is fairly obvious: not only would it not normally be in the interest of a trading bloc to throw away all of its terms of trade gain by reducing external tariffs, it would normally be in the bloc's interest to *raise* its external tariffs.

The reason is that a trading bloc will normally have more monopoly power in world trade than any of its members alone. The standard theory of the optimal tariff tells us that the optimal tariff for a country acting unilaterally to improve its terms of trade is higher, the lower the elasticity of world demand for its exports. So for a trading bloc attempting to maximize the welfare of its residents, the optimal tariff rate will normally be higher than the optimal tariff rates of its constituent countries acting individually.

This implies that the adjustment of external tariffs following formation of a regional trading bloc will not only not eliminate the beggar-thy-neighbor aspect, it will tend to worsen it.

Trading blocs and trade war

An individual trading bloc will tend to gain even in the face of trade diversion by improving its terms of trade at the rest of the world's expense. If one goes from envisioning a single bloc to imagining a world of trading blocs, however, the blocs may beggar each other. That is, formation of blocs can, in effect, set off a beggar-all trade war that leaves everyone worse off.

Imagine a world of *four* countries, A, B, C, and D. Imagine also that A and B enter negotiations to form a free trade area. They find that the area will primarily produce trade diversion rather than trade creation, but that it will still increase their welfare by improving their terms of trade at C and D's expense. Thus A and B will, correctly, form a free trade area; and this area will have an incentive to act as a trading bloc and raise its tariffs on imports from C and D. But suppose that C and D make the same calculation. Then both blocs will raise tariffs in an effort to exploit their market power. Obviously both cannot succeed; one bloc's terms of trade will actually deteriorate, while the other's will improve less than if it were acting on its own. Meanwhile, trade diversion will be taking its toll on world efficiency. The result of the tariff warfare may therefore be to leave all four countries worse off than they would have been had the trading blocs not been formed. And yet the members of each bloc are better off than they would have been if they had not joined their bloc, and thus left themselves at the mercy of the other bloc. So the game of free trade area formation itself may (though it need not) be a form of Prisoners' Dilemma, in which individually rational actions lead to a bad collective result.

This hypothetical example provides a simple justification for those who fear that the indirect costs of the move toward free trade areas will exceed the direct benefits. While it is an extremely stylized picture, it captures at least some of the concern of critics of regional trading arrangements, like Jagdish Bhagwati. The basic logic here is that the regional deals undermine the multilateral system, and that the gains in intraregional trade are more than offset by losses of interregional trade. In effect, bilateralism or regionalism leads to global trade diversion.[3]

Of course, this is only a possibility, not a certainty. Indeed, it is perfectly possible that the gains from free trade between the pairs greatly outweigh the losses from multilateral trade diversion. This is essentially an empirical question, but it is one on which some numerical exercises can shed at least some light.

Trading blocs and world welfare

In an earlier paper (Krugman 1991), I offered a way of making a suggestive back-of-the-envelope calculation regarding the effects of a move toward the formation of regional trading blocs. The formal model is in the appendix to this paper; here I sketch out the approach and its results.

The basic idea is to examine how world welfare changes as a highly stylized world economy is organized into progressively fewer, progressively larger trading blocs. A trading bloc is envisaged as consisting of a large number of small geographic units ("provinces"), each specialized in the export of a different good. (Countries, which presumably themselves consist of one or more provinces, play no explicit role in the analysis.) Each trading bloc chooses an external tariff to maximize the welfare of its members, taking other blocs' tariffs as given.[4]

How does world welfare change as the number of blocs is reduced? There are two effects. On one side, the smaller the number of blocs, the more potential trade is unencumbered by tariffs; in the limit, with only one trading bloc, we have global free trade. On the other side, every time one merges blocs into larger blocs, there will be trade diversion; this effect will be reinforced by the fact that bigger blocs will have more market power and thus normally set higher external tariffs.

Which effect dominates? We know that free trade is best, so as the number of blocs goes from 2 to 1, welfare must rise. On the other hand, in a world of many small blocs nobody would have much market power, and since most of each bloc's consumption would be imported and hence subject to the same external tariff, there would be little trade diversion. So a fall in the number of blocs from a very large number to a somewhat smaller number might well reduce welfare. We would, therefore, expect a U-shaped relationship between the number of blocs and world welfare. While the best of all possible worlds has only one bloc, the worst is not a totally fragmented world but one with a moderate number.

In the simplest version of this story, all provinces stand in symmetric relationship to one another, so that there are no "natural" trading blocs. In this case, as is shown in the appendix, there are only two parameters: the number of blocs and the elasticity of substitution between the products of any two provinces. Figure 3, in the appendix, shows the relationship between the number of blocs and world welfare for three values of this elasticity: 2, a number that implies very large monopoly power in trade (although it is still high compared with empirical estimates, which tend to be not much greater than 1); 4; and 10. Remarkably, for this wide range of elasticities we consistently get the same answer: world welfare is minimized for a world of three trading blocs. The resemblance to the apparent current trend makes this an extremely interesting result!

It is a result that should, however, be treated with considerable caution. Like any abstract model, this one makes a large number of simplifying assumptions; perhaps the most objectionable in this case is the assumption that under free trade any arbitrary pair of "provinces" would have the same volume of trade as any other. This amounts to assuming away geography, the extent to which some countries would be each others' major trading partners even in the absence of preferential trading arrangements. If trading blocs are formed, not with arbitrary membership, but among countries that would be each others' main markets anyway, the consolidation of the world into a limited number of such blocs is less likely to be harmful.

The importance of "natural" trading blocs

If transportation and communication costs lead to a strong tendency of countries to trade with their neighbors, and if free trade areas are to be formed among such good neighbors, then the likelihood that consolidation into a few large trading blocs will reduce world welfare is much less than suggested by the simple numerical example in Figure 3. The reason is straightforward: the gains from freeing intraregional trade will be larger, and the costs of reducing interregional trade, than the geography-free story suggests.

Imagine, for example, a world of six countries, which may potentially form into three trading blocs. If these countries are all symmetric, then three blocs is the number that minimizes world welfare, and hence this consolidation will be harmful. Suppose, however, that each pair of countries is on a different continent, and that intercontinental transport costs are sufficiently high that the bulk of trade would be between continental neighbors even in the absence of tariffs. Then the right way to think about the formation of continental free trade areas is not as a movement from 6 to 3, but as a movement of each continent from 2 to 1—which is beneficial, not harmful.

In practice, the sets of countries that are now engaging in free trade agreements are indeed "natural" trading partners, who would have done much of their trade with one another even in the absence of special arrangements. A crude but indicative measure of the extent to which countries are especially significant trading partners comes from comparison of their trade with what would have been predicted by a "gravity" equation, which assumes that trade between any two countries is a function of the product of their national incomes.

Even casual inspection of such gravity-type relations reveals the strong tendency of countries to focus their trade on nearby partners; that is, in spite of modern transportation and communications, trade is still largely a neighborhood affair.

The magnitude of the strength of natural trading blocs can be crudely calculated from a regression of the following form:

$$\ln(T_{ij}) = \alpha + \beta \ln(Y_i Y_j) + \sum_z \gamma^z D^z{}_{ij}$$

where T_{ij} represents the value of trade (exports plus imports) between some pair of countries i and j; and Y_i, Y_j represent the two countries' national incomes. We suppose that the countries belong to several groups that are or might become trading blocs, and we index these groups by z, with D^{zij} equal to 1 if the pair of countries i and j belong to group z, 0 otherwise. Then we would say that a potential trading bloc is natural to the extent that the estimated γ is strongly positive for that z.

The simplest regression of this kind that one can perform uses the G-7 countries (which after all account for most of world output in any case) and defines the two groupings as $z=1$: the United States and Canada, $z=2$: Europe. The results of that regression are shown in Table 2. To nobody's surprise, they point out very strongly the local bias of trade: the United States and Canada, according to the regression, do thirteen times as much trade as they would if they were not neighbors, while the four major European countries do seven times as much.

Table 2
A G-7 Gravity Regression

	Estimated Value	T-statistic
α	-8.4302	-6.894
β	0.7387	8.966
γ^1	2.6092	6.576
γ^2	1.9823	9.479

$R^2 = 0.7796$

Of course, these results are in part due to the fact that there are already special trading arrangements between the United States and Canada, on one side, and within the EC on the other. Yet the results are so strong that they make it overwhelmingly clear that distance still matters and still creates natural trading blocs.

To reemphasize why this matters: if a disproportionate share of world trade would take place within trading blocs even in the absence of any preferential trading arrangement, then the gains from trade creation within blocs are likely to outweigh any possible losses from external trade diversion.

While the coincidence between potential trading blocs and natural blocs helps allay fears of global immiserization, it also raises a warning flag about the indiscriminate use of the free trade agreement as a weapon of policy. U.S.-Canada free trade is almost certainly a good thing, not just because we like each other, but because the two countries plus Mexico clearly form a natural bloc. U.S.-Korea or U.S.-Israel free trade, to take examples of less neighborly proposals that have been floated, do not share the same virtue; indeed, Israel is, if anything, a natural member of the European bloc. Such "unnatural" free trade areas are highly likely to cause trade diversion rather than creation.

On the whole, however, the fact that geography has already given international trade a strong regional bias makes the concern that allowing free trade agreements at a regional level will lead to a Prisoners' Dilemma a minor one. That is, if governments maximized the welfare of their citizens, prospective moves toward regional free trade would almost surely do more good than harm to the members of the free trade areas.

The major problem with this optimistic statement is, of course, that governments do no such thing. Before turning to the political economy of trade, however, we should also note an important point: while most of the world's output is generated by countries that appear likely to be inside one or another big free trade area, most people live outside. And it is these non-neighbors who are most likely to be beggared.

The innocent bystander problem

A turn to increased protectionism against outsiders by groups of countries that have formed free trade areas and, as a result, start behaving as a bloc toward the outside world is unlikely to leave the members of the blocs worse off. It can, however, quite easily do a lot of damage to countries that, for whatever reason, do not get inside the blocs.

Consider the following back-of-the envelope example. Imagine that the world's industrialized countries plus a few developing countries were, in fact, to consolidate into three blocs, consisting of Europe, North America, and an East Asian collection centered on Japan. On average, these three blocs currently import about 10 percent of gross bloc product from outside themselves. Leaving aside agriculture, the average tariff equivalent they impose on these extra-bloc imports is currently fairly low; call it 10 percent.

Now suppose that because the blocs have more market power than their constituent nations, and, in general, behave more belligerently, they increase their external tariff equivalent to 30 percent. Given typical estimated elasticities, the effect of such a tariff rise would be to reduce extra-bloc imports by about 20 percent. We can use standard methods to come up with an estimate of the welfare loss from this tariff increase. The implied efficiency loss is the average of the initial and final tariff rates, multiplied by the fall in imports: 0.2 times 2 percent of gross bloc product, or 0.4 percent. This is a small, though not negligible, cost; more to the point, it could easily be outweighed by the gains from free trade within the trading blocs.[5]

But consider the same situation from the point of view of a nation that is not part of one of the blocs. This nation simply sees an increase in the tariff its exports must pay to enter the world's major markets. It will, therefore, suffer a terms of trade loss, which may be close to the size of the tariff increase. For example, a country that exports 15 percent of its GNP to the OECD nations, faced with a 20 percent rise in the external tariffs of the newly formed blocs, could suffer a real income loss of close to 3 percent—with no compensating gain in market access elsewhere. The point, then, is that the biggest costs of a consolidation of the world into a few large trading blocs would likely be borne not by the countries in the blocs but by those left out in the cold.

Summary

The purely economic analysis of free trade areas suggests that, in principle, formation of such areas might hurt rather than help the world economy. Trade diversion could outweigh trade creation even with external protectionism unchanged; and the increased market power that countries gain by consolidating into trading blocs could lead optimizing but noncooperative governments to raise tariffs increasing the cost.

While some moves toward free trade surely do produce costly trade diversion, however, it seems unlikely that the net effect on world efficiency will be negative. The reason is geography: the possibly emergent trading blocs consist of more or less neighboring countries, who would be each others' main trading partners even without special arrangements. As a result, the potential losses from trade diversion are limited, and the potential gains from trade creation are large.

The main concern suggested by this economic analysis is distributional: inward-turning free trade areas, while doing little damage to themselves or each other, can easily inflict much more harm on economically smaller players that for one reason or another are not part of any of the big blocs.

The political economy of free trade areas

In a fundamental sense, the issue of the desirability of free trade areas is a question of political economy rather than of economics proper. While one could argue against the formation of free trade areas purely on the grounds that they might produce trade diversion, in practice (as argued above) the costs of trade diversion are unlikely to outweigh the gains from freer trade within regions. The real objection is a political judgment: fear that regional deals will undermine the delicate balance of interests that supports the GATT. Implicit in this concern is the idea that governments do not set tariffs to maximize national welfare, but that they are instead ruled by special interest politics disciplined and channeled by an international structure whose preservation is therefore a high priority.

To discuss the political economy of free trade areas, it is necessary to offer at least a rough outline of how trade policy actually works, and of why free trade areas rather than multilateral agreements seem to be the current trend. Only then can we ask whether such preferential agreements will help or hurt the overall prospects for trade.

GATT-think and trade negotiations

International trade policy has many horror stories. Examples of outrageous policy, like the sugar quota that for a time led U.S. producers to extract sucrose from imported pancake mix, are easy to come by. All microeconomic policy areas, however, offer similar stories of government actions that disregard efficiency and cater to organized interests. Indeed, one may argue that the surprising thing about trade policy is how good it is. Think of the way that the U.S. government handles water rights in the West, or tries to control pollution. These show a disregard for even the most elementary considerations of economic logic or social justice that make trade policy seem clean and efficient. Arguably trade policy is one of our best microeconomic policy areas—largely because it is disciplined by international treaties that have over time led to a progressive dismantling of many trade barriers.

One might be inclined to ascribe credit for this to the economists. After all, economists have for nearly two centuries preached the virtues of free trade. It seems natural to think of the GATT, and the relatively free trading system built around the GATT, as the result of the ideology of free trade.

Yet if one examines the reality of international trade negotiations, one discovers that the GATT is not built on a foundation laid by economic theory. That is not to say that there are no principles. On the contrary, one can make a great deal of sense of trade negotiations if one adopts a sort of working theory about the aims and interests of the participants, a theory that is built into the language of the GATT itself. The problem is that this underlying theory has nothing to do with what economists believe.

There is no generally accepted label for the theoretical underpinnings of the GATT. I like to refer to it as "GATT-think"—a simple set of principles that is entirely consistent, explains most of what goes on in the negotiations, but makes no sense in terms of economics.

The principles of GATT-think

To make sense of international trade negotiations, one needs to remember three simple rules about the objectives of the negotiating countries:

(1) *Exports are good.*
(2) *Imports are bad.*
(3) *Other things equal, an equal increase in imports and exports is good.*

In other words, GATT-think is enlightened mercantilism. It is mercantilist in that it presumes that each country, acting on its own, would like to subsidize exports and restrict imports. But it is enlightened in that it recognizes that it is destructive if everyone does this, and it is a good thing if everyone agrees to expand trade by accepting each others' exports.

GATT-think is also, to an economist, nonsense. In the first place, general equilibrium theory tells us that the trade balance has very little to do with trade policy. A country that restricts imports will indirectly be restricting its exports as well. So even if one agreed with principles 1 and 2, one would argue that countries gain nothing from import restriction.

Nor do economists agree that exports are good and imports bad. The point of trade is to get useful things from other countries, that is, imports, which are a benefit, not a cost; the unfortunate necessity of sending other countries useful things in return, that is, exports, is a cost rather than a benefit.

Moreover, standard trade theory does not see export subsidies and import restrictions as similar policies. On the contrary, in general equilibrium an import tariff is equivalent to an export *tax*. Furthermore, in standard trade theory an export subsidy is a stupid policy but not a malicious one, since it generally worsens a country's terms of trade, and thus benefits the rest of the world. As Avinash Dixit once put it, when the Commerce Department ascertained that European nations had been subsidizing steel exports to the United States, its appropriate response should have been to send a note of thanks.

Finally, standard trade theory generally argues that free trade is the best *unilateral* policy, regardless of whether other countries do the same. That is, in standard theory one does not need to justify free trade in the context of international agreements. (The qualification is the optimal tariff argument, which generally plays no part at all in real-world trade discussion.)

In effect, GATT-think sees the trade policy problem as a Prisoners' Dilemma: Individually, countries have an incentive to be protectionist, yet collectively, they benefit from free trade. Standard trade theory does not agree. It asserts that it is in countries' unilateral interest to be free traders—as Bastiat put it, to be protectionist because other countries are, is to block up one's own harbors because other countries have rocky coasts.

Yet although GATT-think is economic nonsense, it is a very good model of what happens. Indeed, it is embedded in the very language of the negotiations. Suppose that the United States succeeds in pressuring the European Community to stop exporting wheat that costs it three times the world market price to produce, or Japan to take a little rice at one-tenth the cost of domestic production. In GATT parlance these would represent European and Japanese "concessions"—things that they would do unwillingly (and at present appear unwilling to do at all). That is, as GATT-think predicts, countries seem to treat exports—almost any exports, at almost any price—as desirable, and imports—no matter how much better or cheaper than the domestic substitute—as undesirable.

Moreover, over the years a trading system based on the principles of GATT-think has, on the whole, done very well. No amount of lecturing by economists on the virtues of free trade could have achieved the extraordinary dismantling of trade barriers accomplished by lawyers in the thirty years following World War II. If there are problems with the system now, they have more to do with perceptions that some countries are not playing by the rules than with a dissatisfaction of the political process with the rules themselves.

GATT-think, then, is very wrong, yet somehow turns out mostly right. Why?

The hidden logic of GATT-think

GATT-think is not, presumably, the product of a continuing mercantilist tradition, preserved by legislators and lawyers in defiance of economists—although it is probably true that a more or less mercantilist view of trade comes more naturally to the untutored than the economist's blanket endorsement of free trade. The reason why GATT-think works is, instead, that it captures some basic realities of the political process.

Trade policy is a policy of details. Only a tiny fraction of the U.S. electorate knows that we have a sugar import quota, let alone keeps track of such crucial issues (for a few firms) as the enamel-on-steel-cookware case. What Mancur Olson (1965) taught us is that in such circumstances, we should not expect government policy to reflect any reasonable definition of the public interest. Political pressure is a public good, and tends to be supplied on behalf of small, well-organized groups. In the case of trade policy, with few exceptions this means *producers*—producers of exported goods, producers of import-competing goods. The consumers who might have benefited from cheap imports, or the lower prices that would prevail if firms were not subsidized to provide goods to foreigners rather than themselves, count for very little.

This explains the first two principles of GATT-think: We need only append the words "for export producers" and "for import-competing producers," and one has statements with which economists can agree. Add that trade policy is set one industry at a time, so general equilibrium is disregarded, and that consumers are not at the table, and the mercantilist tone of trade negotiations is explained.

The third principle is more complicated. One would like to think that it reflects a residual concern with efficiency. Maybe it does. But it is also true that, on average, a dollar of exports adds more domestic value added than a dollar of imports subtracts, simply because not all imports compete directly with domestic goods. So perhaps the idea of gains from trade plays no role at all.

Yet the result of applying the principles of GATT-think has up to now been pretty good. The reason is the process of multilateral negotiation, which, in effect, sets each country's exporting interests as a counterweight to import-competing interests; as trade negotiators bargain for access to each others' markets, they move toward free trade despite their disregard for the gains from trade as economists understand them. (Notice also that in this context the GATT's harsh attitude toward export subsidies makes a great deal of sense: without such subsidies, export interests become a force for free trade; with free access to subsidies, they are not.)

During the 1980s, unfortunately, the effectiveness of the GATT process seemed to wane, with the focus shifting to regional free trade agreements. We must next ask why.

The erosion of the multilateral process

Everyone who thinks about it has his own list of problems with the GATT process. I would list four main factors that have eroded the effectiveness of the GATT mechanism at channeling special interests.

First is the decline of the U.S. leadership role. There is considerable disagreement among political scientists about the extent to which international policy coordination requires a hegemonic power. What is clear is that the dominant position of the United States in the early postwar period was helpful as a way of limiting free rider problems. The United States could and did both twist arms and offer system-sustaining concessions as a way of helping the GATT process work. With the United States accounting for a progressively smaller share of gross world product, and with U.S. dominance in productivity and technology progressively eroded, the United States has been losing both the means and the desire to serve as global trade hegemon.[6]

A second long-term trend that has undermined the GATT process is the growing subtlety of the issues that must be dealt with. Increasingly, trade negotiations must deal with problems for which regulating the policies imposed by nations at their borders are insufficient. The manufactured goods that enter world trade are increasingly knowledge-intensive; this implies both that traditional criteria for "unfair" trade practices are inappropriate and that domestic policies in support of research and development become issues of trade conflict. The growing role of direct investment blurs the lines between trade policy, which is subject to GATT discipline, and investment policy, which is not. And the role of government itself, and its intrusiveness into the economy, has (in spite of conservative ideological triumph) grown to a point where the distinction between international and domestic policies is difficult to draw.

A third problem is the changing character of protectionism itself, based on the creativity of bureaucrats. In the early postwar period, protectionism was a matter of explicit, unilateral government policies: tariffs, quotas, exchange controls. The great postwar liberalization steadily ratcheted these measures down, to the point where, except in agriculture, they are now fairly unimportant. But the new protectionism that emerged with increasing force after the mid-1970s was more slippery, exploiting the weaknesses of the system. "Voluntary" export restraints, orderly marketing agreements, harassment by countervailing duty cases, red tape barriers, and the like, have all proved much more difficult to police than straightforward tariffs and quotas.

Finally, the legitimacy of the GATT system has been undermined by the growing importance of new players in the world economy—above all, Japan—who are institutionally different enough from the original players to raise questions about what is being negotiated. The GATT is a system largely imposed by the United States, and created in our own image. That is, it is a legalistic system that focuses on process rather than results. Whatever the facts of the (much disputed) case, the widespread perception is that such legalisms are ineffective when dealing with Japan; that the Japanese economy may be as open de jure as one likes, and yet that the collusive institutional structure of Japan's economy will continue to produce an economy that is de facto highly protectionist.

From the economist's point of view, none of these trends should affect the desirability of free trade. Leaving aside some of the recent strategic trade policy arguments, the basic economic argument is still that unilateral free trade is the best policy; it doesn't matter whether there is a hegemon to enforce the rules, whether the rules are inadequate to the new game, whether players have become more adept at cheating, or whether there are new players for whom the rules are meaningless. Given the real political factors that underlie GATT-think, however, these factors do matter very much. And if the evidence of the 1980s is anything to go by, the cumulative effect of these problems has been to erode the effectiveness of the GATT process to the point where further progress has effectively ground to a halt.

The regional answer

The same checklist of frustrations with the GATT process helps explain why regional free trade agreements have gained so much force as an alternative.

First, the decline of the hegemonic role of the United States at a global level can be ignored in regional agreements where there either is a local hegemon or a special correlation of forces that makes such a hegemon unnecessary. In North America, the United States obviously remains and will remain for the indefinite future the overwhelmingly dominant player; and U.S. political interest in helping Mexican reformers gives the U.S.-Mexico deal, at least, some of the national security gloss that used to be attached to the idea that free trade helped fight Communism. In Europe, the case is somewhat more complex: in effect, the idea of a single market is being pushed by a Franco-German entente, in which Germany for historical reasons needs to be seen as a good European nation, and France sees its national influence best served by being part of a European whole. In the EC enlargement, as in the U.S. embrace of Mexico, politics played a large part: the wealthy EC nations wanted to reward and safeguard the Southern European transition to democracy.

Our second and third problems with the GATT—the complexities of dealing with modern trade and with modern trade barriers—are also, on the evidence, more easily dealt with at a regional level than at a global level. Europe's 1992 is not so much a trade agreement as an agreement to coordinate policies that have historically been regarded as domestic. That is, it is, in effect, a mutual sacrifice of national sovereignty. The Canada-U.S. FTA also involves significantly more than free trade: it is a pact over investment rules, and involves creation of dispute settlement mechanisms that limit the ability of the countries to act unilaterally.

Why can regional pacts do what global negotiations cannot? The answer appears to be that neighbors understand and trust one another to negotiate at a level of detail and mutual intrusiveness that parties to global negotiations cannot. One does not hear U.S. businessmen raising the arguments against free trade with Canada that they raise against Japan—nobody claims that Canada is so institutionally different from the United States, so conspiratorial a society, that negotiated agreements are worthless and ineffective. We think that we understand and can trust the Canadians; apparently the European nations have reached a similar point of mutual understanding and trust. North Americans and Europeans have not reached a comparable state with regard to one another, and both deeply distrust the Japanese.

And this is the final point. Whether or not Japan is really a radically different kind of player from other advanced nations,[7] the perception that it is has done a great deal to undermine the perceived effectiveness and legitimacy of the GATT in the United States and Europe. So the great advantage of regional pacts is that they can exclude Japan.

One could argue that the surge of interest in regional free trade agreements is actually a godsend to world trade. Given the loss of momentum in global trade negotiations, regional pacts offer a route through which trade can still increase. Of course this trade increase might, in principle, be diversion rather than creation, and hence make the world worse rather than better off. As argued in the first part of this paper, however, the importance of natural blocs is such that this is unlikely.

The real case against free trade agreements is that they may undermine the effort to deal with the problems of the multilateral system.

Free trade agreements and the international system

In the past two years there has been a schizophrenic mood in Washington regarding trade policy. On one side, the dismal prospects for the Uruguay Round, and the perceived lack of public spirit by the Europeans, have led to disillusionment with the prospects for the GATT—and, to at least some extent, a resigned acceptance of the likelihood of greater U.S. protectionism against Japan. On the other side, prospects for free trade with Mexico have brought out the traditional export sector support for liberalization with full force. It has been noted by a number of observers that the U.S. business community has put much more effort into supporting Mexican free trade than into any other trade area, even though Mexico remains a considerably smaller market than either the EC or Japan.

European enthusiasm over 1992 has similarly gone hand in hand with a rather sour attitude toward trade with non-European nations, and in particular, with a fairly notable failure to make any concessions on agriculture that would help make the Uruguay Round a success and thus help sustain the GATT's credibility.

Suppose that one could make the following two-part argument:

(1) By focusing on regional free trade, the United States and the EC have diverted political energies away from working on the problems of the GATT.

(2) Had they committed themselves to working within a multi-lateral framework, they could have achieved a solution to the GATT's difficulties that would have led to better results than the local solutions they have achieved instead.

If one believed this argument, one could then believe that the rise of free trade agreements has had an overall negative effect.

Part (1) of the argument clearly has some validity. Free trade agreements in Europe and North America have diverted some political, administrative, and intellectual capital away from the multilateral negotiating process. They have also reduced the sense of urgency about getting on with that process.

But would the GATT process really have done much better in the absence of moves toward regional free trade? This does not seem too plausible. The GATT's problems are deep-seated; it is hard to imagine achieving anything at the global level remotely approaching what the EC and the Canadian-U.S. pact have accomplished. And the problem of Japan seems extremely intractable.

It is understandable that economists and trade negotiators who have grown up in a world in which multilateral negotiations were the centerpiece of trade policy would be disturbed by a shift in emphasis toward regional agreements, especially if that shift seems to impair the effectiveness of the multilateral process—which it does. But while the move to free trade areas has surely done the multilateral process some harm, it is almost surely more a symptom than a cause of the decline of the GATT.

The impact of the move toward free trade zones

An unsophisticated view would see Europe 1992 and the move toward North American free trade as unadulterated good things. Global free trade would be better still, but these moves at least are in the right direction. And even if one is dismayed by the disappointments of the Uruguay Round, one may still take comfort in the continuing integration of markets at a more local level.

A more sophisticated view sees both economic and political shadows. Free trade areas are not necessarily a good thing economically, because they may lead to trade diversion rather than trade creation. In the highly imperfect politics of international trade, regional free trade zones could upset the balance of forces that has allowed the creation of a fairly liberal world trading system.

The basic message of this paper is that the unsophisticated reaction is wrong in theory but right in practice. The prospects of trade diversion from free trade areas are limited, because the prospective trading blocs mostly fall along the lines of "natural" trading areas, countries that in any case do a disproportionate amount of their trade with one another. While regionalism does to some extent probably undermine the political force behind multilateral trade negotiations, the problems of the GATT are so deep-seated that it is unlikely that a world without regional free trade agreements would do much better.

The world may well be breaking up into three trading blocs; trade within those blocs will be quite free, while trade between the blocs will at best be no freer than it is now and may well be considerably less free. This is not what we might have hoped for. But the situation would not be better, and could easily have been worse, had the great free trade agreements of recent years never happened.

Appendix: Trading Blocs and World Welfare

This appendix lays out a simple model of the relationship between the number of trading blocs in the world economy and world welfare. It is based on Krugman (1991); as discussed in the text, it is intended as a guide to framing the issue rather than as a realistic tool for calculating the effects of free trade zones.

We imagine a world whose basic units are geographic units that we will refer to as "provinces." There are a large number N of such provinces in the world. A country in general consists of a large number of provinces. For the analysis here, however, we ignore the country level, focusing instead on "trading blocs" that contain a number of countries and hence a larger number of provinces. There will be assumed to be B<N trading blocs in the world. They are symmetric, each containing N/B provinces (with the problem of whole numbers ignored). In this simplified world, the issue of free trade zones reduces to the following: how does world welfare depend on B?

Each province produces a single good that is an imperfect substitute for the products of all other provinces. We choose units so that each province produces one unit of its own good, and assume that all provincial goods enter symmetrically into demand, with a constant elasticity of substitution between any pair of goods. Thus everyone in the world has tastes represented by the CES utility function

$$U = \left[\sum_{i=1}^{N} c_i^{\theta} \right]^{1/\theta},\tag{1}$$

where c_i is consumption of the good of province i, and the elasticity of substitution between any pair of products is

$$\sigma = \frac{1}{1-\theta}.\tag{2}$$

A trading bloc is a group of provinces with internal free trade and a common external ad valorem tariff. We ignore the realistic politics of trade policy, and simply assume that each bloc sets a tariff that maximizes welfare, taking the policies of other trading blocs as given. This is a standard problem in international economics: the optimal tariff for a bloc is

$$t^* = \frac{1}{\varepsilon - 1} \, , \tag{3}$$

where ε is the elasticity of demand for the bloc's exports.

In a symmetric equilibrium in which all blocs charge the same tariff rate, it is possible to show that (see Krugman 1991)

$$\varepsilon = s + (1 - s) \, \sigma \, , \tag{4}$$

where s is the share of each bloc in the rest of the world's income measured at world prices. The optimal tariff is therefore

$$t^* = \frac{1}{(1 - s) \, (\sigma - 1)} \, . \tag{5}$$

It is apparent from (5) that the larger the share of each bloc's exports in the income of the world outside the bloc, the higher will be the level of tariffs on intra-bloc trade. This immediately suggests that a consolidation of the world into fewer, larger blocs will lead to higher barriers on inter-bloc trade.

One cannot quite stop here, however, because the share of each bloc in the rest of the world's spending depends both on the number of blocs and on the worldwide level of tariffs. Again after some algebra it is possible to show that this share equals

$$s = \frac{1}{(1 + t)^{\sigma} + B - 1} \, , \tag{6}$$

so that the share of each bloc's exports in the rest of the world's income is decreasing in both the tariff rate and the number of blocs.

Equations (5) and (6) simultaneously determine the tariff rate and the export share for a given number of blocs B. In Figure 1, the downward-sloping curve *SS* represents (6); it shows that the higher is the worldwide level of tariffs, the lower the share of each bloc in the spending of other blocs. The curve *TT* represents (5); it shows that the optimal tariff rate is higher, the smaller that export share. Equilibrium is at point *E*, where each bloc is levying the unilaterally optimal tariff.

Now suppose that there is a consolidation of the world into a smaller number of blocs. We see from (6) that for any given tariff rate, the effect of the reduction in B is increase *s*; thus *SS* shifts up to *S′ S′*. As a result, tariff rates rise, as equilibrium shifts from *E* to *E′*.

Clearly this change will reduce the volume of trade between any two provinces that are in different blocs. Even at an unchanged tariff, the removal of trade barriers between members of the expanded bloc would divert some trade that would otherwise have taken place between blocs. This trade diversion would be reinforced by the rise in the tariff rate.

Figure 1

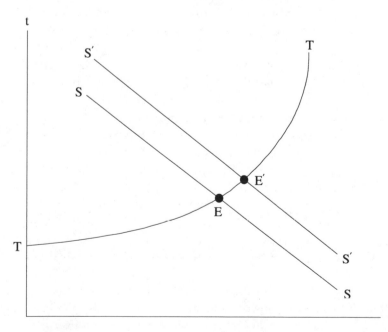

We now turn to welfare. Given the utility function (1), it is possible to calculate the welfare of a representative province as a function of the total number of provinces N, the number of blocs B, and the tariff rate *t* on inter-bloc trade. Since N plays no role in the analysis, we can simplify matters somewhat by normalizing N to equal 1. Again after considerable algebra, given in Krugman (1991), we find that the utility of a representative province is

$$U = \left[\frac{B}{(1+t)^{\sigma} + b - 1} \right] [(1 - B^{-1}) + B^{-1}(1 + t)^{\sigma \theta}]^{1/\theta}. \qquad (7)$$

If trade were free, this would imply a utility of 1. Since the tariff rate *t* is also a function of B, we can use (5), (6), and (7) together to determine how world welfare varies with the number of trading blocs.

The easiest way to proceed at this point is to solve the model numerically. This grossly over-simplified model has only two parameters, the number of trading blocs and the elasticity of sub-stitution between any pair of provinces; it is therefore straightfor-ward to solve first for tariffs as a function of B given several possible values of the elasticity, and then to calculate the implied effect on world welfare. Here the values of ε considered are 2, 4, and 10.

Figure 2 shows how world tariff rates vary with the number of blocs. Two points are worth noting. First, the relationship between tariff rates and the number of blocs is fairly flat. The reason is that when there are fewer blocs, trade diversion tends to reduce interbloc trade, and thus leads to less of a rise in each bloc's share of external markets than one might have expected. Second, except in the case of an implausibly high elasticity of demand, predicted tariff rates are much higher than one actually observes among advanced nations. This is not an artifact of the economic model: virtually all calcu-lations suggest than unilateral optimum tariff rates are very high. What it tells us, therefore, is that actual trade relationships among advanced countries are far more cooperative than envisaged here.

Finally, we calculate welfare. Figure 3 shows the results. World welfare is, of course, maximized when there is only one bloc, in

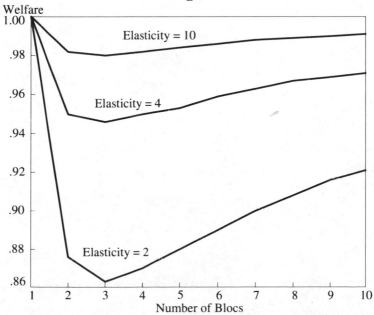

Figure 2

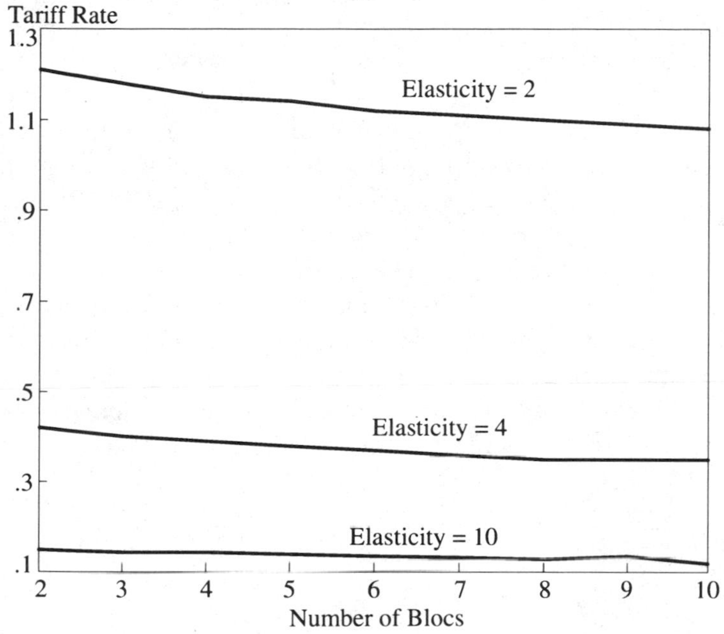

Tariff Rate
1.3
1.1
.9
.7
.5
.3
.1
Elasticity = 2
Elasticity = 4
Elasticity = 10
2
3
4
5
6
7
8
9
10
Number of Blocs

Figure 3

Welfare
1.00
.98
.96
.94
.92
.90
.88
.86
Elasticity = 10
Elasticity = 4
Elasticity = 2
1
2
3
4
5
6
7
8
9
10
Number of Blocs

other words, global free trade. As suggested informally in the text, however, the relationship between welfare and the number of trading blocs is not monotonic but U-shaped. World welfare reaches a minimum when there are a few large blocs, and would be higher if there were more blocs, each with less market power.

The figure also shows a startling result: for the full range of elasticities considered, world welfare is minimized when there are three blocs.

As pointed out in the text, however, this result is an artifact of the assumption that under free trade any two provinces will trade as much as any other pair. That is, it ignores geography, which gives rise to natural trading blocs; as argued there, in practice, the strength of this natural linkage is strong enough to make it unlikely that consolidation of the world into regional blocs would actually reduce welfare.

Endnotes

[1] Indeed, this is one of those concepts that tends to get lost if one uses anything more high-powered than a numerical example.

[2] Hopes for large benefits from both the U.S.-Canada free trade agreement and Europe 1992 rest largely on increased competition and rationalization. In the North American case, the estimates of Harris and Cox (1984), which attempt to take account of competitive/industrial organization effects, suggest a gain for Canada from free trade that is about four times as large as those of standard models. In Europe, the widely cited, although controversial figure of a 7 percent gain due to 1992, presented in the Cecchini Report (Commission of the European Communities, 1988) rests primarily on estimates by Alasdair Smith and Anthony Venables of gains from increased competition and rationalization.

[3] Bhagwati and others have, of course, a much subtler view than this. They are not so much concerned with the fear that trading blocs will pursue optimal tariff policies as with the fear that regional trade negotiations will shift political resources away from the task of defending global trade against special interest politics. So this approach is only a rough metaphor for a real political story to be described in the paper's second part.

[4] This setup is clearly both too cynical and not cynical enough about the political economy of trade. The internal politics of trade are not nearly this benign. Governments do not simply (or ever) maximize the welfare of their citizens. At the same time, the external politics of trade show far more cooperation than this. An attempt at more realism follows later in the paper.

[5] The cost of an increase in protection here may seem surprisingly small. It is a familiar proposition to those who work with quantitative trade models, however, that the estimated costs of protection usually turn out to be embarrassingly small.

[6] It is surely also not irrelevant that with the collapse of the Soviet empire, the national security argument for fostering free trade among U.S. allies has suddenly lost its force.

[7] I believe that concerns that Japan is fundamentally different, and that negotiated trade liberalization is largely ineffective for Japan, are justified; but what is important here is not what is true but what is believed.

References

Commission of the European Communities. *The Economics of 1992, European Economy,* No. 35. Luxembourg: Commission of the European Communities, 1988.

Harris, R., and D. Cox. "Trade Liberalization and Industrial Organization: Some Estimates for Canada," *Journal of Political Economy,* 1985. pp. 115-145.

Kemp, M., and H. Wan. "An Elementary Proposition Concerning the Formation of Customs Unions," *International Economic Review,* 1976. pp. 95-97.

Krugman, P. "Is Bilateralism Bad?" in E. Helpman and A. Razin, eds., *International Trade and Trade Policy*, Cambridge: MIT Press, 1991.

Viner, J. *The Customs Union Issue.* New York: Carnegie Endowment for International Peace, 1950.

Commentary: The Move Toward Free Trade Zones

C. Fred Bergsten

There are three central strands to Paul Krugman's analysis of free trade areas (FTAs):

—that they are considerably better in practice than in theory;

—that this is particularly the case when they are viewed as *alternatives* to multilateral trade liberalization because "half a loaf is better than none;"

—which is how they should be viewed because of the demise of the GATT and the poor prospects for the Uruguay Round .

My view is fundamentally different on all three counts:

—that FTAs are considerably less desirable than Krugman suggests, especially in practice;

—that this is *particularly* true if they are seen as alternatives to an effective global trading system;

—but that, fortunately, they need *not* be seen as alternatives because the Uruguay Round is quite likely to succeed, thereby restoring the credibility and central role of the GATT and making the world safe for FTAs which, as *complements* to such a global system, are acceptable and even desirable.

The big picture

Before discussing FTAs in detail, it is essential to place the issue of trade (and currency) zones—the topic of this conference—within the context of the sweeping structural changes that will dominate the world economy in the 1990s and beyond.

The first of these historic transformations is the onset of full economic tripolarity. By sometime in this decade, if not already, the three economic superpowers—uniting Europe, Japan, and the United States—will look much more alike than different.

—In terms of absolute economic size, Europe will be bigger than the United States. Japan, already the largest creditor country and most competitive national economy, will match the GNP of both early in the twenty-first century even on conservative assumptions concerning growth rates and exchange rates.

—In terms of economic openness, defined as the share of exports plus imports of goods and services in GNP, the three are already virtually identical. This ratio has changed very little over the past two decades for Japan and the European Community as a group but has risen sharply for the United States.

Hence, *there is no longer any economic basis for American hegemony,* rightly described by Allen Meltzer in his paper as a major element in bringing relative prosperity and stability to the postwar world.

This outcome is reinforced by the second historic transformation: the end of the Cold War. The Cold War provided a "security blanket" over the trans-Atlantic and trans-Pacific relationships for almost half a century, suppressing potential conflicts on economic and other issues in the overriding interest of maintaining firm alliances against the Soviet threat. That security blanket has now been pulled aside: neither Europe nor Japan any longer needs much American protection, and the United States no longer needs to strengthen its allies—who also happen to be its chief economic competitors. Hence, *there is no longer any security basis for American hegemony either.*[1]

The Gulf War reinforces the conclusion that America's economic dominance is a thing of the past despite its new status as the only military superpower. The United States had to insist that other countries pay for the war—the first admission of such economic dependence by a military leader in modern history. And, despite American efforts to lever its leadership of the Gulf coalition into greater foreign cooperation in the Uruguay Round and G-7 policy coordination, there appears to date to be zero transferability of military power into economic payoff (beyond the payments for the war itself).

The policy choice: globalism or blocs?

Economic (and other issues) are now much more likely to produce conflict among the Big Three because of the onset of equal tripolar economic power and the elimination of the Cold War glue that bound the allies together. Hence, these historic transformations are central to the question of trade and currency zones. In broad strategic terms, the Big Three—who together will clearly dominate the world economy for at least the next few decades—can evolve in only two directions:

—into an informal steering committee (G-3) to revitalize and subsequently maintain a *globally oriented economic system* based largely on the existing institutional framework or

—into the poles of *regional blocs* where, for the reasons posited by Andrew Crockett in his paper, the dynamics would move from trade arrangements into deeper economic integration and then monetary zones and, as Krugman himself notes, the resulting entities would likely become exclusionary and discriminatory.

Hence, the issue of trade (and currency) zones is far more important than welfare triangles or even dynamic gains from trade. The outcome of the current trade debate will go far to shape the course of the world economy for the coming decades. There will be significant political effects as well—especially if, as Krugman suggests, trade zones were pursued partly to discriminate against a major economic actor (Japan).

There is a widespread view around the world, sufficiently powerful that it is rapidly becoming a self-fulfilling prophecy, that we are headed toward the second outcome: regional blocs. The deepening and widening of European economic unity—toward "completion of the single market" in 1992, Economic and Monetary Union (EMU), and the addition of more members and associates (including Eastern Europe)—generate defensive reactions in the Americas and Asia. Initiatives by the United States toward a North American Free Trade Area (NAFTA) and the Enterprise for the Americas Initiative (EAI) produce Asian fears that "the Western Hemisphere is going regional too," both generating proposals for exclusionary regional groupings there (notably Malaysia's East Asian Economic Grouping) and making it harder for Japan and others to resist such calls. The resulting "evidence" of burgeoning Asian regionalism reinforces advocacy of similar steps in the Americas. Some Europeans then cite both to justify the inward-looking focus of their own initiatives. The critical importance of renewing the postwar momentum of trade liberalization on a *global* basis, the only alternative to eventual realization of the prophecy, is shunted aside in the rush toward regionalism. Krugman's paper unfortunately supports this spiral by prematurely writing an obituary for the Uruguay Round, which he rightly suggests is essential to restoring momentum and credibility for the multilateral system.

A revitalized global system managed collectively by the Big Three is far superior to a devolution into regionalism. Within such a system, regional arrangements would still take place but they would complement the global order rather than substitute for it. I believe that it is still eminently possible to forge such a global approach:

—As pointed out by both Allan Meltzer and Jacob Frenkel and Morris Goldstein, the trade patterns of the Americas and Asia are quintessentially multilateral. They have experienced *no* long-run trends toward increased reliance on intraregional trade. Indeed, the trade patterns of both the United States and Japan—the core countries of the supposed blocs—are split into almost equal thirds. These countries have no interest in substituting regional for global arrangements. Europe is now the only bloc but the share of extraregional trade in its GDP is even greater than for the Americas or Asia, so it, too, needs a multilateral world.[2]

—The markets of the three economic superpowers (and much of the rest of the world) are deeply intertwined. There would be enormous economic costs from any significant erosion of global trade and financial openness, and resulting political costs for those who let it happen.

—The Big Three are democracies, have been allies for more than four decades, and have a habit of working closely together on economic issues. Despite the absence of historical precedents for effective cooperative leadership, they should be able to provide it.

—Though the Uruguay Round has clearly faltered, multilateral trade negotiations always resemble "the Perils of Pauline." The prospects for both the Kennedy and Tokyo Rounds looked extremely grim at key points before their eventual successes. The "failure" to conclude the Uruguay Round at Brussels in December 1990 should have come as no surprise because the only real deadline for such talks is the expiration of the negotiating authority extended to the U.S. Administration by the Congress—a deadline set for June *1993* by the Trade Act of 1988 and duly reaffirmed by extension of the 1990 "fast track" authority in May 1991. The Uruguay Round is quite likely to achieve major success, probably greater than either the Kennedy or Tokyo Rounds, if only because the costs of failure would be so high in both economic and political (especially United States-Europe) terms.

Does it matter?

The central issue is whether global or regional trade liberalization

is superior and, in particular, whether there need be any conflict
between them. Krugman recognizes that trade blocs are decidedly
second best because they generate trade diversion and because
"they would upset the balance of forces that has allowed the creation
of a fairly liberal world trading system." He attacks the "proposals"
for "unnatural" (that is, non-neighborly) free trade agreements,
such as U.S.-Israel (which has been in place since 1985) and
U.S.-Korea. He himself points out that "world welfare is *minimized*
(my emphasis) for a world of three trading blocs."

But Krugman goes on to endorse blocs, arguing that prospective
diversion is modest because they are likely to take place mainly
among geographical neighbors and thus the blocs "mostly fall along
the lines of 'natural' trading areas." This is an empirical question
on which Krugman offers little supportive evidence. There are four
reasons why I believe the view is flawed.

First, the impact of geography on trade has declined dramatically
in recent decades. Geographical propinquity is no longer central to
trading patterns.[3] For example, American trade is much denser with
Korea and Taiwan—"unnatural trading partners" in Krugman's
view—than with Argentina and Brazil, even adjusting for the different size of the respective economies.

Second, partly as a result (and as already noted), there are no major
"natural trading areas" anyway except for Europe and possibly
NAFTA. United States and Japanese trade is split into almost equal
thirds. The Americas and Asia as a whole are highly diversified. The
concept of "natural trading areas" rationalizes the EC and NAFTA
but provides no guidance beyond.

Third, it must be candidly recognized that trade diversion is a *goal*
of many contemporary proposals for trade blocs. Canada sought
primarily to achieve preferential treatment (that is, exceptions) under
any new protectionist steps by the United States. Mexico is driven
importantly by a similar motive. As already noted, and stressed by
Krugman, anti-Japanese sentiment lies near the surface of many FTA
initiatives. Such a desire for discrimination suggests that it could
very well occur.

Fourth, Krugman's supposition that neighboring countries would be the primary beneficiaries of trade liberalization anyway—so why *not* proceed on a regional basis?—does not stand up in practice, at least in the case of the Western Hemisphere. The hypothesis can be tested by assuming U.S. liberalization on an MFN basis and asking which countries would "naturally" get the business. Tariffs are already so low that their elimination would not make much difference. Hence, the outcome would be determined primarily by the new trade patterns generated by liberalization of the seven large U.S. import quota regimes:[4]

(1) Textiles and apparel: East Asian, South Asian and some other developing countries are far more competitive than Latin America.

(2) Steel: Brazil and Mexico could take some advantage but the major increases would accrue to Europe and Japan.

(3) Automobiles: Mexico and perhaps Brazil could expand sales of parts but the overwhelming increases would come from Japan, Korea and possibly Europe.

(4) Machine tools: virtually all new imports would come from Europe, Japan and Taiwan.

(5) Dairy products: the bulk of the increased trade would emanate from Australia, New Zealand and Europe.

(6) Sugar: several Latin American countries could compete effectively if U.S. quotas were lifted, but Australia and several others outside the Hemisphere would also be major beneficiaries.

(7) Meat: several Latin American countries could gain markets but the bulk of the increased imports would derive from Australia and New Zealand.[5]

The lesson is that trade liberalization by the United States on a regional basis would almost certainly generate much more trade with uncompetitive countries than with efficient suppliers. Economic welfare would be reduced to the extent that current (efficiently produced) imports were supplanted by less efficiently produced imports. For example, the United States has already unilaterally increased Mexico's share of its textile quotas while deducting a like amount from the quotas of Hong Kong and other Asian suppliers. Since the latter are considerably more efficient, the shift has further increased the welfare costs of the textile quotas to the American economy.[6]

Beyond this central point, there are a number of additional reasons why Krugman's advocacy of trade zones does not stand up in practice:

—His conceptual case for free trade arrangements, akin to the optimal tariff argument, is that they can strengthen the region's terms of trade by increasing its weight in the global economy and permitting it to extract better prices from its trading partners. This would, however, by definition hurt other countries. Moreover, it has very little to do with the contemporary world: "EC 1992" and EMU emphasize deepening rather than broadening of Europe's economic zone, and the creation of NAFTA would add less than 15 percent to the weight already exercised by the United States in the world economy.

—He is simply wrong to argue that regional trade deals produce bigger results than global deals. The United States-Canada FTA, contrary to his assertion, was a mouse in terms of liberalization: on the biggest issues, like agriculture and subsidies, the countries explicitly deferred to the Uruguay Round because there was not enough benefit on other issues in the bilateral context to justify taking on the domestic opponents.[7] Is it conceivable that America's textile quotas could be liberalized more meaningfully in NAFTA than in GATT, where the offsetting "gains" (in GATT-think terms) would at least give the effort a fighting chance?

—He notes that, to an economist, unilateral liberalism is best but fails to observe that countries all over the world are practicing it: Australia and New Zealand, Eastern Europe and many in both Asia and Latin America. A successful Uruguay Round can induce these countries to bind their new regimes and thus obviate the risk of reversal. On the other hand, a withering of GATT would make it much easier for them to reverse gears—and could even compel them to try to strike defensive deals with one or another bloc instead that would include the erection of new barriers against outsiders.

—This would clearly include "unnatural" alignments of the type that Krugman himself denounces. In particular, few Asian countries want to join a bloc led by Japan. The United States is unlikely to "settle for" Latin America, both because such insulation from the most dynamic world markets would erode its own competitiveness over time (as Britain's preferences within the Empire and, later, Commonwealth, undermined its economic strength) and because all the other countries in the Hemisphere are also debtors and cannot help the United States improve its trade balance. Moreover, the United States could hardly push for a Western Hemisphere bloc and oppose Japan's pushing for an Asian bloc—as it clearly would—without offering the Asians a place in its own "regional" arrangement. Hence there would almost certainly be an "unnatural" trans-Pacific dimension to a world of trading areas.

—The increasingly central global role of multinational enterprises adds to the potential for a negative dynamic if a world of blocs were ever to get seriously under way: once positioned within each bloc to hedge themselves, the companies would enjoy relative gains from the erosion of interbloc trading freedom and would, at a minimum, no longer espouse global liberalization. Other constituencies within member countries of a bloc also acquire a distaste for global liberalization and thus add to the exclusionary dynamic.

—Krugman strangely ignores the historical absence of any successful free trade agreements between industrial and developing countries, despite the centrality of this issue to any meaningful construction of blocs in Asia and the Americas. The difficulties in combining Japan and China, or even the United States and Mexico, loom considerably larger than meshing Greece and Portugal with the EC—and even that arrangement includes transfers of public capital equal to 5 percent of the GNP of the LDC partners.

—Indeed, as Krugman notes, the biggest losers from a world of regional blocs would be those left outside—which, in practice, would be primarily the poorest developing countries which could least afford it.

—One can only cringe when Krugman argues that "the great advantage of regional pacts is that they can exclude Japan." Many Americans and Europeans certainly do "deeply distrust the Japanese," as he asserts. It does not take much knowledge either of history or of contemporary thinking in Japan, however, to conclude that steps to institutionalize, rather than combat, that distrust would run enormous risks. History teaches that failure to accommodate rising powers in the systemic structure is a sure recipe for serious conflict.

—On the political economy plane, both the United States and Japan have sufficient national power to be world leaders without forming blocs around them. No individual European country does; hence bloc creation was essential to restore that area as a global player but such considerations hold nowhere else.

—It would be particularly tragic if the countries that created and nurtured the global trading system and the GATT, notably the United States and to a degree the EC, were to turn their backs on it now when (a) virtually all of the countries which have heretofore rejected that regime are now clamoring to get in (the USSR, China, East Europe, and most of Latin America) and (b) the developing countries have, in the Uruguay Round, for the first time become active participants in it.

Would FTAs undermine globalism?

Regional trading arrangements are clearly going to happen: further deepening and eventually broadening in Europe, NAFTA, and perhaps the Enterprise for the Americas Initiative in this hemisphere, Australia-New Zealand, and even conceivably an East Asian Economic Grouping per the current Malaysian proposal. Another possibility is a Pacific Basin construct, growing out of the recent Asia-Pacific Economic Cooperation initiative.

The crucial question is whether these arrangements take place within the context of an effective and credible *global* system. If so, they will be—and will be viewed as—*supplements* to that system between countries that choose to liberalize further together, perhaps providing a constructive challenge for emulation at the global level.

Indeed, it is the existence of tariff bindings under GATT (along with the proscriptions of Article XXIV itself) that prevent bloc members from raising barriers toward the outside world to exploit the potential gains described by Krugman. Even more importantly, it was the major liberalizing negotiations under the GATT—the Kennedy Round in response to the creation of the Common Market itself and the Tokyo Round in response to its broadening to include the United Kingdom and others—that achieved the reductions in the common external tariff of the EC that, as he correctly notes, were essential to convert the European Community from a beggar-thy-neighbor arrangement into a positive force for the world economy.[8] At a minimum, a strong GATT system is essential to avoid the costs that Krugman acknowledges are quite likely to result from FTAs.

If there is no effective GATT system, FTAs would almost certainly come to be viewed as *alternatives* to globalism. In that case, they would almost certainly evolve over time—as Krugman suggests —in an exclusionary and eventually discriminatory direction. The economic costs would be significant and growing. The political effects would, at a minimum, be worrisome.

The present stalemate in the Uruguay Round has sharply raised the prospect of the regional path. If the Uruguay Round were to fail, the trend toward regionalism almost certainly *would* accelerate. And it will be much harder to avoid "failure" of this multilateral negotiation than in the past because a modest agreement that tries to paper over the major problems would be denounced as such by the growing corps of proponents of regionalism as well as others; world leaders and trade officials can no longer " declare victory and go home."

The United States usually plays the pivotal role on international trade issues. It will do so even more in this case. Europe is already a bloc and Asia is clearly not, so the United States will tip the balance. It is thus imperative for the United States to continue to make clear that its priority is a successful outcome to the Uruguay Round.

The United States was motivated to negotiate the FTA with Canada, in the wake of the failed GATT Ministerial of late 1982, primarily to spur the launch of what became the Uruguay Round.[9] It fully intended to complete the Uruguay Round before negotiating NAFTA, reaffirming the primacy of the global system. It has held back on any substantive negotiations with Latin American countries, other than Mexico, despite the eagerness of Chile and others to commence such talks.

The "failure" at Brussels in December 1990, however, means that NAFTA may now be concluded before—or simultaneously with— the Uruguay Round. Hence the United States will be characterized as "joining the rush toward regionalism." This will reinforce the self-fulfilling prophecy, as noted above, making it harder for Japan and others in Asia to resist blandishments such as Malaysia's to pursue defensive arrangements of their own.

As important as continued American fealty to a successful Uruguay Round is full support for such an outcome from Europe and Japan. Europe bears a special responsibility in this context. As the only trade bloc, it has done much to stimulate similar developments in other parts of the world. Its current inward orientation, while unlikely to produce a "Fortress Europe," has raised anxieties elsewhere and intensified the risk of realization of the self-fulfilling prophecy. The EC has been the key partner of the United States in achieving successful outcomes of the last two global trade negotiations; it has both a major interest in, and major responsibility for, doing so again.

The stakes are even higher than the future of the international trading system, however. As noted at the outset, the overarching issue for world economic policy in the decade or more ahead is whether the Big Three can effectively co-manage a reinvigorated global order. The Uruguay Round is one of the first test cases. If the Big Three cannot deal with a few farmers and other recalcitrant interest groups, they will hardly be able to provide global leadership on the wide array of issues—including money, macroeconomic cooperation, energy, and the environment as well as trade and the GATT—where it will be needed.

The monetary dimension

Finally, it is necessary to note that the one monetary bloc now extant and potentially expanding in the near future—again, in Europe—could also raise significant problems for the global system.

A successful move to EMU will convert Europe from a series of small and medium-sized open economies into one large and much less open economy. This change alone will have several effects:

—It will tend to increase the extent of currency fluctuations among Europe, America, and Japan—generating greater international financial instability and potentially misalignments that would distort trade and add further to the tendencies toward trade protection outlined above.

—It will tempt Europe to practice "benign neglect" from time to time, as the other large and relatively closed economy has done, or at least to try to force the costs of adjustment onto others as the United States has also done.

—If it fails to achieve a unified fiscal policy to go with its unified monetary policy, there will be a strong possibility of a Europe-wide repetition of Reaganomics from the early 1980s and the German policy mix of the early 1990s: large fiscal stimulus,

very tight money, a sharp appreciation of the currency, big
trade deficits, and resultant protectionism.

—Without a political master, the European Central Bank will
be particularly likely to foster such an outcome. This will be
especially true in its early years, as it seeks to prove its fealty
to the goal of price stability and to discipline recalcitrant
governments into fiscal rectitude.

Moreover, achievement of EMU—even without the final step of a
single currency, but especially with it—will propel the ECU to a
central role in a new multiple reserve currency system. This will
both reflect and produce a substantial portfolio adjustment from
(mainly) dollars into ECU, reinforcing the likely appreciation of
European currencies with attendant trade balance and protectionist
problems. This effect would be further accelerated if the EMU
pooled Europe's monetary reserves and attempted to dispose of some
of the "excess," identified by the EC Commission as on the order
of $200 billion.[10]

The policy implication is that the United States and Japan should
engage Europe in negotiations on the global monetary system while
the latter works out its regional arrangements—particularly as both
of the basic blueprints for EMU, the report of the Delors Commission[11] and Karl Otto Pöhl's design for a Eurofed,[12] totally ignored
the external dimension thereof. American strategy in the trade area
has been to engage Europe in a global negotiation at each key
milestone in its evolution: the Kennedy Round when the Common
Market was created, the Tokyo Round when it expanded to bring in
the United Kingdom and others, the Uruguay Round as it moved
toward "1992." A similar approach is needed in the monetary area
to avoid the risk that EMU will destabilize global arrangements and
that, once its details have been put in place, it will be too late. This
should be feasible now that the G-7, by successfully placing a floor
under the dollar in February 1991 and (so far) effectively capping
the dollar in July 1991, seems to be returning at least de facto to
reference ranges among the major currencies à la Louvre.

Epilogue

There is still time to restore the effectiveness and credibility of the global approach to world economic policy and its existing institutional framework. Contrary to Krugman's assertions, the Uruguay Round is still alive—and, if not totally well at this juncture, with reasonable prospects for meaningful success. EMU can still be channeled in directions that are fully compatible with global monetary stability.

The Big Three must seize leadership on both issues (and several others) and make a conscious effort to restore a global focus, however, or the regional drift will continue and perhaps accelerate. The costs of permitting such an outcome could be extremely high in both economic and political terms. Reversing it is the first major test the Big Three face in the tripolar, post-Cold War world economy of the 1990s and beyond.

Endnotes

[1]A detailed analysis of these historic transformations on the world economy can be found in C. Fred Bergsten, "The World Economy After the Cold War," *Foreign Affairs*, Summer 1990, pp. 96-112.

[2]Robert Z. Lawrence, "Emerging Regional Arrangements: Building Blocks or Stumbling Blocks?" June 1991, mimeo.

[3]The downsizing of economic activity accelerates that trend. See Alan Greenspan, "Remarks at the Annual Dinner of the Japan Society," New York, May 22, 1989.

[4]See the discussion of the impact of FTAs on nontariff barriers in Paul Wonnacott and Mark Lutz, "Is There a Case for Free Trade Areas?" in Jeffrey J. Schott, ed., *Free Trade Areas and U.S. Trade Policy*. Washington: Institute for International Economics, 1989, p. 64.

[5]These U.S. quota regimes are largely implemented through "voluntary" restraints administered by the exporting countries which are enormously costly to the United States because they transfer most of the quota rents to the exporting countries and firms. See C. Fred Bergsten, Kimberly Ann Elliott, Jeffrey J. Schott, and Wendy E. Takacs, *Auction Quotas and United States Trade Policy*. Washington: Institute for International Economics, September 1987.

[6]These costs are estimated in William R. Cline, *The Future of World Trade in Textiles and Apparel*. Washington: Institute for International Economics, Revised 1990.

[7]See Jeffrey J. Schott and Murray G. Smith, eds., *The Canada-United States Free Trade Agreement: The Global Impact*. Washington: Institute for International Economics, 1988.

[8]Excluding, of course, its agricultural component which, however, resulted from the EC's decision to create a customs union rather than a free trade area and where liberalization was severely hampered by the United States' decision to take agriculture out of the GATT in 1955 to protect its own farmers.

[9]The difference between that situation, when a regional initiative by the United States clearly promoted global liberalization, and that of today is emphasized in Jeffrey J. Schott, *More Free Trade Areas?* Washington: Institute for International Economics, 1989.

[10] See *One Market, One Money: An Evaluation of the Potential Benefits and Costs of Forming an Economic and Monetary Union*. Brussels: Commission of the European Communities, European Economy, No. 44, October 1990, Chapter 7.

[11]*Report on Economic and Monetary Union in the European Community,* prepared by the Committee for the Study of Economic and Monetary Union, April 1989.

[12]"Basic Features of a European Monetary Order," a lecture by Karl Otto Pöhl, president of the Deutsche Bundesbank, organized by *LeMonde,* Paris, January 16, 1990.

The Transformation of Trade and Monetary Regimes in Europe

Michael R. Emerson

One approach to the relationship between trade and monetary zones is through recalling the three uses of money: means of settlement, numeraire, and store of value. The first two of these bring money and trade together, but the third is a separate matter. The rate of inflation can be chosen apart from the trade regime. For this reason it has not been self-evident whether the frontiers of monetary and trade regimes should coincide.

This choice, of coincidence or not, of regimes involves a tradeoff. It is not quite the same tradeoff as the familiar Phillips curve between unemployment and inflation. But it is a cousin tradeoff, in this case between the microeconomic efficiency gains of coincidental regimes and the macroeconomic costs of not being able to pursue an independent monetary policy.

In federal countries it is taken for granted that the monetary and trade frontiers coincide. This is true not only of those with stable constitutions. It is also seen today in the USSR, where debate over the new Union-republic Treaty rightly recognizes the maintenance of the single money and single market as the litmus test of whether the Union survives or not. This is because the political structures required to manage the market and the money are at the heart of the civil functions of federations.

In the textbooks of international economics much attention is given to the opposite case of noncoincidence of frontiers: the liberal-monetarist paradigm of free trade coupled to a floating exchange rate. While this does not attract much support in practice today for intra-European affairs, it is more relevant for intercontinental economic relations.

Europe today is neither of these cases. It is a seething mass of integrationist, disintegrationist, and regime change movements. The transformation of trade and monetary regimes is the concern of virtually every government.

The options in the choice of trade and monetary regimes are in fact numerous and permit fine graduations. They are listed in Table 1 under three distinct regime variables: trade regime, currency convertibility, and exchange rate. Each of these offers a choice matrix, with degree of openness or convertibility or fixity in one dimension and the extent of regional to global coverage in the other. Several of these many combinations are being tried or considered by one government or another. Is there a pattern or trend in regime development? Let us first recall what is actually happening and then try to interpret.

What is happening to Europe's regimes?

Much is happening to the trade and monetary regimes in each of Europe's four regional groups—the European Community, EFTA, the countries of East and Central Europe (PECOs for short, to use the French acronym which appears to gain usage), and the USSR.

Within the EC the single market bulldozer maintains its momentum to the end-1992 finishing line. With one and one-half years to go, the scorecard reads 201 acts of EC legislation finally adopted out of the total of 282 required.

On the monetary side, the long march to monetary union was effectively resumed in 1988, soon after the single market program had, itself, become credible in the eyes of public and political opinion. The overall design of the monetary union campaign was established in the Delors Committee report, which became a landmark document. This led to the convening of an Inter-governmental Conference to draft a new Treaty of Economic and Monetary Union. A complete institutional infrastructure is now in an advanced state of preparation. This should be concluded by the

Table 1
Hierarchies of Trade and Monetary Regime Choices

Trade
T1 Bind trade policy internationally
T2 Free trade
T3 Customs union
T4 Single market

Currency Convertibility
C1 Current account convertibility for residents (internal convertibility, means eliminating multiple exchange rates)
C2 idem, for nonresidents too
C3 idem, plus capital account convertibility for residents
C4 idem, plus for nonresidents too = total convertibility

Exchange Rate
E1 Float
E2 Crawl or soft peg
E3 Hard peg
E4 Monetary union (really fixed exchange rate or single currency, requiring total convertibility)

Notes:
Countries beginning their integration into the world economy may choose regime T1+C1+E1 or E2, and this may well be at a global rather than regional level.

Countries that are fully integrated will operate regime T4+C4+E4, necessarily at a regional level. This usually means political federation, but there are also examples that combine small dependencies with larger powers.

As the trade regime becomes more integrated with elements of T2, T3, and T4, it will certainly become broken up in geographic coverage (except for the case of unilateral free trade), with a two-or-more-tier system (also sharing a T1 regime with other regions). The monetary regime may also become a two-tier system, in the case that there is pegging to a regional system with E2 or E3, and must do so with E4.

end of 1991, ready for ratification by all national parliaments in the course of 1992. A second, parallel Treaty on Political Union is also being prepared, which will mature somewhat the powers of the EC institutions in several domains of microeconomic policy as well as foreign and security policy. Both treaties should be available for use by the beginning of 1993, coinciding with the completion of the single market. The date of commencement of the monetary union is so far unknown, and will remain a politically controlled rather than automatically triggered decision. It might be expected in the second half of the 1990s. Meanwhile there have been some important steps consolidating the European Monetary System, Spain and the United Kingdom joining the exchange rate mechanism with the wider 6 percent margins, and Italy graduating to the narrower margins of the core group.

The EFTA countries negotiate with the EC a "European Economic Space," which would mean being practically within the single market, but without full membership of the EC. Designed as a stopgap measure before either side was ready for another enlargement of the European Community, these negotiations are proving not particularly easy to conclude (rather like a contract to get 90 percent married). The stickiest points seem to be fishing rights, financial contributions to EC regional policy, and trans-Alpine transport rules. Meanwhile Austria and Sweden became impatient and tabled full EC membership applications (in mid-1990 and mid-1991, respectively), but without wishing to interrupt the Economic Space negotiations which have a more immediate time-horizon in any case. The Commission of the EC, late in July 1991, decided to recommend to the council the opening of accession negotiations in 1993. It is widely expected that Norway will follow Austria and Sweden in lodging a membership application, and political taboos over considering such a move appear to be evaporating in Finland and Switzerland.

Monetarily, Austria and Switzerland have long pegged to the deutsche mark. The Nordic countries until recently all pegged to their own preferred baskets. Norway, which had been considering various forms of association with the European Monetary System for some time, switched unilaterally to peg on the ECU in 1990.

Sweden and Finland followed in 1991.

Before moving to the PECOs, let us not overlook the special case of the ex-East Germany. In 1990, we saw the biggest bang regime change in peacetime history, with total and virtually instant change for the domestic economy coming under the law of the Federal Republic and the EC, the trade regime as part of the EC, and money with extension of the deutsche mark area. Creative destruction proceeds with little compromise but much budgetary support from the federal budget, as industrial production collapsed to the extent of 60 percent in the first year. The beginnings of a building boom may now be a leading indicator of recovery and, eventually, a new *Wirtschaftswunder.*

For the regular PECOs the regime changes are also decisive but less immediately clear-cut. Nonetheless liberalization, privatization, and stabilization measures flow in rivers. Some surprises emerge on the speed of reform by country, with Bulgaria moving ahead fast (Commission of the EC 1991).

The predominant external trade and monetary systems of the PECOs collapsed simultaneously in the first half of 1991. While Comecon was legally wound up in this period, the economic collapse of these extraordinarily deep trade relations (50 to 60 percent drop in trade volumes) was precipitated by the USSR's insistence that from January 1, 1991, all transactions should be contracted and settled in world prices and hard currency. Economic historians may take a while to sort out quite what happened amid contributing causes (lack of hard currency liquidity, other sources of disruption in the USSR, and so on). In any event, major PECO enterprises such as URSUS tractors in Poland and ICARUS buses in Hungary are on the brink of bankruptcy. Within the USSR the chronic shortages of industrial inputs from the PECOs contributed to the loss of 10 percent of GDP in the first half of 1991, compared with a year earlier. For students of linkages between trade and monetary regimes, here was a case of radical disintegration of both together.

The trade regimes of the PECOs see two important tendencies. First, the leaders of the group are scrapping quantitative restrictions and administrative licensing systems, replacing them with relatively uniform tariff levels averaging around 20 percent. Second, Poland, Hungary, and the Czech and Slovak Federative Republic (CSFR) have all set their sights on eventual membership in the EC. While political objectives here are obviously important, the economic point is to establish a firm reference and discipline for their internal market policies. The EC has accepted to enter already into negotiations with these countries over a new form of association agreement, in which the ultimate objective would figure in the preamble (even if the EC discourages hope for prematurely rapid accession).

Monetarily the PECOs have been moving fast to establish some kind of internal convertibility for their currencies, coupled to price liberalization. Two countries have not been able to avoid episodes of hyperinflation (Poland and Yugoslavia). Stabilization policies have made some use of exchange rate pegging, usually to baskets. Inflation performances now see these countries in three groups: the CSFR and Bulgaria in single digits, Poland and Hungary at around 30 percent, and Romania and Yugoslavia at around 100 percent.

Within the USSR there have been both trade disintegration and monetary disintegration. Early this year inter-republican trade barriers began to proliferate in the form of export controls and refusals to supply. Some republics prepare or consider introducing their own currencies (the Baltics and the Ukraine). Ration coupon systems also proliferate, and these become in some cases, quasi-currencies. The Ukraine embarks now on overstamping rubles with a "U" in order to have an own currency more efficient than ration coupons. These tendencies became so alarming in early 1991 that the leaders of nine republics and the Union resolved to work constructively together to agree on a new Union-republic Treaty. This culminated in a large degree of agreement on a text late in July, which is now to be open for formal signing.

The USSR's external trade and monetary regime is now characterized most sharply by the massive gap between the official, commercial exchange rate of the ruble ($1=1.6R) and the market rate (official tourist rate, auction rates, black market), which range from 26 to 36 to the dollar. This discrepancy of between 15 to 20 times is much wider than even the maximum observed in Poland before the monetary reforms there of 1990 (seven times). The USSR authorities have rightly come to give prominence to the objective of eliminating these multiple rates with internal convertibility of the ruble, as of January 1, 1992 according to official plans. However, the necessary accompanying measures are not yet clearly established, while President Gorbachev's submission to the London Summit argued that external financial aid would be required to make this possible at all quickly.

What are the driving forces?

The EC began the 1980s with a high but incomplete degree of market integration. The young European Monetary System also marked an intention to become more integrated monetarily. One could imagine, replaying history, that the EC could have been content with this as a status quo. Instead, integration ambitions were radicalized with the 1992 program and now that also for Economic and Monetary Union. Why did this happen, noting also the time lag of the monetary action about five years behind that for the market?

The single market program was a reaction to the period of Euro-pessimism of the early 1980s. The EC felt itself falling behind both the United States (then enjoying the Reaganomics boom) and Japan. The intuitions of the politicians and business interests coincided: to create a truly frontier-free EC market of more than 300 million consumers would result in a dynamic impetus, boosting investment and efficiency. Economists were invited to examine how this might be so (Commission of the EC, 1988). The conclusion was that indeed only a market of at least this size could combine the advantages of economies of scale, product diversity, and competition. When the 1992 program became credible, in part because of new treaty powers to expedite the needed legislation by majority voting on many such matters, it appears that there was indeed a dynamizing effect on the strategic plans of many enterprises, both European and multinationals, who scrambled to position themselves in expectation of this new market environment.

But also, as soon as the 1992 program became credible, debate began over whether the single market needed a single currency (or other form of monetary union) as its handmaiden. The crucial argument that emerged was that the status quo of the European Monetary System risked being disturbed by the elimination of capital controls required for the single market (see the contribution of Krugman to Padoa-Schioppa and others, 1987). The European Monetary System at that time was showing some signs of increasing monetary stability and inflation convergence. But the imperfections in this convergence coexisted with exchange rate stability partly because of the insulating properties of capital controls. With their elimination, the EC faced the prospect either of renewed exchange rate instability or the need to heighten the degree of monetary policy to the point that monetary sovereignty at the national level had little substance left. The bicycle theory of integration had asserted itself again. Either you keep moving or you fall off.

The politicians elected to push ahead to Economic and Monetary Union, albeit at a measured pace, with several stages and check-points on the way. Economists were again invited to go to work, this time to analyze the benefits and costs of adding a single money to a single market (Commission of the EC, 1990, and Emerson and Huhne, 1991). They reviewed evidence of the advantages of price stability itself, which a well-designed, independent, federal central banking system, inheriting a reputation for stability from some of its members, might offer. They produced evidence on the benefits of eliminating currency transaction costs and of having a leading inter-national currency. In these respects the linkage between the single market for financial services and single money was evident. The full benefits of an integrated market require a single currency, at least at the level of microeconomic effects.

The major cost, or risk of cost, in moving to the single money would be the loss of the exchange rate as a policy instrument. How important is this risk of cost? The research done on the EC case suggests this to be an empirical rather than a categorical matter. It hangs upon the extent to which economic shocks that call for adjustment policies tend to be national in character (rather than common, or regional, or sectoral), or otherwise asymmetrical (in the sense that nations may react differently to common shocks). It also hangs upon the efficiency of the exchange rate instrument in remedying such shocks. For the EC the findings were that the value of the exchange rate instrument was rather substantially reduced, compared to some preconceptions and doubtless other regions of the world that are less integrated or adjusted to market conditions.

The EC's case for its own market and monetary integration, and for linkage between the two, thus turns out to be quite strong on purely economic grounds. To go from free trade to a single market adds substantial benefits, but politically it requires a much greater concession to the needs for common legislation and law enforcement than international regimes seem capable of (indeed this involves the very distinction between international and federal regimes). To go to monetary union also offers substantial benefits, and the risks of costs seem in the EC case to be acceptably reduced. Monetary union also makes strong requirements for federal rather than just international institutions, unless one accepts a hegemon, which is not the case between EC countries. Finally, to do the one without the other (market or money) means either failing to exploit the full benefits of each or, worse, creating new risks of costs.

We may also note in passing a tentative conclusion. The prereq uisites for a mature and stable regional bloc, combining trade and monetary structures, seem very demanding. Politically it means moving out of the arena of international relations and into the different arena of federalism.

How do these arguments apply to the other three regional groups in Europe?

The EFTA countries, as dependent on trade with the EC as the member states of the EC themselves, had clear reasons to react quickly to the EC's 1992 program. The new industrial-structuring dynamic of 1992 threatened their countries to become less-favored locations for their own multinational corporations as well as internationally mobile investment generally. For example, Sweden's multinationals swung powerfully into the EC. It became vital for EFTA governments to persuade business that their countries were "as if" in the EC single market. So began the "European Economic

Space" negotiations. The institutional implications of being "as if" in the EC single market proved to be an important issue. In being prepared to compromise over matters of sovereignty in this process, in the sense of accepting virtual extra-territoriality of EC jurisdiction, these countries also seemingly began to overcome their reluctance to seek full membership. This reinforces the point made above about moving from the international arena to that of federalism.

On the monetary side, the recent moves of the Nordic countries closer to the ECU appear to have been motivated by two factors. The first is to reduce exchange rate variability in relation to the EC market caused by dollar and yen movements in their former baskets. Such movements confused the industrial logic of the European Economic Space. The second is to enhance the credibility of their macro-economic policy commitment to price stability. One might wonder why the ECU should be better than their former baskets for this purpose. It seems to be more of a political institutional point. The baskets were highly anonymous and technical things. By comparison the ECU represents growing political commitment to ties with the EC, and a monetary bloc led by the deutsche mark. Also, the risks of macroeconomic cost in reducing the degree of exchange rate flexibility for these countries is almost certainly no greater than for the EC countries themselves. Here too, then, readiness to step onto the integration train is an important part of the story. In so doing, the geographic organization of their trade and monetary regimes converge.

These West European case studies in trade and monetary regime linkages amount to no more than a fine-tuning of systems, by comparison with the issues at stake in the revolutions under way to the east. The very topic of the relationship between trade and monetary regimes has an academic ring to it, seemingly far removed from the desperate battlefields of regime change in the PECOs and the USSR. How wrong one could be. The key to executing these regime changes, if one is to single out a particular action, is the convertibility of the currency. This is the pivotal action linking trade and monetary systems.

In practice, we are talking here of current account, or internal, convertibility (for a taxonomy of different forms of convertibility and an excellent discussion of the issues for Eastern Europe, see Asselin, 1991 and Bofinger, 1991). Westerners may be inclined to yawn at the subject, since, for example, the EC has seen many of its countries approach full convertibility of their currencies at a leisurely pace over decades. The history of the European Payments Union offers a more exciting episode in the conjunction of trade and payments initiatives.

Even this latter example is not comparable in importance to the convertibility reforms now undertaken or envisaged in the PECOs and the USSR. Only through assuring internal convertibility—that is, current account convertibility for residents—can price reform and liberalization be achieved with the information and discipline of world market prices; only in this way can multiple exchange rates and currency rationing systems be efficiently swept away; only in this way can the overwhelming incentives for corruption be eliminated. Let us be clear on this last point. We are talking about a social poison much more serious than a marginal black market sector. When exchange rate distortions of the order of multiplies of 7 to 15 exist as Poland knew and the USSR still knows, then any economic agent making international trade or monetary transactions is invited to concentrate on the opportunities for illegal arbitrage of some kind. This is not good for the political reputation of the market.

Convertibility assures that money can fulfill two of its functions at least, as numeraire and means of settlement. What about the third function, store of value? This was suggested at the beginning to be something that could be disconnected from the choice of trade regime. This is normally so, but not in the special situations today of the regime revolutions of Eastern Europe. If convertibility is introduced before macroeconomic stabilization and elimination of the monetary overhang, then the result is an excess depreciation of the currency to the point of risking hyperinflation. This, in turn, risks capsizing the political viability of the reform process, including (history suggests) the viability of democracy. These problems return our attention to the advisability of securing external and credible anchors to market reform and stabilization policies.

Where are these countries going to get their external anchors?

Poland, Hungary, and the CSFR have all been quick to raise the issue of ultimate EC membership. The economic point here is to borrow the policy rules and credibility of a third party, given the initial fragility of political conditions at home. With an opening of the prospect (even undated) of EC membership, these countries can more easily make the strategic decision to shadow the rules and regulations of the internal market of the EC. Why take the EC's rules for this purpose? Clearly not because the EC's laws are thought to be better or worse than those of the United States, but because of a strong politico-historical desire to "rejoin Europe." Many things are confused in these countries in the aftermath of revolution, but this point is not. Noneconomic sentiments can thus be used to help carry the economic reform process through the difficult transitional period (see Portes, 1991 on these questions).

Similar issues are, if anything, even more relevant in the monetary domain, where for stabilization policy, the strong or weak institutional credibility of the authorities is vital in determining whether there be low or high transitional costs. The use of conditional credits from the International Monetary Fund (IMF) and other Western donors (including the EC itself) is already important for almost all the PECOs and looms on the horizon for the USSR. But these credits are only of a few years' duration. The long-term question of adherence to some zone of monetary stability is also posed. Here the PECOs do not yet have clear positions. Their present practices see a predominant preference for homemade currency baskets as numeraire, with an uncertain degree of commitment to exchange rate parities. The impression is mostly one of soft pegging to the basket, with fairly frequent devaluations. Alternative numeraires are the dollar (which Poland tried for a while before switching to a basket), the deutsche mark (chosen by Yugoslavia), and the ECU. One could imagine the PECOs following the Nordic countries in switching from their anonymous and technical baskets to peg on the ECU. But that is not the case for the time being.

There is a particular reason why the PECOs may in due course choose to coordinate their choices of monetary regime. All of them will be striving to succeed in creating internationally competitive industries in similar segments of the world hierarchy of industrial technologies. They will not want to add to their difficulties by indulging in wild, unpredictable swings in competition with one another. The EC itself may also become interested in this question, as the PECOs and the USSR overcome the stage of creative destruction of their old regimes and start coming on stream with large-scale export production. When the 400 million population of this group become active members of the world economy, the EC will know about it first and foremost. Let us recall the Swedish 16 percent devaluation out of the blue in the early 1980s, which ruffled the feathers of its free-trade partners in the EC and EFTA, and imagine that sort of thing happening twice a year on a scale ten times as important. One could imagine the association agreements between the EC and PECOs providing for issues of competition policy (subsidy control, price decontrol), currency convertibility, and monetary cooperation.

To summarize on the PECOs, one may imagine a two-stage evolution of their trade and monetary regimes, and of linkage between them. In the first stage, already under way, the accent is on open-economy fundamentals. World price structures are imported, trade policies are normalized in the GATT, current account convertibility toward the world is established, and the exchange rate is loosely pegged on some international numeraire while the search for the equilibrium level is made. In a second stage, these regimes are more fine-tuned, with an importing also of EC internal market policies and cooperation with the EC on monetary policy for both stabilization and competition policy purposes, consistent with the wider framework of the GATT and IMF.

These PECO cases are simple, compared to that of the USSR. The country spans two continents, with a deep cultural attachment to Europe in the West but no less affinity, for ethnic and economic reasons, for Asian connections in the five central Asian republics and eastern parts of the Russian federation. Moreover, as a land of wide open spaces and big horizons, one also senses a natural affinity of Russians toward Americans. These simple but basic facts are cautions for advocates of trilateralism in the West. When the USSR enters the international economy, it does so at a world and not at a regional level. The G-7 summit is not the only illustration of this. There is also the European Energy Charter which quickly came to embrace the United States and Japan when it became clear that the USSR was interested, even though this is an EC-sponsored initiative.

To the USSR, the EC offers something of a role model rather than membership prospects, even though the latter question crops up surprisingly frequently in nonofficial conversations in Moscow. The 9+1 Treaty of Sovereign States, now ready for ratification at the level of major principles, is in the economic field closer to the confederal constitution of the EC presently under negotiation in the two intergovernmental conferences, than the strongly federal constitutions of the United States or Germany. Most republics of the USSR are in fact now more restrictive in agreeing economic powers to the center than most member states of the EC. The current organization of Western Europe offers several ideas for the USSR. The EC itself warns that the 9+1 should not go too far in emasculating the legal competences of the center, if the single market and single money are to be restored (indeed restoration, because today the market and money of the USSR are fragmented). For the secessionist six republics, or however many (it seems that Moldavia and Armenia might rejoin the fold), the EC-EFTA relationship offers an example of how a large and small pair of groups of states can reconcile together deep economic integration and political independence.

The biggest challenge of any surveyed in this paper, however, is that of achieving the macroeconomic stabilization of the ruble, in a setting marked today by uncontrolled budgetary decentralization and populism, and a lack of political independence and credibility of the monetary authorities. With a 20 percent GDP budget deficit, a 100 percent inflation rate, and terribly reduced consumption levels, the task is appallingly difficult.

For reasons already stated, the internal convertibility of the ruble has to be the pivot of the operation as a matter of economic policy. But there is the no less urgent task of institution building. For the central bank, the Federal Reserve, the Bundesbank, and draft statutes of the European Central Bank offer a well-honed pedigree model. But this means that the governments of the republics as well as the center have to learn to do without the prerogative to order the supply of bank notes. The budgetary model will have to be one, de facto, of coordination between five major players: the Union, Russia, the Ukraine, White Russia, and Kazakhstan. The Union of Sovereign States is condemned to sharing with the EC the trials and tribulations of seeking cooperative behavior among a small group, where game theory is more important than legal rules.

Summarizing on the USSR and trade and monetary regimes, three points are to be stressed. First, the survival of the Union clearly depends upon the linked dismantling of trade barriers and achieving the internal convertibility of the ruble. Second, the same convertibility of the ruble must be the pivot of a set of reforms to introduce the USSR into the world economy. Third, the next task will be to refine the internal market and monetary regimes of the USSR, perhaps along the lines being pursued by the EC. Fourth, the USSR seems clearly destined to integrate with all the main regions of the world economy, not primarily with just one region; the model of a three-region world soon encounters limits to its adequacy and acceptability.

Conclusions

The contemporary European scene offers four different case studies of the relationship between trade and monetary zones.

(1) The EC is the classic case of integration, which the GATT statutes recognized as warranting the formation of a customs union. The member states are deeply integrated economically, compact as a geographical group and rather homogeneous in terms of political values and interests. The EC now passes up the integration hierarchy from customs union to single market, and so on to economic, monetary, and political union. Both market and monetary integration are shown by studies to be beneficial in their own right but also in ways that are significantly interdependent. The integration process reveals an endogenous dynamic—that is, intermediate degrees of integra-

tion do not appear to have been steady-state regimes in this case.

(2) The EFTA countries are also classic examples of the small open economy next to a large neighbor; together, they are comparable to Canada in relation to the United States. They opted during many years for regional free trade with the EC, with a mixed history on the monetary side, sometimes (in some cases) joining the EC (or deutsche mark) monetary zone as well, sometimes not. Recently, however, the integration dynamic of the EC has spilled over to affect their perceptions of their own interests. Thus, increasing association with the EC's monetary zone and its single market and some full membership applications are observed. The economic case for these developments seems very much the same as for the EC. They become sufficiently strong to override traditional preferences for political independence.

(3) The PECOs make revolutionary changes to their systems, joining the world market economy. In a first stage they join the international and not a regional system for both trade and monetary relations. To import world price structures with the aid of a convertible currency is the first priority. For a second stage of refinement of their new systems, questions of special regional market and monetary relations emerge. The issue here is to borrow from robust nearby systems so as to buttress the fragile reform and stabilization process. This concerns tying more closely to the EC internal market with the eventual prospect in at least some cases of political integration (negotiations are already begun with three), and closer monetary relations with the European Monetary System could become attractive for the same reasons as the EFTA countries found.

(4) The USSR also proceeds with its revolution. Trade and monetary system linkages are dramatically evident everywhere: negatively, in the disintegration of Comecon trade and payments, in the proliferation of inter-republican trade barriers and nonconvertible quasi-monies such as ration coupons; and positively, it is to be hoped, with the crucial need

for at least partial convertibility of the ruble as pivot of a comprehensive set of liberalization and stabilization measures. The size of the USSR makes it fundamentally interested in the world, rather than a regional system or two. Debate over a new federal constitution in the USSR follows the classic pattern of all existing or EC incipient federations; the combination of a single market and single money is the litmus test of federal union.

Reflection on the case of a Euro-Asian USSR already suggests that, to some, ideas of a world model of a small number of trade and monetary regions are too simple. Moreover, the political integration properties of the EC case are not visible elsewhere. The Pacific area looks like being also, like the USSR, most interested in as open trade relations as possible with both North America and Europe as well as among themselves. In the Americas there are many questions still over the plausible extent and depth of hemispheric integration.

For those parts of the world where the case for classic integration—economic, monetary, and political—is not yet evident, it seems unlikely that a neat pattern of coincidence of trade and monetary zones will emerge.

The rumblings in the Americas and the Pacific about regional systems may be interpreted in part as a warning to the EC not to abuse Article XXIV of the GATT, as much as precursors of fully developed regional blocs. The GATT article permits customs unions and free trade areas on condition that substantially all trade is covered and external tariffs for the rest of the world are not raised. All countries are free to choose whatever monetary regime they wish to accompany their trade policy. To opt for a coincidence of trade and monetary zones is thus also largely a free one from the standpoint of international agreements.

But what is a regional bloc? Is the EC going to be any more of a "bloc" than the United States, which usually does not answer to this name? If by "bloc" we mean something less than an outright federation, actual or envisaged, it is not self-evident that a world of large regions of trade-plus-monetary systems is the way to go. The

GATT and IMF have increasingly globalwide geographic coverage and are highly significant organizations for all except those who are looking fancifully for a system of world government. Their limits are really only those inherent in international relations as opposed to federations or integration movements in that direction. The case of coincidental trade-plus-monetary zones may justify itself from time to time but should not be viewed as the new paradigm.

Editor's Note: Michael R. Emerson prepared this paper for delivery at the Federal Reserve Bank of Kansas City's Symposium on "Policy Implications of Trade and Currency Zones," Jackson Hole, Wyoming, August 1991. Though Mr. Emerson was unable to be present, his paper is being published with the proceedings.

References

Asselin, J. " Convertibility and Economic Transformation," *Commission of the EC.*, 1991.

Bofinger, P. " Options for the Payments and Exchange-Rate Systems in Eastern Europe," *Commission of the EC,* 1991.

Commission of the EC. " The Economics of 1992," *European Economy,* no. 35, Luxembourg: Office for Official Publications of the EC, March, 1988. (Also published by M. Emerson and others, 1988. Oxford University Press.)

_____" One Market, One Money," *European Economy*, special ed. 2. Luxembourg: Office for Official Publications of the EC, October, 1990. (Also published by M. Emerson and others, 1991. Oxford University Press.)

_____" The Path of Reform in Central and Eastern Europe," *European Economy*, special ed. 2. Luxembourg: Office for Official Publications of the EC, 1991.

Emerson, J., and C. Huhne. *The ECU Report: The Single European Currency and What It Means to You.* London: Pan Books, 1991.

Emerson, M., K. Shigehara, and R. Portes. " Europe After 1992: Three Essays," in T. Padoa-Schioppa, ed., *Essays in International Finance,* no. 182. Princeton: Princeton University Press, 1991.

Padoa-Schioppa, T., and others. *Efficiency, Stability and Equity.* Oxford: Oxford University Press, 1987.

Portes, E. " The European Community and Eastern Europe After 1992," in T. Padoa-Schioppa, ed., *Essays in International Finance.* Princeton: Princeton University Press, 1991.

Does One Market Require One Money?

Martin Feldstein

Much of the current European discussion about monetary union, especially the discussion in official circles, assumes that the adoption of a single currency is necessary to perfect the free trade in goods and services that is called for in the European Community's 1992 plan. The European Commission has summarized this official view in the title of its publication *One Market, One Money.*

In contrast, no one seriously suggests that the United States, Canada, and Mexico should form a currency union as part of the process of establishing a North American Free Trade Area.

I believe that this difference does not reflect anything about the economic requirements for efficient free trade zones or the potential usefulness of a single currency in Europe or North America. Instead, it reflects very different political goals in Europe and in North America.

European monetary union is sought by those who want to move to a political union among the current members of the European Community (EC). They seek a common currency both as a public symbol of super-nationhood and as an effective way to shift government decisions on monetary and eventually fiscal policy from national capitals to Brussels or some other single European location.

Although I shall have more to say today about the political motivations that are driving the European move toward a single currency,

I think it is important for economists to evaluate the economic case for a European currency union. Political officials and voters who must make the decisions about future steps toward monetary union should understand whether a monetary union really is important for economic reasons.

In my judgment, the economic case for a currency union is not persuasive. Although there may be some economic advantages to adopting a single currency, the disadvantages are likely to outweigh the advantages. A single currency is certainly not necessary to obtain the advantages of free trade within Europe and may be counterproductive. The loss of independence in the management of monetary policy at the national level and of potential exchange rate flexibility within Europe may have more serious adverse consequences than the trade-promoting benefits that are claimed for establishing a single currency.

To support this conclusion, I will begin by reviewing the economic arguments advanced in favor of any monetary union and will then consider the associated economic costs that weigh in the opposite direction. I will then discuss whether Europe as such is an appropriate unit for a currency area. After this review of the economic case, I will look at the political motivations that, in my opinion, explain why some Europeans are so eager for the establishment of a monetary union and a single currency. Here too there are costs and benefits that should be identified in the interest of informed decision-making.

The economics of monetary union

The primary economic case for moving to a single currency is that elimination of currency fluctuations within Europe would increase trade among members of the community. Those who hold this view argue that currency fluctuations inhibit businessmen from developing markets in other countries and from buying from foreign producers because the fluctuations in exchange rates can more than wipe out the normal profits from individual transactions. More generally, in an environment of fluctuating exchange rates, international transactions involve an uncertainty that is not present in domestic transactions.

It is not clear, however, whether this is of any importance in practice. The several econometric studies that have tried to measure the effect of exchange rate volatility on trade in Europe have failed to find any impact. If businesses really care about the exchange rate risk, they can hedge future outlays and receipts in the market for foreign exchange futures. Although businessmen often complain that such hedging is "expensive," I suspect that they are confusing what is really a very low cost of avoiding uncertainty by buying or selling currency futures with the discount on forward sales or premium on forward purchases that prevails when the market expects the value of the currency to change. After all, it is when the value of a currency is expected to fall that businessmen are most eager to protect themselves and it is then that they find that forward sales of that currency are "costly".

Further evidence that currency volatility may not inhibit trade is the very sharp increase in the volume of exports to the United States during the decade of the 1980s when the dollar gyrated sharply. And certainly the Japanese have not found that the fluctuations of the yen relative to the dollar and the European currencies have been a serious barrier to their ability to increase exports.

A fixed exchange rate zone may in some cases even be an obstacle to expanded trade. Consider a manufacturer in England who contemplates expanding his marketing efforts in France. He knows that he will compete in that market with producers from the United States as well as from France. If the dollar falls relative to the franc, the American producers will gain an advantage. Since this will be a problem for all British exporters, the British government might respond by devaluing the pound in line with the dollar if it is free to do so in order to maintain British exports. With a fixed exchange rate vis-à-vis the French franc and other EC currencies, such devaluation would not be possible. For a British manufacturer, the idea of developing a market in France is in this way less attractive when the U.K.-French exchange rate is fixed than when it is flexible. Fewer resources may therefore go into the manufacture of tradeable goods and more into the production of services and goods for the local market. In short, while a world in which all exchange rates are fixed may encourage trade, fixing the exchange rates among a subset of currencies may actually discourage trade.

Quite apart from its effect on trade, the shift to a single currency can be helpful in creating a larger financial market. There is a simple convenience when more of the people with whom you deal use the same currency. In addition, with more securities and transactions quoted in a particular currency, it may be less costly to make financial transactions. This may be a reason for very small countries to tie their currencies together or to a larger currency but it is not relevant for countries as large as Britain, France, Germany, and Italy.

Against these possible but uncertain advantages of a currency union must be set the disadvantage of losing an independent national monetary policy—that is, losing the ability to respond to changes in the demand for local products by changing interest rates and the exchange rate. If the demand for the products of a country falls, it will suffer a decline of employment and output unless money wages and prices are completely flexible. Although this adverse effect on employment and output could be mitigated by a reduction of domestic interest rates, such a local interest rate reduction is not possible when there is a single currency or an absolutely fixed exchange rate. With multiple currencies and flexible exchange rates, the favorable offsetting expansionary effect of an easier monetary policy on interest rates is reinforced by the decline of the exchange rate that the lower interest rate induces.

For the past thirty years economists have considered these issues in the context of a theory of optimal currency areas first proposed by Robert Mundell. The basic idea is that it is worthwhile for a group of independent "countries" to adopt a single currency when the demand shocks that hit the countries are similar and when labor is highly mobile among the countries in the area. The similarity of the demand shocks means that there is little to be gained by changes in real exchange rates within the proposed currency area and that the appropriate monetary policy is the same for all of the countries. A highly mobile labor force among the countries in the proposed currency area means that to the extent that there are different shocks in different parts of the currency area, the workers will move from regions of declining demand to regions of stronger demand. Just how similar the shocks must be and how mobile the labor must be to justify a currency union depends on the potential gains, usually thought of in terms of the convenience of transactions and the increased size of the market for financial dealings.

It is hard to argue that the European Community satisfies either of the two requirements of an optimal currency area to any appreciable extent. The individual countries suffer substantially different shocks because of differences in the mix of the products that they produce, in their dependence on imported oil, and in the foreign markets to which they sell. (Barry Eichengreen has recently shown that the real exchange rate changes in the 1970s and 1980s have been far greater among the countries of Europe than among the major regions of the United States, a reflection that the shocks have differed more among European countries than among U.S. regions.) Labor mobility among European nations will inevitably be limited for a very long time to come by differences in language and by a culture that, unlike that of the United States, regards geographic mobility with suspicion.

The politics of monetary union

If economic analysis does not provide support for a shift to a single European currency, why are there such strong voices in Europe calling for a monetary union that will replace national currencies with a single European currency? There are, I think, three distinct political reasons behind this advocacy.

First, there are those who see a single currency and a European central bank as a way of restricting the ability of national governments to pursue inflationary monetary policies. European central bankers in particular who must now answer to their finance ministers see the move to a single currency and a European central bank as a chance to make monetary policy with much less political interference. They argue that although each government could by itself pursue a noninflationary monetary policy, it is politically easier for a European collective to do so than it is for individual governments. Although a European central bank would still be accountable to some political body like the European parliament, distance from national capitals and national parliaments is assumed to reduce the pressure of domestic electoral politics on monetary policy.

They and others who make this argument would accept a much restricted scope for good monetary policy in each nation in order to reduce the political temptations for bad national policies. Quite apart from the question that this raises about the making of monetary policy in democratic states, it implies a possibly very large sacrifice of potentially good monetary policy in order to reduce the risk of a bad policy being chosen.

Moreover, although this argument is logically sound, as a practical matter it is very much weakened by the success of the current EMS arrangement in which German hegemony has encouraged other countries to pursue a German-style anti-inflationary policy. Why force every country to give up the possibility of stabilizing monetary adjustments in order to prevent inflationary policies that are only hypothetical?

Indeed it is the success of the German hegemony that creates the second of the political motivations for European monetary union. Put simply, nobody but the Germans is fully in favor of letting the Bundesbank make monetary policy for all of Europe. For many non-Germans, the creation of a European central bank that manages a European currency is a matter of national pride. For non-German central bankers, it is an opportunity to play an active role in the making of monetary policy.

But the reasons for wanting to replace the Bundesbank with a European central bank goes beyond national pride and the wishes of European central bankers. Not everyone shares Germany's strong anti-inflationary preferences. A European central bank might today adopt a more expansionary monetary policy that accepts permanently higher inflation to avoid a period of slow growth in the 1990s.

It is ironic that while some advocates of a single currency and a

European central bank argue that they want this to reduce the risk of inflation, others see it as a way of relaxing the very tough German anti-inflationary policy now "forced" on Europe by the Bundesbank.

All of which reinforces my belief that the strong advocacy of European monetary union does not reflect the political economy of monetary policy any more than it does a technical belief in the ability of monetary union to enhance trade within the community. Those who fervently advocate monetary union do so because they see it as a step toward a political union, and a particular type of political union at that.

Those who want to see Europe evolve into a political union see a monetary union as a helpful point along the way. A single currency would give the people of Europe a sense that they are part of a single country even though they speak different languages and remember different national histories. A single currency and European central bank would transfer substantial power away from national governments and to the nascent European central government. Many expect that this would be followed by limits on national fiscal policies and by enhanced centralized taxation.

The events in Eastern Europe have complicated this scenario. The economic costs of a single currency union for all of Europe increase as the number of countries with their different economic situations increases. As a practical matter, the single currency and the European central bank would not include many of those nations that are not currently in the EC. Although there is much talk about a single all-encompassing European Community that would welcome the countries of Eastern Europe, the move to a European monetary union now would create a two-class Europe in which those countries excluded from the proposed monetary union would be second class Europeans. With the Eastern Europeans and probably some of the northern countries excluded, Germany would be on the edge of the primary European Community and France would be in the center.

Let me end by reiterating my principal conclusion that monetary union is not needed to achieve the advantages of a free trade zone.

On the contrary, an artificially contrived European monetary union might actually reduce the volume of trade among the member countries and would almost certainly increase the average level of unemployment over time.

Although a European monetary union will accelerate the formation of a federalist political union among its members, those countries that are not part of the monetary union will be political outsiders. The consequences of this for the future stability of Europe, while difficult to contemplate with any certainty, may well not be favorable.

One Market, One Money?
Well, Maybe . . . Sometimes . . .

David E.W. Laidler

The slogan "One Market, One Money" is European. It sum-marizes the view that, as the European Community (EC) evolves into a single supranational economic union, the adoption of a single currency should be an integral, indeed natural, element in that evolution. But North America is developing into a supranational free trade area. An agreement between the United States and Canada is already in place, and one including Mexico is soon to be negotiated. Nor should we rule out the possibility of similar arrangements coming into being with other countries in the Western Hemisphere. If the Americans are emulating Europe in the matter of trade arrangements, should they not also be reconsidering the matter of monetary arrangements? Does not the evolution of a single market in goods and services also point to the desirability of some sort of monetary union: if not initially to a single currency, then at least to a system of fixed exchange rates?

I shall argue here that the foregoing conclusion does not follow, at least not yet, and probably not in the foreseeable future either. The "one market" of Western Europe, and that of North America, are very different entities, and the differences between them are, not altogether coincidentally, particularly relevant to the question of monetary unification. To put it simply, perhaps over-simply, the one European market is part of a broader, albeit as yet quite loose, political union, and the one North American market shows no sign of developing in such a direction. Monetary union, however, is at

85

least as much a political as an economic matter. It may be an appropriate aim for the EC—though I am not well enough informed to take a firm position here—but it is not an appropriate aim for North America. In what follows I shall discuss in the abstract the pros and cons of the maintenance of separate national currencies, and then I shall attempt to weigh these with reference to the above mentioned similarities and differences between the European and North American cases.

The nation is a political, not an economic, entity, and if there was any general and always compelling argument that it is economically desirable for a nation to maintain its own currency, and reserve the right to have its exchange rate against other currencies fluctuate, then that argument should be applicable to other political entities too. Why should states or provinces not each have their own currencies, and if states, why not cities and counties, or wards within cities, and so on? This *reductio ad absurdam*, which could be carried to the ultimate silliness of asking why each agent should not issue his or her own personalized money, forcefully draws attention to the fact that the social purpose of money in the first place is to act as a common means of exchange and unit of account in order to facilitate market activity.

It would be ridiculous for city wards to have their own monies because city wards are extremely open economies whose inhabitants trade extensively across their borders. The information and transactions costs, not to mention exchange rate risks, agents would face in the presence of a multiplicity of city ward monies would be prohibitive. But trade does not stop at national boundaries, and agents engaged in international trade do face information and transactions costs and exchange rate risk. Why not, then, set the boundaries of a single currency at the boundaries of the area over which a substantial amount of trade takes place, at the economic borders of the market, rather than at the political borders of the nation-state? Or, failing that, why not at least minimize the costs generated by the existence of national currencies by maintaining fixed exchange rates within the market area? What, in short, does a nation-state get out of having its own currency, and what does it get out of permitting the exchange rate of that currency to fluctuate? The standard answers to these questions are well known.

To begin with, within the typical nation-state, some symbolic importance is still attached to the maintenance of a distinct national currency, which is a traditional trapping of national sovereignty. Economics does not help us to understand this matter, but it should not, for that reason, be ignored. I suspect, for example, that much popular suspicion within the United Kingdom of a common European currency stems from this source. Curiously, however, in debates currently going on in Canada, the advocates of Quebec sovereignty seem to find no attraction in a separate currency. Be that as it may, this advantage of a separate national money is to be had under a rigidly fixed exchange rate. So, too, is the ability which a separate national money confers upon the government to raise revenue through seigniorage. This is not necessarily a trivial matter, even in conditions of reasonable price stability. If the non-interest-bearing monetary base amounts to one month's income, and the nominal interest rate is equal to, say, 6 percent, then this source will raise revenue at a rate equal to a little less than 0.05 percent of national income. Only to the extent that foreign exchange reserves are held in non-interest-bearing form, as they would be, for example under a commodity standard, is this source of revenue shut off by a fixed exchange rate.

The ability to vary seigniorage income by varying the domestic inflation rate is, of course, limited by a fixed exchange rate; and quite apart from this aspect of the matter, the ability to control inflation is of political significance. Here indeed lies the very core of the case for maintaining separate national currencies linked by flexible exchange rates. Though I believe neither that the inflation tax is an efficient source of revenue, nor that any long-term inflation-unemployment tradeoff exists, I do believe that the inflation rate is a legitimate and important matter of political concern and debate, and that those who control it, namely the monetary authorities, should be accountable to the general public for their performance.[1] So long as the political institutions through which such accountability can be ensured exist only at the level of the nation-state, this consideration argues strongly in favor of maintaining a national currency, and an exchange rate regime that gives the monetary authorities the necessary room to maneuver.

The final element in the traditional case for a separate national currency also requires a flexible exchange rate. I refer to the help which such an arrangement gives to an economy which faces so-called real shocks, either changes in the terms of trade, or variations in capital flows, that require adjustment of domestic real factor incomes relative to those ruling abroad. To the extent that money incomes, particularly wages, are sticky—and downward stickiness is usually regarded as being particularly relevant here—then exchange rate movements brought about by market forces can help with such adjustments and mitigate adverse employment consequences.

A number of comments on this argument are in order. To begin with, the very same money-wage-price stickiness which makes a flexible exchange rate desirable in the face of real shocks underlies the mechanisms that lead exchange rate fluctuations to amplify the consequences of monetary shocks. Thus, to deploy wage-price stickiness in defense of a flexible exchange rate is to imply a certain empirical judgment about the relative frequency and seriousness of the shocks to which the economy is vulnerable. It might, therefore, be a valid element in the special case for a particular country to maintain a flexible exchange rate, but it cannot be part of any blanket defense of the general superiority of such a regime. Second, one cannot help but wonder whether the degree of wage-price stickiness which characterizes an economy is going to be completely independent either of its exchange rate regime or of the shocks to which it is normally subjected. Finally, a flexible exchange rate can be used as a policy instrument by a central bank intent on fine tuning the economy. All the usual arguments against fine tuning apply here, and the opportunity to indulge in it conferred by a flexible exchange rate is not an advantage.

Terms of trade changes and capital flow fluctuations take place within, as well as across, national boundaries, and so the above argument about smoother adjustment can be advanced (and in the case of western Canada sometimes *is* advanced) to support the proposition that the boundaries of currency areas might be drawn more narrowly than those of nations. The usual counter to this point, that the opportunities for labor mobility and the capacity for inter-regional fiscal transfers that exist within a nation-state provide alternative means of cushioning the impact of real shocks, has obvious relevance to the question of the desirability of any supranational monetary union. If the union is part of a broader economic union, with provision for ensuring international labor mobility, and the implementation of international fiscal transfers, it is more likely to be viable.

In the light of the above arguments, then, is it desirable that the one European market should have one money, and that the one North American market should emulate it, at least to the extent of moving to fixed exchange rates? The reader will forgive me if I do not come to definite conclusions about all aspects of these questions. Suffice it to say that it is easier to make the case for a single money for Europe than for North America, and that I am extremely dubious that it can be made at all in the latter case. From the outset, the EC was a *common market*, and it became an *economic community*. A common market, by definition, maintains a common external tariff. In the European case it has also maintained a common agricultural policy, along with some capacity to make fiscal transfers to depressed regions. The administration of these arrangements has required the existence of a marketwide bureaucracy, and has led to the creation of a European parliament too, albeit with very limited powers, to oversee the substantial budget involved. The EC has a common passport, and few legal or administrative restrictions on labor mobility within the community for its holders.

In North America we have a *free trade area* (FTA) from which several important sectors—for example, agriculture—are exempted. The extent of the supranational institutions created by the Canada-U.S. FTA goes no further than ad hoc dispute settlement panels, and an agreement to negotiate a common policy on what constitutes subsidies. National rules, made by national governments, still govern trade across national borders. The FTA has left immigration laws untouched—apart from making the transborder provision of professional services a little easier—and surely the desire to reduce cross border labor mobility is not altogether absent as Canada and the United States seek to include Mexico in a broader agreement.

The point of all this is, first, that there exist in Europe, but not in North America, alternative mechanisms of adjustment to real shocks which can, in principle, take the place of exchange rate flexibility. Even within Europe, the existence of such mechanisms was insufficient to persuade Britain, a large oil producer and center of an important capital market and hence a potential recipient of differential real shocks, to give up a flexible exchange rate until very recently. Why should Canada whose terms of trade vis-à-vis the United States can be volatile, and for whom transborder capital movements are extremely important, give up the exchange rate adjustment mechanism in the absence of any alternative?

More generally, and more important, European countries have already surrendered a certain amount of political sovereignty to Brussels and Strasbourg, and the institutions already exist through which, perhaps, the seigniorage generated by a European central bank might be collected and allocated, and through which the bank might be held accountable for its performance. Moreover, it should be noted explicitly that, during the 1970s, the EC encountered serious difficulties in maintaining its CAP in the face of large and frequent exchange rate fluctuations among the currencies, of members. Much is often made of the discipline which the European Monetary System (EMS) has imposed on members in the 1980s, but surely some of the discipline needed to keep the EMS in place and to move the system toward a closer union has come from a deeper desire to protect the CAP which, if not quite the EC's raison d'être, is its most important single institution. No comparable institutions exist in North America.

A new common currency for North America seems beyond the bounds of possibility, therefore, though fixed exchange rates on the U.S. dollar for both Canada and/or Mexico are not. If, however, the exchange rate were rigidly and perpetually fixed, the dominant size of the U.S. market and currency area would involve either or both of the others in surrendering control of inflation, a matter of domestic political concern, to a central bank responsible to another electorate. It is hard to believe that this would be politically acceptable in either country, or that the alternative, namely permitting foreign representation in the policymaking bodies of the Federal Reserve System would be acceptable in the United States.

What about a potentially adjustable peg, then? Such an arrangement certainly would meet the above political objections, but the trouble here is that all of those traditional arguments to the effect that an adjustable peg brings with it the worst features of a fixed rate, and of a flexible rate too, have to be faced. Argument from the example of the EMS seems barely relevant to the case of North America. The same worries about terms of trade and capital account fluctuations that kept Britain out of the ERM for so long, are, as I have argued, present in the North American economy; and crucially, the verdict is by no means in yet as to whether Britain was wise to change her policy last year. If that verdict should in the end be favorable, that will, in part, stem from the coincidence of Britain's entry with the monetary disturbances associated with German reunification, but also in more important part, from the possibility that entering the mechanism will appear to have been a step toward catching up with an altogether more broadly based movement toward economic and political integration. There is no counterpart to this movement discernible in North America.

Be all that as it may, voices are now being heard in Canada that urge the adoption of a fixed exchange rate, partly at least because the appreciation which the Canadian dollar has undergone since the signing of the free trade agreement has swamped the gains that Canadian producers hoped to obtain from easier access to U.S. markets. These arguments should, I believe, be treated with suspicion. To begin with, no one in Canada is urging that the exchange rate be fixed at its current level—though U.S. beneficiaries of the free trade agreement might find such a measure attractive! Canadian advocates of a fixed rate are arguing for a deliberate devaluation. Though I am as puzzled as anyone about the current level of the exchange rate, I nevertheless believe that a deliberate policy of trying to reduce it would be inflationary, and hence would not restore the competitive position its advocates are hoping for.[2] Some of them would like to accompany devaluation with "effective" wage and price controls; but they ignore two issues, namely how to ensure that such controls would indeed be effective; and, if that hurdle for once is cleared, how to prevent their success breathing new, and in these circumstances unwelcome, life into negotiations about what does and does not constitute a subsidy! I cannot imagine U.S. legislators failing to react if Canada were to attempt to gain competitive advantages through a policy of devaluation and wage-price controls.

But for all that, the more transborder trade in goods, services, and capital takes place, the greater are the transactions costs and the exchange rate risks to which agents are exposed. Absent the political institutions that could make a common currency or rigidly fixed exchange rate regime viable, more exchange rate stability would still be better than less. Stability, however, is not the same thing as fixity, and there are certain market mechanisms tending to produce it anyway, though I have no idea how important they are in practice. I refer to the phenomenon of currency substitution. Though national currencies predominate in domestic transactions as a result of custom, reinforced perhaps by legal restrictions, agents engaged in international transactions have a choice of which currency to use. If stability in purchasing power is important, and I would not want to dispute that for a moment, then a more stable currency will be preferred to a less stable alternative. This very fact gives an incentive to national authorities on both sides of any border to deliver stability in the purchasing power of the money for which they are responsible, and if they respond to those incentives, then apart from the effects of real shocks, exchange rate stability should result. The market for the means of exchange, that is to say, is contestable at the national frontier, and the fewer restrictions there are on transborder transactions, the more likely is it that competitive mechanisms will deliver, if not one money for the whole market, then at least rather stable exchange rates between the currencies circulating in various parts of it.

To sum up: it is certainly the case that there are benefits, in terms of lowering transactions costs, to be had from using one money in one market; but it is also true that certain political factors, involving the management of inflation and, less important, the economy's response to real shocks, argue in favor of maintaining separate national currencies, even when countries are deeply involved in mutually beneficial and only lightly regulated international trade in goods, services, and capital. There can be no single rule telling us how to balance off these factors in each and every instance. In the case of the EC, it may well be that the development of supranational bureaucratic and political institutions has already been carried so far forward that the politics of monetary and stabilization policy can be accommodated within them. If that is so, then "one money for one market" is a defensible slogan for Europe. For North America, the institutional framework to justify such a move seems completely absent; and in any event, the one market in this instance is an altogether more modest arrangement than its European counterpart. In the North American case, a more appropriate slogan, at least for the medium term, is probably "three markets, becoming more closely linked, with three monies, all converging on stable purchasing power and hence on rather stable exchange rates, too;" not pithy perhaps, but accurate!

Endnotes

[1]Let it be clear, though, that by "accountable", I do not mean "under direct control". As I have argued at greater length elsewhere, it seems to be important to insulate those in charge of monetary policy from any interest in maximizing seigniorage, or in attempting to fine tune the unemployment rate, while ensuring that they are simultaneously given strong incentives to aim for a low inflation rate, and are answerable for their performance on this score. See D. Laidler, "Price Stability and the Monetary Order" (paper presented for the 1991 Bank of Japan Institute of Economic and Monetary Studies Conference, mimeo).

[2]It is important here to distinguish between a policy of driving down the exchange rate, which would be inflationary, and one which permits it to fall, if that is where market forces wish to take it, while maintaining domestic monetary stability.

Characteristics and Implications
of Different Types of Currency Areas

Miguel Mancera

First let me say that Mexico's possible participation in one or more free trade zones does not imply that we anticipate the formation of monetary unions in these zones. Furthermore, currency areas are not necessarily essential to a free trade zone's good performance, nor are the benefits from the formation of such areas self-evident. It must also be pointed out that formal monetary unions, that is, currency areas established by international treaties, are so complex that for now it would be virtually impossible to establish them in the free trade zones in which Mexico will probably participate.

It is not my intention to propose the adoption of any specific monetary scheme for trade zones. Rather, I would like to offer some reflections on the characteristics and effects of various types of currency areas.

The concept of a currency area can be understood in several ways. The broadest concept is that of a group of two or more countries whose currencies' exchange rates follow predetermined patterns. These patterns result from the exchange rate policies of the countries which are part of the currency area, although the exchange rate policy of the country whose currency serves as reference for the others may be entirely independent.

This type of currency area does not require an international treaty. It can simply stem from the desire and the ability of a country to unilaterally peg its currency's exchange rate (or the rate of change of the same) to another country's currency.

The other extreme might be represented by a currency area formed by a group of countries which adopt a common currency. However, even in this case, there are at least two variants: The United States and Panama, for example, use the same currency, but this is a decision made by Panama alone; in contrast, several European countries are considering the adoption of a common currency to be issued by a community central bank.

Between these extremes, there are several types of currency areas. Some do not require international treaties, tantamount to law, but may nonetheless involve monetary cooperation agreements. Other currency areas, such as the so-called monetary unions, are usually based on international treaties, the scope of which varies from case to case.

Now I would like to review the characteristics and the implications of various types of currency areas. First, I will discuss the most informal types, and last, I will make a few comments about those with a common currency.

Again, the broadest notion of a currency area is that attained by a country unilaterally pegging its currency's exchange rate to a foreign reference currency (or by fixing the speed of the crawl thereof). This policy can have considerable advantages for the country that fixes its exchange rate, but only if certain conditions are met. The first and by far the most important prerequisite is that the reference currency's purchasing power be reasonably stable. Other conditions are: that prices as well as nominal and real personal income be generally flexible; that the country whose currency is used as a reference be an important trade partner, or that the country that has pegged its currency's exchange rate conduct most of its international trade in the reference currency; that there are no serious obstacles for the international mobility of merchandise; that the country which has fixed its exchange rate is not overly exposed to large external shocks; and, crucially, that sustaining the exchange rate is a real and credible possibility. If this last condition is not met, there will eventually be speculative attacks against the currency, which may lead to an abrupt devaluation. In this case, the public may expect further devaluations, and such expectations imply among other effects, high interest rates, which dampen economic growth.

If all of these conditions are met, especially that of the reference currency's reasonably stable purchasing power, and that of the peg's sustainability, it is very likely that fixing the parity will yield considerable benefits. The country's inflation rate should converge with that of the reference currency, at least in the realm of internationally tradable goods. At the same time, the risk involved in international transactions would be reduced. This implies greater certainty and confidence, which are essential for economic development.

The danger of pegging the exchange rate stems from the risk that these preconditions may not be satisfied due to circumstances beyond the control of the country which fixed the rate. For example, if the exchange rate remains fixed and the country experiences an external shock or the reference currency becomes unstable, the country may face undesirable consequences. In fact, if the country which has a pegged exchange rate undergoes a severe external shock, it could suffer a deep recession, or if the reference currency country has an outbreak of inflation, this would imply general price hikes in the former.

Thus, we might question whether exchange rate rigidity is better than flexibility. Of course, I cannot do justice to such a broad topic within the scope of this discussion; I will, however, offer a few comments.

First, a flexible exchange rate regime does not offer the same results in the case of revaluations as in the case of devaluations. When a currency is revalued to isolate the country from imported inflation, this would not normally have negative effects. Should there be negative effects, they would be minimal compared to the benefits of preserving domestic price stability.

On the other hand, currency devaluations tend to cause inflation and, therefore, ongoing uncertainty, which is very costly in terms of economic development and social equity. However, it is rightly argued that in certain situations, devaluations may in fact be a lesser evil. For example, consider a country where the income of the general population is flexible in real terms, but downwardly rigid in nominal terms. Suppose it has pegged its exchange rate, and then it suffers a massive external shock. In this case, a devaluation and the ensuing higher prices permit the external shock's absorption through a reduction in the real income of a large part of the population, rather than through bankruptcies and public sector program cutbacks, both of which result in unemployment and lower production.

Thus, the most justifiable devaluations are in response to an external shock in the context of downwardly rigid nominal incomes. However, given that devaluations have inflationary consequences, one must ask whether there are not other means of handling the problems caused by, say, a sudden deterioration of the terms of trade or a natural disaster. In this sense, it might be convenient, for example, to remove nominal income rigidities.

An adverse shock inevitably has negative effects; yet a response conducive to inflation creates obstacles to economic growth and causes a chaotic redistribution of real income, which are both much worse than an explicit reduction in nominal income. It is regrettable that when economic reality dictates real income adjustments, these cannot always take place in an orderly and, indeed, civilized fashion. Sometimes the misguided step is taken, although surely with the best of intentions, of making reductions in workers' wages illegal, except in extreme circumstances which may be invoked only with great difficulty. And other times, noninflationary adjustment is problematic since people are misguided by money illusion—they are more willing to tolerate price increases than explicit reductions in their incomes. Such legal provisions, as well as money illusion, cause an unfortunate inflationary bias, the degree of which varies among national economies, but is present in all.

As I mentioned, one of the conditions for successfully pegging an exchange rate is that such action be viable and credible. With this in mind, we might consider establishing legal limits to primary credit expansion. At one extreme, the central bank's statutes may only allow currency to be issued against the purchase of a specific foreign currency or international assets in general. Under a fixed exchange rate regime, such a rule is highly appropriate since it makes it almost impossible for the domestic currency's value to erode with respect to the reference currency. The rule is equivalent, in a certain sense, to adopting the reference currency as the domestic currency, but with the advantage that the reference currency need not circulate within the national territory and, importantly, "seigniorage" can be earned from the issuing of domestic currency. Indeed, the central bank may invest the foreign exchange it purchases overseas, while not paying interest on the domestic currency it issues, and perhaps not paying interest, or only at a reduced rate, on its other monetary liabilities such as the commercial banks' deposits.

A few countries, such as Hong Kong and Singapore, have successfully adopted schemes of this sort. However, in spite of the evident advantages for fixed exchange rate regimes, this is unusual for several reasons: First, it is clear that even under a fixed exchange rate regime, the judicious use of primary credit can, in some measure, influence the evolution of monetary aggregates and interest rates, without jeopardizing exchange rate stability; second, it is obvious that the central bank's function as lender of last resort is nullified or severely limited if it cannot grant credit; under this scheme, the central bank could lend only as long as it had more foreign assets than liabilities. Third, although this is not always acknowledged, with this sort of scheme the government renounces a source of financing which can be very expedient. Of course, expediency as the only motive is questionable, as it has been precisely central banks' abuse of their power to grant primary credit which in many countries and on too many occasions has caused persistent inflation and recurring devaluations. Some countries have therefore relinquished the benefits of a moderate use of primary credit in exchange for the advantages of the monetary stability that results from an absolute confidence in the exchange rate.

Currency unions established by international treaties could be divided into three basic categories: The first is characterized by fixed exchange rates (or exchange rates which fluctuate within a band), but which are revisable and supported by a system of reciprocal credit. The European Monetary System's exchange rate mechanism is an example of this type of currency union. The second type of currency union is the same as the first, but the exchange rates are permanently fixed. The third type of currency union establishes a common central bank and a single currency.

The first type of currency union resembles Bretton Woods, which, you will recall, established an international monetary system characterized by pegged exchange rates. This type of currency union diminishes the member countries' monetary sovereignty in the sense that exchange rate variations cannot be determined unilaterally but must be agreed upon by the union. In exchange for this restriction, an important benefit is obtained: member countries agree to combine credit resources to finance temporary, nonfundamental balance of payments disequilibria and, therefore, support their exchange rates. This is further backed by member countries' efforts to coordinate their fiscal and monetary policies.

The second type of currency union, in which exchange rates are permanently fixed, implies very strict policy coordination among the member countries. In reality, this kind of coordination is closer to that required for the third type of currency union, with a common central bank and a single currency, than it is to the first type. In fact, permanently fixing exchange rates is in almost every sense tantamount to monetary unification. It could also be said that the requirements for policy coordination are virtually the same. However, under permanently fixed exchange rates, since the various domestic currencies would continue in circulation, with some transactions costs in exchanging one currency for another, there would be smaller benefits vis-à-vis a single currency system; this is also true to the extent that the population perceives some possibility, however small, that exchange rates could be modified by "force majeure."

Permanently fixing exchange rates requires that the national monetary authorities cede their prerogative to decide the amount and timing of currency issues to a common monetary authority. The implications of this are profound. National governments give up to an untested agency their de jure or de facto privilege to manage or at least influence their central bank's primary credit. Furthermore, the recognition of a common monetary authority raises questions that are difficult to answer: whether this authority should be independent of the national governments; to whom should it be accountable; how should voting power be allocated among the different countries within the common agency; and who should be responsible for the regulation and supervision of financial intermediaries.

The third type of currency union, in which member countries adopt a single currency, implies the creation of a common central bank. By adopting an organizational framework similar to that of the Federal Reserve System of the United States, a common central bank could take advantage of the various original member country central banks' human and operational resources without incurring the costs of a full-scale merger. This third type of currency union confronts the same problems as the second type of union, as well as some others: for example, how to allocate among the member countries the seigniorage derived from issuing the single currency. On the other hand, the benefits of this third type of union can be impressive. Benefits include the reduction of investment risks, the practical unification of leading interest rates, and considerable savings in the costs of international transactions within the union, all of which are highly favorable for economic development.

Belonging to a currency area has advantages and disadvantages which depend both on the type of currency area being addressed and the circumstances of each country. When it becomes necessary to make a decision concerning this subject, as with many others, it is advisable to adopt an eclectic rather than a dogmatic position. Moreover, considering the enormous variations in the rates of inflation within and among most countries, as well as price and wage rigidities, it is not unreasonable to argue in favor of floating exchange rates, notwithstanding the marked trend toward free trade and currency areas.

The Relationship Between Trade and Currency Zones

Salvatore Zecchini

The subject under consideration, the relationship between trade and currency zones lends itself to a variety of interpretations. When I was asked to speak on this subject, I wondered what kind of interpretation I should discuss, not knowing the contributions of the other speakers. After all, one can historically observe the relationship as going from a trade zone to a currency zone or from a currency zone to a trade zone. Given the various configurations of this relationship, I decided to speak briefly about what I still consider to be a core issue of this economic debate: must a trade zone inevitably evolve into a currency zone? Also I will touch upon some previous remarks concerning such an evolution in the context of the European Economic Community.

First, we must recognize that exchange rate policy can be used as a tool for trade protection. We are not in a system of fixed parities with specified rules for exchange rate flexibility and adjustment. Rather, we are in a system of floating exchange rates. This floating is not a free floating or a clean floating. It is a sort of managed floating—one without a clear set of guidelines that are internationally agreed upon and enforced for the purpose of regulating exchange rate management, preventing "beggar-thy-neighbor" policies and spurring a country to enact measures for macroeconomic and structural adjustment as soon as imbalances begin to emerge.

The basis of a trade zone is that the exchange of goods, services, and, under certain conditions, factors of production is free not only from tariff barriers but also from other protectionist maneuvers such as exchange rate manipulation. Countries in a trade zone cannot disregard what happens on the exchange rate policy front. Trade policy does not take place in a vacuum. Trade policy is one component of a whole set of policies that have to be considered altogether.

Some argue that, apart from considerations related to the safeguard of the attributes of national sovereignty, it is essential for countries participating in a trade zone to retain autonomy and flexibility in exchange rate management in order to minimize the economic costs of dealing with demand or supply shocks. Excluding this policy tool would lead, in their opinion, to higher output losses and unemployment. But those who argue in this sense fail to explain the reasons why in several countries, regions that are not endowed with the power to adjust the exchange rate of the currency used in their territory, and that face downward rigidity in nominal wages, have nontheless been successful in minimizing the costs of dealing with demand or supply shocks. Why should it be preferable for these regions to have at their disposal the possibility of varying their exchange rate? Does such flexibility allow a given country to lessen or avoid the need for structural adjustment?

Taking an historical perspective, there were significant supply shocks in the Organization for Economic Cooperation and Development (OECD) area during the 1970s, but exchange rate flexibility did not provide a lasting solution for dealing with these shocks. For instance, in the European Community, some currencies floated downward for a number of years in the 1970s, but the resulting sizable depreciations did not eliminate the need for sizable adjustments in both macroeconomic management and economic structures. Although policies accommodating depreciations appear an easy solution to macroeconomic or structural imbalances, in fact they are a deceptive solution because they do not eradicate the root cause of the problem but end up only in buying time.

At the same time, such policies tend to shift, via corresponding currency appreciations, adjustment costs onto countries that have applied financial discipline and/or achieved structural productivity advances. Unless countries participating in a trade zone are willing to accept such an unfair sharing of the costs, a free trade zone with countries pursuing independent exchange rate policies cannot survive. Over the long term, in order to prosper, a trade zone inevitably has to lead to some form of currency zone.

The next issue is what type of currency zones might emerge in this process. Miguel Mancera has given a good account of the various possibilities, ranging from a loose pegging policy to some form of monetary union. How can one identify what could be a viable solution? To this end, one has to take into account the differences in policy objectives and economic conditions among the various countries participating in the trade zone.

First, one objective in moving toward a currency zone could be to prevent any participating country from easily accommodating failures in domestic policy by making its exports cheaper and its imports less competitive.

Second, another objective can be derived from the recognition that the free movement of goods and factors of production within a trade zone tends to reduce the degrees of freedom that a member country has in policy orientation. In such a context, it is preferable for a participating country to aim at the introduction, within the zone, of some rules for exchange rate policy, and possibly for macroeconomic management, rather than being subject to the policy discretion of the major partner countries.

Third, member countries might find it in their mutual interest to reach a common policy, vis-à-vis major currencies of the rest of the world so as to command some degree of seigniorage in international monetary relationships.

Fourth, some participants in a trade zone might belong to the category of small, highly open economies. Such an economy is actually highly dependent on other economies' policy orientations and its ability to pursue divergent policies is very limited, if not nonexistent. Under these conditions, this country has a clear interest in extending the trade zone arrangement to a binding exchange rate arrangement in which it can have some say.

Of course, the range of options in currency zones is large and there is no reason to assume that the free trade zone is bound to evolve into a currency unit. Whether this does occur will depend on the characteristics of the participating economies, such as economic, geographic, or cultural contiguity, and on additional objectives these countries might have. There are at least four additional objectives.

First, member countries might share as a common goal not just the establishment of a free trade zone, but a complete integration of their economies. This is now the case of the European Economic Community.

Second, these countries could consider it important to reduce the uncertainty stemming from the fact that even in a system of permanently fixed exchange rates, currency realignments are still possible. Such an uncertainty can stand in the way of maximizing trade opportunities within a zone and can distort capital movements. To obviate these effects, it is not sufficient to resort to futures or forward markets for foreign exchange. With the exception of a few major economies such as the United States, these markets are generally thin and not well developed. Since they cover only a limited range of maturities and currencies, they do not offer hedging facilities to investors interested in long-term investment or in investing in countries lacking such markets for their currency.

Third, participating countries might aim at counterbalancing their loss of autonomy in macroeconomic policymaking, a loss which is due to the presence within the area of partner countries with an overwhelming economic weight. In this context, it is appropriate for these countries to pursue the establishment of institutions and mechanisms for deciding jointly, that is, with the participation of all member countries, common policies that apply across the entire zone. Thereby, they could share some influence in shaping monetary or financial policies for the area, or could obtain a less uneven distribution of the benefits resulting from freedom of movement of goods and capital by means of a system of fiscal federalism.

If the set of objectives and conditions that have been described are met within a free trade area, then the single currency approach is preferable to a looser exchange rate arrangement, even if it is not a necessary complement to the freedom of trade. It is actually hard to see the advantages of a permanently fixed exchange rate system over a single currency area, because in the latter context, all member countries can have the opportunity of sharing responsibility for the common monetary policy within an appropriate institutional framework.

A single currency will also do away with the costs of currency conversions and, by reducing transaction costs, will maximize the potential of trade liberalization to promote trade. Moreover, in a currency union it would no longer be necessary for a country to curb domestic absorption in order to meet the constraint of balancing the external deficit to a financeable position. In this respect there would be only one currency and only one monetary policy for the whole area, and savings and credit would flow freely across countries within the area, responding mainly to differences in productivity and after-tax profitability among regions. As a result, the notion itself of balance of payments inside the zone would lose policy relevance.

Of course, not all these objectives and conditions that have been mentioned are present in all free trade zones. For instance, there is good reason to doubt whether these elements are present in the North American free trade area. Even in the EEC, one can doubt that all participating countries share these objectives or conditions.

Before concluding, some comments are needed on three points that were raised by previous speakers. One is related to the argument that a European currency union would reduce the scope for potentially good monetary policy in member countries. This argument appears rather unreasonable since it assumes that some countries would always gear their monetary policy to only one objective, namely, price stability, therefore downgrading or excluding other traditional objectives such as to allow their economy to reach a sustainable rate of growth. That argument also appears excessive because it implicitly assumes that in the future European currency union, the model of monetary policy management that will prevail will be too lenient toward member countries with a high inflation propensity. It is actually too early to assert which institutional model for monetary policymaking will be established in this union as well as which country, or group of countries, that have specific policy objectives will prevail in the management of the new monetary institutions.

The second point is related to the discussion concerning first-class/second-class citizens in the evolution of the European Community. It is clear that a number of EC countries are not ready to undertake all the obligations of a currency union. They need a longer time to prepare themselves to fulfill these requirements and responsibilities. But this should be seen as a purely transitory phenomenon, not a permanent one. This transitory stage does not necessarily have to lead to discrimination or separation among member countries since there are no institutional hindrances to prevent some economies from catching up with the leaders. Such a difference among countries is a matter of economic reality that must be overcome rather than accommodated. In particular, it must be overcome through the determination of first-class and second-class countries to cooperate in raising the second-class countries to the same level of economic development and price stability achieved by the first-class countries at an earlier date.

The third point concerns the contention that "half a loaf" is not better than "no loaf"—namely, that the diffusion of free trade regions is inimical to further progress toward full, multilateral trade liberalization. Although under certain conditions such a conclusion might be warranted, these conditions do not correspond to the reality of today's world economy. Today, as a result of several rounds of multilateral tariff reductions that have taken place in the last three decades, the average level of tariffs is quite low, at least among the advanced, industrial countries. Consequently, there is relatively little room left to bring the average tariff level close to zero.

The majority of the remaining trade barriers or obstacles is thus concentrated in the nontariff areas. They stem from regulations that are justified on grounds extending far beyond the economic domain. These regulations may reflect public safety concerns, social factors, or cultural aspects. In order for such nontariff barriers to be lower, they must first be identified, and this requires deeper and longer examinations than in the case of tariff barriers. Second, their reduction requires intervening in areas much broader than tariffs, thereby introducing far-reaching limitations to the powers of national sovereignty of each country. An illustrative example of the complexities involved in curtailing nontariff barriers to trade is provided by the Structural Impediments Initiative that was agreed upon by the United States and Japan in the 1980s.

Most of the current difficulties in reaching a successful conclusion of the Uruguay Round are due to the same complexities. In the face of these difficulties, the creation of new, large free trade areas such as in North America might be seen as a step forward in multilateral trade liberalization, provided that these zones do not raise trade barriers and continue cooperating for the success of multilateral trade negotiations. After all, the articles of the GATT agreement include in some cases (Articles XXIV and XXVIII) a commitment to avoid raising tariffs. An enforcement of such a commitment would suffice to ensure compatibility of regional trade agreements with worldwide trade liberalization. By another token, it could eventually be easier to negotiate a very high degree of trade freedom on a global scale if all the countries of the world were to belong to very few regions with no inside trade barriers. In conclusion, under these conditions it can be said that "half a loaf is much better than no loaf at all."

Financial Market Implications of Trade and Currency Zones

Andrew D. Crockett

Recent developments have focused renewed attention on the implications of trade and currency unions. In Europe, the single market is scheduled to be fully operational by the beginning of 1993. By that date, the countries of the European Community (EC) should be virtually free of all formal barriers to the movement of goods, services, labor, and capital. Meanwhile, in North America, the Canada-U.S. Free Trade Agreement is removing tariff barriers to trade in goods and services between the United States and Canada. Negotiations have recently begun for the creation of a North American free trade area which would embrace Mexico, as well as Canada and the United States.

There are also moves toward strengthening currency links, especially in Europe. For more than a decade, the European Monetary System (EMS), through its exchange rate mechanism, has linked participating currencies in a "zone of monetary stability." Now, after a flurry of activity initiated by the Delors Report (1989)[1] two intergovernmental conferences are under way, aimed at concluding draft amendments to the Treaty of Rome that would eventually transform the European Community into a single currency area. Some of the more ambitious proponents of Economic and Monetary Union (EMU) in Europe envisage a move to locked exchange rates and a single monetary authority as early as the late 1990s.

These various trends have led a number of observers to see the world economy evolving in a tripolar direction, with the United States, Japan, and the European Community serving as the focal point of trade and currency zones of North America, East Asia, and Europe respectively.

This is a considerable simplification of the forces at work, however. For one thing, the three main "zones" in the world economy vary enormously in the tightness of the links among their constituent economies. Europe is on the way to becoming a true economic and monetary union, in which the economies of the EC members will be almost as closely integrated as regions within individual national economies. North America has very close trade links, but has no plans to move forward from the rather informal leadership role occupied by the U.S. dollar. And in East Asia, despite the regional weight of Japan, many of the countries of the region look more toward their trading and other economic links with the United States than to those with Japan.

Another reason why the "tripolar" paradigm can be misleading is that it overlooks the importance of the trend toward greater economic integration at the *global* level. The postwar period has seen the dismantling of much of the network of trade barriers that had been built up during the 1930s and the wartime period. This process has continued in the 1970s and 1980s, albeit at a slower pace and with some backsliding. So the development of closer trading links within the three main areas of the industrialized world, as well as in other smaller regional trading areas, has not been at the expense of trade growth *between* trade zones, or with the rest of the world.

Nevertheless, the growing significance of trade and currency zones poses a series of analytic and policy issues that command attention. This paper will attempt to deal with five of them:

(1) Is there an *inherent dynamic* in regional economic integration? Does increasing trade among national economies lead naturally to a formal trade zone? And does this process tend to spill over into the financial sphere, with growing links involving currency and financial markets?

(2) Will integration lead to changes in *financial structure*? Will institutions and markets become more homogeneous among countries belonging to trade and currency zones? Will transnational financial conglomerates become the norm, or will financial markets remain more segmented, and financial institutions more specialized or localized?

(3) As economies become more closely integrated, how do *supervisory and regulatory* arrangements need to evolve so as to both promote efficiency and competition in the financial sector and at the same time provide adequate prudential safeguards?

(4) What are the implications of trade and currency zones for *monetary and other macroeconomic policies*? Do new instruments of control need to be developed to compensate for the autonomy that is lost as a result of economic integration?

(5) What are the implications for the *management of financial relations between major economic zones*? How is it possible to ensure that greater liberalization *within* regions is not accompanied by the erection of greater barriers to trade and financial relations with the outside world?

This is rather a long list of questions. Each one of them could be the subject of a paper in itself. The following analysis will do no more, therefore, than touch on a number of the key issues that arise. First, however, it is worth a brief digression to define terms.

A definition of terms

At its least formal, a *trade zone* could be said to comprise an area within which trading links are closer and more important than they are with the outside world. Trading relations do not need to be formalized for there to be a recognized mutuality of interest in the trading flows that occur. More usually, however, analytical attention is focused on situations where *preferential trading arrangements* exist between member states in a trade zone. This usually involves understandings that tariffs among members of the preferential trading area will be levied at reduced or zero rates, and/or that quotas and other nontariff barriers will be waived or applied on a less discriminatory basis. Finally, countries can enter into a *single market arrangement* in which goods, services, and factors of production can be exchanged across national boundaries within the union on exactly the same terms as they can be sold domestically. This involves not just the removal of tariffs, but also the elimination of barriers to factor mobility (explicitly excluded in the classical theory of international trade) and the dismantling of administrative barriers that are found in the form of product specifications and labeling requirements, health and safety standards, marketing arrangements, and so on.

Table 1

Increasing Currency Integration	Increasing Trade Integration		
	Preferential Trade Zone	Trading Arrangements	Single Market
Currency Zone	Japan (1991)	U.S. (1991)	
Mutual Currency Management		Europe (1991)	Europe (1993)
Single Currency			Europe (2000+?)

In the domain of currency zones, it is similarly possible to distinguish three broad classes of relationship. The least formal may be called a *currency zone*, and is characterized by the predominant use of a single currency for invoicing trade within the area, as well as the use of that currency as a standard for the management of other currencies within the zone. Such a situation would not involve any formal rights or obligations among members of the zone. A more formalized set of obligations exists in a currency zone with *mutual currency management arrangements*. In such a situation, countries enter into arrangements to maintain the value of their currency in a certain relationship with that of other members of the zone, and to provide and receive the financial resources necessary to meet this obligation. They retain, however, the ultimate responsibility to decide on their internal monetary policy, and have the right to negotiate changes in the external peg for their currency. Lastly, countries can decide to turn such arrangements into a thorough-going *currency union*, in which the countries concerned have, in effect, a single currency with a single monetary authority.

The international economic scene offers examples of all of these types of trade and currency zones. Using the definitions given above, North America has long been a *trade zone*, in the sense that trading relations between the United States and Canada have always been much closer than with other trade partners. But North America has for some time been moving in the direction of becoming a *preferential trading area*. Agreements such as that related to automobiles were formalizing trading links before the Canada-U.S. Free Trade Agreement came into existence in 1989. It seems unlikely that the United States and Canada will become a full *single market* in the foreseeable future, however.[2] Nor is it likely that a formal relationship between the U.S. and Canadian dollars will be established. In the taxonomy developed above, North America is a *currency zone*, because of the central importance of the U.S. dollar, and the fact that Canada (along with many other countries in the Western Hemisphere) gives heavy weight in its own monetary management to its exchange rate with the U.S. dollar. But it seems unlikely that Canada and the United States would contemplate reciprocal obligations in the currency sphere, still less that they would move toward the use of a single currency.

Europe presents a picture of gradual movement in the direction of closer integration, both in the trade and in the currency sphere. In the immediate postwar period, it would have been hard to consider Europe as being either a trade or a currency zone. Several European countries (notably France and the United Kingdom) had closer trading links with suppliers and markets in the developing world than they did with their geographical neighbors and competitors in Europe. Reconstruction, and the gradual removal of payments barriers, strengthened trading links. *Preferential trading arrangements* were established in the late 1950s with the formation of the European Economic Community (EEC) and the European Free Trade Area (EFTA). Thirty years or so later, the passage of the Single European Act (1986) represented an attempt to move the enlarged EEC for-

ward to the status of a genuine *single market*. Similarly, the negotiations on Economic and Monetary Union have the goal of going
beyond the mutual currency arrangements of the EMS to a full
monetary union.

   East Asia has much less closely interlinked economies than either
Europe or North America. Despite the economic weight of Japan,
most economies in the region still depend very heavily on the United
States (and to a lesser extent Europe) as markets for their manufactured goods. Nevertheless, supplier-customer relationships between
Japan and raw-material producing East Asian countries have always
been strong. And they are increasingly being complemented by
investment links, as Japanese manufacturing corporations seek to
use the relatively cheap labor that is still available in other Asian
countries to displace Japanese production of labor-intensive
products.

   The trade and currency zones of the industrial world will be the
principal focus of this paper. Before going on to analyze the questions identified in the introduction, however, it is worth noting that
there are several trade and currency zones in the developing world,
some of which are of quite long standing. The CFA franc zone, for
example, is a fairly highly developed economic union, whose members enjoy preferential trading arrangements and use what is, in
effect, a common currency.[3] The Andean Pact countries have coop-
erated for more than 30 years and tariff-free internal trade is expected
by 1992. Other examples of regional trade arrangements include the
Caribbean Common Market (Caricom) and Mercosur—the recently-
established pact between Brazil, Argentina, Uruguay, and Paraguay
which aims at establishing a free trade zone by the end of 1995.

   Trade and currency zones in the developing world differ from
those among industrial countries in that they generally have the aim
of developing trading links among countries whose existing trade
relations are rather meager. They often represent an attempt to move
away from dependence on trade links with developed countries, and
an effort to enlarge the market for infant industries behind protective
barriers. Trade zones in the industrial world, however, particularly
those in North America and Europe, reflect an attempt to strengthen

further trade linkages that are already strong.

The dynamics of trade and currency zones

The example of the European Community suggests that there is an inherent dynamic to regional economic integration. In Europe, trade linkages became formalized into preferential trade arrangements, and the tariff-free *common* market gave way to a demand for a *single* market, in which administrative as well as formal barriers to trade would be removed, and where factors of production and services would be as free to cross national boundaries as manufactured goods.

From a financial standpoint, an interesting question is whether the benefits of free trade require parallel progress in the field of capital liberalization and financial market integration. Traditionally, freedom of capital movements has been accorded a lower priority in the process of liberalization than freedom of payments for current transactions. This is reflected in a variety of international pronouncements, from the Articles of Agreement of the International Monetary Fund down to the recommendations now being offered to the formerly centrally planned economies as they embark on the process of economic restructuring and reform.

This advice is perhaps understandable. Trade integration brings more obvious benefits in the international specialization of labor, and the linking of the domestic economy with the international price structure. And freedom of payments to finance trade does not have the potentially disruptive effects on currency relationships of freedom of capital transactions.

There are, however, at least four reasons why the removal of controls on capital flows can be important in improving efficiency and welfare in a trade zone.

First, freedom of capital flows is an important complement to the cross border provision of financial services. While exchange controls remain, banking, investment, and insurance services face barriers in international competition. Together, such services represent

some 5-10 percent of GNP in Organization for Economic Cooperation and Development (OECD) countries, and are an important
intermediate input to the production process in the industrial sector.
The principles of specialization of function and comparative advantage are no less important in the area of services than they are in trade
in manufactured goods.

Second, capital liberalization can promote *dynamic efficiency* in
the financial services sector. Not only will liberalization lead to the
displacement of relatively inefficient by relatively efficient suppliers, it will increase competitive pressure on a continuing basis,
and thus promote innovation and productivity improvement.

Third, the removal of capital controls is necessary to improve the
channeling of resources from savers to investors. For a variety of
reasons (demographic, developmental, cyclical, and policy-in-
duced) some countries will be net savers, and others net absorbers
of saving, at a given world rate of interest. Capital account restrictions tend to keep national savings bottled up in each national
economy, and thereby prevent flows of financial and real resources
from economies with a high propensity to save to those with a high
propensity to invest.

Fourth, related to the above, the removal of capital controls of
investment improves the allocation of a given volume of investment.
It can facilitate two-way investment through which enterprises with
technological or managerial know-how in a particular sector can
diversify abroad, and promotes the spread of best-practice techniques
in foreign countries.

Most economists would accept that free capital movements have
potential benefits for international resource allocation. These are
comparable to the benefits that a national economy derives from a
unified capital market and financial system. But capital liberalization
also carries one important drawback. It can facilitate large scale
speculative capital movements that undermine exchange rate
stability. So long as exchange rate stability is felt to be important for
the promotion of trade, and so long as trade in goods is thought to
be more important than trade in services and international invest-

ment, capital account liberalization is likely to be accorded a secondary priority.

To reconcile this conflict requires arrangements that can contain or absorb speculative currency flows, as the freedom of economic agents to move their financial resources is enlarged. The recent success of the European Monetary System's exchange rate mechanism (the last substantive realignment was in January 1987) suggests that it is possible to achieve sufficient policy convergence for fixed exchange rate margins to contribute to exchange rate stability, rather than to provide a focus for speculative attack. This occurs when the belief in the authorities' willingness to do what is necessary to defend a parity is such that private economic agents tend to *buy* currencies at the bottom of their fluctuation margin (to profit from subsequent appreciation) rather than sell them (to profit from eventual realignment).

The contention that the ERM is *inherently* unstable in the absence of capital controls[4] is belied by the experience of the past four and a half years. But it could still be argued that it is *potentially* unstable, if exogenous disturbances or endogenous shifts in policy preferences were to call in question the willingness of monetary authorities to sustain the existing parity grid. It is to deal with this potential instability that some observers believe it is necessary to go forward to full monetary union. Once the members of the EC use a single currency, it will become impossible to envisage realignment, and capital flows within the union will perform the same equilibrating function that they do in, say, the United States.

Of course, the arguments for moving to a single currency are not just to avoid the potentially destabilizing effects of capital flows. It has been argued that the continued existence of difficult national currencies will represent "the last nontariff barrier" once the single market is achieved in 1992. In a thorough study of the costs and benefits of moving to a single currency, the EC Commission has argued that there will be a substantial positive welfare effect from reducing uncertainty and eliminating transactions costs.[5] The Commission's estimate of the benefit may be exaggerated,[6] but the potential trade promoting consequences of currency union nevertheless have a powerful appeal.

The general conclusion of this section is that there is, indeed, a natural evolution within economic zones whereby trade arrangements lead to a perceived need for capital liberalization, and capital liberalization creates the need for closer cooperation on currency arrangements. It would be wrong to suggest that trade zones in North America and Japan will copy the path that Europe has followed at any time in the foreseeable future. But it is perhaps not fanciful to expect that the issue of how to make capital liberalization compatible with the desired degree of regional exchange rate stability is one that will receive increased attention in the years ahead.

Financial market structure

Another financial issue that is raised by the formation of trade and currency zones is how the structure of financial institutions and markets will respond in a situation of greater economic integration. Historically, financial structures have developed differently in different countries. In North America and Japan, for example, there remains a fairly strict segregation of banking and securities business, the product of the Glass-Steagall Act in the United States and Article 65 in Japan. In much of continental Europe, by contrast, the "universal bank" has been the norm. The United Kingdom occupies an intermediate position.

There are also significant distinctions with respect to geographical diversification. In the United States, branching by banks has traditionally been closely circumscribed, while in Europe, banks have branched freely in their respective national economies.

It has been argued earlier that a natural extension of regional free trade in goods is a free market in services, including banking services. Does this mean that financial structures will tend to converge in the member countries of a single market area? Will large multinational conglomerates tend to absorb smaller institutions? And will a single major financial center exert a centripetal force on financial activity in the whole area?

Concerning the long-run development of institutional structures, it seems inevitable that there will be a tendency to converge on the most efficient and low-cost means of providing financial services. To that extent, market forces are bound to bring about some increase in the homogeneity of financial structures within a currency zone. However, most studies do not suggest that there are major differences in efficiency resulting directly from the different structures.[7] Moreover, customs and traditions take time to change, and established relationships between financial institutions and their customers have the character of "sunk capital." All in all, therefore, it seems unlikely that Europe will see rapid changes in existing financial structures as a direct result of single market legislation.

What is perhaps more likely is that capital markets throughout Europe will become increasingly integrated. Improvements in payments systems will link markets for banking services, and the removal of remaining restrictions on cross border investment will promote harmonization in securities market practices. This will inevitably be a gradual process, however. At present, the main financial centers in Europe are in competition with each other for securities business, and attempts at inter-European collaboration have not so far met with great success. The differences in market practice which have been referred to, reflect long-standing differences in tradition between different centers, which will take some time to dissipate. But exposure to free competition will undoubtedly catalyze that process.

Another issue concerns whether the expansion of the market for financial services will eventually lead to a smaller number of larger institutions, as mergers occur to reap economies of scale. Some observers note that the number of banks in the community far exceeds the number of major suppliers in other sectors of economic activity. Just as international trade in goods has led to concentration in steel or chemicals or automobiles, will not the same process lead to mergers in the banking and financial services industries?

Recent research suggests that economies of scale in financial services are significantly smaller than was once thought.[8] The need for size in order to service the borrowing needs of major industrial clients has diminished as large corporations have increasingly found it cheaper to raise finance in their own name. Banking has become increasingly involved with the provision of *services*, rather than *capital*, except in the case of small and medium-sized customers. This has diminished the need for size, and put a premium on the flexibility that smaller financial institutions are able to offer.

Diversification also seems less popular than several years ago. Some attempts to develop financial services conglomerates (Sears Roebuck, American Express) have encountered difficulties in the attempt to manage businesses with different characteristics. The prospect of "Chinese walls" separating different aspects of the business of a single financial enterprise also diminishes the potential attractiveness of diversification.

This does not mean, of course, that diversification will not occur. In particular, it seems likely that the repeal or reform of the Glass-Steagall Act and Article 65 will be accompanied by a movement on the part of banks and securities houses into each other's areas of specialization. In Europe, there has been a pronounced trend toward links between banks and insurance companies. But this does not seem likely to be a trend that will transform the nature of financial intermediation within a short period.

What of the issue of geographical concentration? Will the creation of a single financial area in Europe accentuate the trend toward a world of one dominant financial center in each major time zone? Two conflicting tendencies will come into play. On the one hand, there are clearly economies of concentration in financial markets.[9] These will tend to benefit the position of London, as the restrictions and habits that have kept certain activities in continental centers are abolished or die away. On the other hand, certain restrictions have tended to drive business to the more liberal environment and these activities may be repatriated as restrictions are released. Moreover, technology is diminishing the importance of concentration and making it easier to conduct financial business on the basis of screen and telephone. This may weaken the pull of London as a center of *employment* in the financial services industry, especially if congestion continues to raise employment costs.

The implications of trade and currency zones for financial market structures are therefore difficult to predict with precision. It has been argued here that major changes are unlikely in the short term, given the absence of major disparities in unit costs, and the inertial forces of existing habits and relationships. Over time, forces of convergence could well become more apparent, but even in the long term, complete homogeneity is not to be expected.

Regulatory and supervisory issues

The extension of free trade to financial services, and the progressive elimination of barriers to capital flows, raises the issue of how to structure regulatory and supervisory controls on an appropriate international basis. The basic rationale of regulation and supervision of the financial system is threefold: *first*, to assure prudent management of financial institutions, so that the stability of the financial system is safeguarded; *second*, to ensure that the interests of depositors and investors are protected; and *third*, to foster competitive efficiency, so that the requirements of users of financial services arc adequately met.

These objectives are equally valid when the domain of competition in the provision of financial services is extended to the international level. But the complexity of the issues involved is considerably increased.

Traditionally, the responsibility for the health of financial institutions and markets has lain with the authorities of the country in which financial activity takes place. Institutions that did not meet required standards could be excluded from undertaking business in the country concerned. This basic approach has been somewhat modified over the years as banks and other financial institutions have become increasingly global in their approach. Understandings among regulators provided that certain elements of supervision should be undertaken by "home country" regulators (that is, those in the country of an institution's head office) while others would continue to be undertaken by the "host" country (the country where business is done). But it was always clear that the *host* country had the ultimate right to decide which institutions it would permit to undertake business within its boundaries.

The advent of the single market in Europe will change this situation. The principles of free movement of goods, services, and factors of production mean that individual member states will no longer have the ultimate authority to regulate access to their financial markets.

In the financial services area, the Single Market Act seeks to achieve three broad objectives: *first,* to allow consumers of financial services free access to providers, in whichever member state the latter are located; *second*, to give properly authorized and supervised providers of services the freedom to offer them on equal terms throughout the European Community; and *third*, to ensure that financial service providers compete on a "level playing field."

The first of these objectives can be met by the removal of exchange controls. This is already complete in most member countries. The second will be met by the introduction of the principle of "mutual recognition." The principle of mutual recognition has enabled the European Community to avoid time-consuming and unnecessary harmonization of regulatory structures across all member countries. Instead, countries agree to accept the regulatory decisions of other member states as meeting the requirements for authorization. This approach naturally requires agreement on minimum common standards if it is not to lead to "competition in laxity" and regulatory arbitrage.

The need to agree on minimum common standards is the key practical question in a trade or currency zone where financial services are authorized and regulated on the basis of mutual recognition. All countries have restrictions or regulations about the placement of assets invested on behalf of consumers. There can be no dispute in principle about the need for such restrictions. However, their application in practice can result in a tilting of the playing field against institutions from one or another member country. For example, rules that the assets of insurance companies or pension funds must be invested to a specified minimum extent in instruments issued by governments of their respective home states have an obvious prudential rationale—namely, to protect policyholders from credit and exchange risk—but interfere with the establishment of a true single market.

The various directives designed to give effect to the single market seek to specify appropriate minimum standards for the European Community as a whole, while leaving member states free to apply nondiscriminatory additional standards, where this is appropriate for the conditions of their particular markets. This means that, for a single institution with branches in different member states, portfolio constraints relating to capital adequacy and risk concentration are specified centrally, since it is not sensible to think of branches having capital of their own. "Conduct of business" rules, however, which govern such aspects as relations with customers arc to bc sct by host countries with the important proviso that they must not be disproportionate to the goals they are designed to achieve and thus must not be protectionist in nature.

Deposit protection is an awkward issue. Deposit protection schemes vary quite widely in the degree of formal insurance they provide to depositors. At present, deposit protection is a host state responsibility which means that depositors in the same country are not faced with competing deposit insurance arrangements. But logically it should be a home state responsibility, so that the home country supervisor is forced to bear the financial consequences if an institution it supervises fails. This could, however, lead to deposit protection becoming a competitive factor within individual states unless there were a considerable degree of harmonization. Moreover, to the extent that deposit protection is implicitly subsidized (for example, the expectation that a government would not allow a nationalized bank to fail) there is an issue of competitive equality to be faced.

In Europe, agreement has now been reached, in the Second Banking Coordination Directive, on the mutual recognition of banks in all countries of the European Community. Authorization in one country will permit the institution to operate throughout the European Community. The home country will be responsible for supervising the financial soundness of the institution, and will be entitled to monitor compliance with locally established "conduct of business" rules. Supervisors will, of course, cooperate with each other through the usual channels in Brussels (the Banking Advisory Committee) and Basle (the EC Central Bank Governors Committee).

Rather less progress has been made in the establishment of common standards for the securities business. Indeed, it seems possible that no agreement may be reached, in which case, there will be no automatic mutual recognition for securities firms.

Why should it be proving more difficult to reach agreement for securities than for banking? Part of the answer may be in the relative importance of markets as against institutions in different financial activities. In the securities business, *markets* are more important than *institutions*, while in banking, it is the other way round. In markets, the interests of consumers are protected by conduct of business rules, whereas for institutions, customers must rely more on portfolio constraints. Conduct of business practices vary significantly from market to market. Some countries favor rules to enforce concentration of trading in a single market, so as to improve liquidity; others believe that markets with different operating techniques should be free to compete with one another. Some favor maximum transparency (that is, immediate publication of all trades); while others would prefer to limit or delay publication, so as not to inhibit large transactions. *Last,* some markets operate on a quote-driven system, while others operate on an order-driven system.

It is not necessarily inconsistent with the spirit of the single market to allow the coexistence of different financial markets operating according to different practices. However, the relevant directive (the Investment Services Directive) seeks to achieve agreement on market practices as well as on institutional standards. Failure to agree on the former may prevent agreement on the latter. It will be unfortunate if, as a result, investment services companies do not have access to markets throughout the community, especially as, under the terms of the Second Banking Directive and in line with the universal banking model common in Europe, banks are permitted to engage in the full range of securities activities. Competition among providers of financial services would be undermined, to the detriment of consumers' interests.

What conclusions can be drawn about supervision and regulation in a trade and currency zone?*First*, the concept of a single market implies that providers of financial services (whether institutions or markets) should have the right to offer their services throughout the single market area. This implies, *second*, a single license, whether this is issued by a central regulatory authority or at the country level with mutual recognition throughout the area. *Third*, harmonization of market practices is harder, and arguably less important, than the harmonization of capital standards for credit institutions. Since there are different views about the optimal organizational framework for securities markets, a case can be allowed for allowing different structures to coexist and compete.

Monetary policy in a trade and currency zone

Perhaps the most significant aspect of monetary integration lies in the constraints that it imposes on monetary policy. It is a well known theoretical proposition that, of the three policy objectives—stability of exchange rates, freedom of capital movements, and independence of monetary policy—only two can be achieved continuously. When countries pursue independent monetary policies, differential inflation rates will lead to a trend movement in the equilibrium nominal exchange rates. This movement will quickly be perceived by speculators who, in the absence of capital controls, will undertake capital movements in anticipation of the exchange rate movement. Stable exchange rates will therefore be undermined.

For many years, a solution was sought by making compromises in each of the three objectives listed above. Under both the Bretton Woods system and the ERM, for example, exchange rate stability is an important objective, but parity changes are allowed when situations of "fundamental disequilibrium" occur.[10] Capital movements have generally been allowed when they are in support of direct investment flows or other welfare-enhancing transactions, but have been restricted to the extent necessary to prevent a fixed exchange rate being overwhelmed by short-term speculative flows. And domestic monetary policy has typically not been completely independent. It has been formulated in the light of external constraints, though with the choice of exactly how to respond to these constraints remaining in the hands of national authorities.

Despite this broad characterization, there have clearly been shifts over time in the priority accorded to each of the three objectives. In the Bretton Woods system, fixed exchange rates were seen to be of key importance, and the main objective of monetary policy was to ensure the sustainability of established parities. Capital controls were also important in helping maintain parities, while domestic economic balance was regarded as the task of fiscal policy.[11] By the early 1970s, the benefits of fixed exchange rates were increasingly questioned—at least if that meant fixed *nominal* exchange rates which had to be defended by the use of monetary and intervention policy. Greater priority was accorded to the right of each country to pursue its own stabilization policy, with the exchange rate being the residual, or "shock-absorber" in the system. Capital controls had a limited role to play, although some saw them as useful in dampening speculative excesses.

Those who favored monetary independence for national authorities did so because they assumed that this would increase the freedom of maneuver for stability-oriented policies.[12] They also expected that the common pursuit of stability-oriented policies would, in a world of exchange rate flexibility, ultimately lead to greater, not less stability in *real* exchange rate relationships.[13]

Experience has not borne out the hopes entertained for flexible exchange rates. Real and nominal exchange rates have been highly volatile, both in the short and medium term. And the record on inflation, despite a considerable improvement in the early and mid-1980s, has left much to be desired. (See Charts 1 and 2.)

It is partly this experience that led the European Community to search for arrangements to help create a "zone of monetary stability." The objective is both to create a conducive environment for regional economic integration, and to provide a credible exchange rate "anchor" for domestic monetary policy. Although the empirical literature has generally failed to discover much of an effect of exchange rate volatility on trade, much of the investigation has focused on the effects of short-term exchange rate movements.[14]

Chart 1
Exchange Rate Volatility

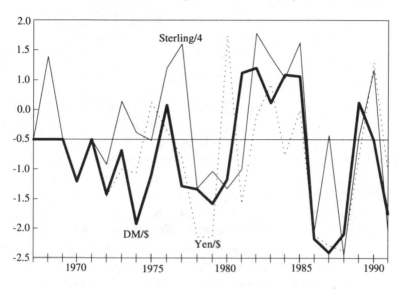

Chart 2
Consumer Price Inflation

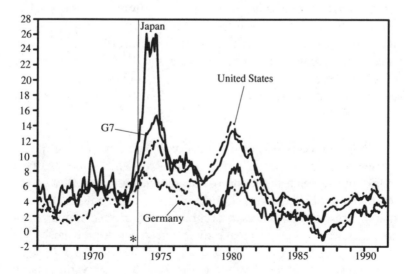

*Denotes move to floating exchange rates

When longer-term swings in competitiveness are considered, economic intuition suggests that such volatility must have adverse resource allocation effects, even if these prove hard to capture using standard econometric techniques.

Europe is now in a situation, therefore, in which exchange rate stability and capital liberalization are avowed priorities. What does this mean for the formulation of national monetary policies?

The existence of the European exchange rate mechanism (ERM) means that costs and price trends must be consistent among ERM members if realignments are to be avoided. In the shorter term, growing confidence in the ERM parity grid means interest rates, too, will tend to converge. However, there remains scope for interest rate divergences, which is provided by two factors: *first*, the existence of exchange rate bands, which even with full credibility of parities would allow interest rates to diverge cyclically among participating countries; and *second*, the existence of residual uncertainty concerning the possibility of realignment, which means that some countries have to pay a "premium" over the interest rates prevailing in the anchor country.

Interestingly, interest rate divergences in Europe, which used to be explainable mainly in terms of the "premium" paid by inflation-prone currencies, are now increasingly the result of cyclical divergences in economic conditions. Chart 3 shows that the spread of short-term interest rates among currencies participating in the ERM has narrowed considerably over the period since the realignment of January 1987.

This has led to a so-called "paradox" whereby high inflation countries tend to be strong within the ERM. This is not really a paradox, but rather a reflection of the increasing credibility of the ERM parity grid. If markets do not expect a realignment, then the higher interest rates needed to combat inflation in countries with excess demand will tend to make their currencies appreciate.

Still, notwithstanding the scope for intercountry variations in monetary conditions, there is little doubt that Europe is gradually

Chart 3
ERM Short-Term Interest Rates[1]

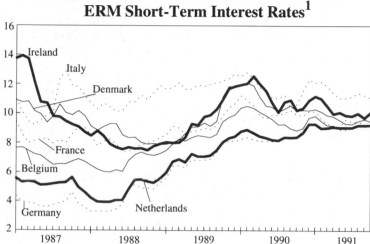

[1]Rates are three month euro-market rates

moving toward a single monetary policy. Since this trend, perhaps in attenuated form, could well occur in other trade and currency zones, it is of interest to consider the manner in which European monetary policy has been framed.

For much of the 1980s, the ERM was a *hegemonic* system, in which the monetary environment was established by the Bundesbank.[15] This was beneficial for the other members of the European Community because of the anti-inflationary orientation of German monetary policy, and the credibility of the Bundesbank. Adherence to the ERM enabled other countries to "borrow" some of the Bundesbank's credibility, and thus to achieve a reduction in domestic inflation at lower cost than might otherwise have been the case.

Despite these successes, however, a hegemonic system has certain disadvantages. *First*, in purely political terms, it is difficult to justify such a role for an institution of one country in a multinational community. *Second*, despite the successful record of the Bundesbank thus far, it cannot be guaranteed that this record will continue in the future. *Third*, the monetary policy suitable for Germany will not necessarily be appropriate at all times for the European Community at large. This is more likely to be an issue when adequate price stability has been restored and combating inflation is no longer an adequate focus, in itself, for the European Community's monetary policy. *Fourth*, if a single currency managed by a newly created institution is to emerge in the future, the continued dominance of the Bundesbank will not allow experience to be gained of communitywide monetary management.

For these reasons, attention has been given to the question of how responsibility for monetary policy can be shared more widely. The Delors Committee concluded, correctly, that ultimate responsibility for monetary management of each currency must be unambiguous. Nevertheless, within this constraint, European central bank governors have increased their cooperation through their regular monthly meetings in Basle. As capital controls have been dismantled and the stability of the ERM has been reinforced, currency substitution has made the growth of *national* monetary aggregates a less reliable guide to policy. The central bank governors have therefore begun to study the use of communitywide indicators as a guide to analyzing policy interactions at the European Community level.

So long as Europe retains twelve separate currencies, none of this will detract from the ultimate responsibility of each national monetary authority to manage its own currency. This situation will change, of course, as soon as the twelve currencies are formally and irrevocably locked. From that time onward, there will be no national monetary autonomy, and all monetary powers will be transferred to an EC institution.

Relations between currency and trade zones

The analysis in this paper so far has been concerned mainly with the financial market implications of trade and currency zones for institutions and markets *within* each zone. But questions also arise of how to manage relations *between* zones. Three sets of issues can be distinguished:

(1) how to ensure that regional economic integration is made compatible with increasing *global* integration and the promotion of a liberal world trading order,

(2) how to preserve equitable market access for institutions coming from outside a particular trade zone, and

(3) how to promote macroeconomic policy coordination aimed at providing the best global environment for stable noninflationary growth.

There is no reason why the development of closer trading and financial links within an economic zone should involve the erection of higher barriers against institutions from nonmember countries. Spokesmen for the European Community, for example, have been at pains to emphasize that the creation of the single market is not intended to lead to "Fortress Europe."[16] Still, it would be naive to deny that trade zones can lead to trade diversion as well as trade creation. Moreover, if there is a given quantum of political "capital" which politicians are prepared to expend to promote freer trade, the more that is spent in supporting regional trade and currency zones, the less there is left over for use in global negotiations.

It is important, therefore, for all governments to be aware of this danger, and for continuous efforts to be devoted to ensuring that the multilateral discussions of the Uruguay Round are a success. From an economic standpoint, regional free trade is a second-best to global free trade.

The issue of *market access* in the financial services sector is one which will increasingly involve negotiations between trade zones. In Europe, questions of financial market access had been, naturally enough, the province of national governments. National authorities had undertaken bilateral discussions with their counterpart authorities in the United States, Canada, and Japan. With the advent of the single market, and the inclusion of financial services within the framework of the Uruguay Round, negotiations on market access will increasingly fall within the competence of the European Community taken as a whole, and in practice, become the province of the

EC Commission.

There are two broad approaches to reciprocal market access. *"Mirror image"* treatment involves the negotiation of identical conditions of establishment for financial institutions in different markets; *"National treatment"* involves the nondiscriminatory treatment of all financial institutions in each national market, but without requiring that each market necessarily offer the same privileges and regulations as its competitors.

Mirror image reciprocity is obviously a considerably more restrictive requirement than national treatment. There is now general agreement that issues of reciprocal market access should be based mainly on the principle of national treatment. This principle is a useful basis for financial relations, but it is not always sufficient to ensure a "level playing field" in competition between domestic and foreign financial institutions. For example, if a foreign financial institution is required to establish a subsidiary rather than a branch, this could be held to be inequitable since it does not take account of the availability of head office capital to domestic institutions conducting the same business. In a similar vein, the imposition of interest rate ceilings may hamper the ability of foreign banks to compete, if they do not have access to the retail deposit base available to indigenous banks. In other words, the playing field must be level de facto, as well as de jure.

Lastly, as the global weight of the three main trade and currency zones increases, and as the financial links between the zones become closer, the question arises of how *macroeconomic interactions* among the zones should be managed.

The large and prolonged appreciation of the U.S. dollar in the early 1980s, and its substantial depreciation thereafter, show that currency relationships can undergo substantial medium-term swings in the absence of policies to limit or avoid them. These swings have resulted from policy changes that shift relative savings/investment balances in individual countries. Since swings in exchange rates have major effects on economic growth and inflation, as well as on the virulence of inflationary pressures, it is natural that consideration should be given as to how to limit them.

There are two broad approaches to avoiding the damaging consequences of medium-term exchange rate swings. One involves the establishment of some form of "target zones" for key exchange rates. The expectation is that the policies required for a country to keep its currency within the target zone will help correct savings/investment imbalances, and thus make economic fundamentals consistent with the established target zone. The other approach involves an attempt to deal with macroeconomic imbalances directly through a process of multilateral surveillance and peer pressure.

There are two crucial drawbacks to a process of international policy coordination based on target zones. The first is that it is not easy to identify what is an "equilibrium" exchange rate, around which a target zone would be set. The second is that there can be no guarantee that the policies used to maintain an exchange rate within a target zone will, in fact, be the appropriate ones. For example, if a currency is appreciating because of a loose fiscal/tight monetary policy mix, the desirable solution is to tighten fiscal policy. But the exchange rate constraint could equally be satisfied by an easing of monetary policy—a solution that would tend to exacerbate the original demand/supply imbalances.

If exchange rate rules are impractical as a way of organizing relations among the major economic regions, other means of policy coordination have to be found. Thus far, this has been in the form of the "G-7 process," which involves continuous consultation among the seven major industrial countries on matters of joint policy interest. Although the G-7 process has its defenders, it also has acknowledged shortcomings.[17] These range from the political objections to the exclusivity of the group, to the more technical complaint that there is no satisfactory model of international economic relationships underlying the coordination process. It is obviously unsatisfactory that policy coordination should rest on such an incomplete structure, yet it is not easy to see how it could be developed and formalized.

Conclusions

This paper has argued that the growing economic linkages within trade and currency zones have important implications for financial markets. These implications have to be considered along with the impact of technical innovations that are already exerting pressures for the globalization of financial relations.

The intensification of trade relations, whether regionally or globally, leads to increased pressure to reduce tariffs and then to reduce remaining barriers to trade. Freer trade in goods in turn creates pressures for financial liberalization. This is necessary both to complete the process of trade liberalization, and to lay the basis for a more effective international use of savings and investment.

Capital liberalization accelerates the integration of financial markets and thereby raises issues of prudential and regulatory control, as well as those of macroeconomic policy coordination, to a different level. Policymakers within a trade or currency zone face two sets of questions: how to coordinate regulatory and macroeconomic policy *within* the zone, so as to maximize the benefits of market integration; and how to manage relations with *other* countries and zones, so as to preserve a liberal and mutually beneficial world trade environment.

There can be little doubt that the emergence of trade and currency zones is having a profound effect on financial markets. It is to be hoped that they are only part of a wider picture of liberalization, in which the benefits from global economic integration will come to exceed those from integration on a regional basis.

Endnotes

The author thanks Michael Foot, Tony Latter, Lionel Price, Alan Crawford, Stephen Collins, Phil Davis, Stuart Iles, and Robin Webster for helpful comments on an earlier draft.

[1]Delors Report, "Report on Economic and Monetary Union in the European Community," EC Commission, April 1989.

[2]Even the United States is not a true single market in this respect. Different regulations at state level (for example, with respect to car emissions) mean that the same product cannot be sold without modification throughout the union. Moreover, in the financial sector, banks are limited in their interstate activities, and insurance services are regulated at state level.

[3]IMF, "A Review of CFA franc arrangements," SM/90/136, July 9, 1990.

[4]See Alan A Walters, "Britain's Economic Renaissance."

[5]EC Commission, "One Market, One Money," European Economy, 1990.

[6]"Exchange Rate Volatility and World Trade," IMF Occasional Paper No. 28, 1984.

[7]Comparative work on bank margins, such as Revell J., "Costs and Margins in Banking: An International Comparison," 1980, as well as analysis of more recent OECD data on the same subject reveal few systematic differences between bank margins and bank profitability in countries with universal banks, as compared with those that separate commercial and investment banking. Such divisions as occurred could be related to factors such as the division of banking business between retail and wholesale, and competitiveness of the financial system.

[8]"Competition in Banking," OECD, Paris 1989.

[9]See E. Philip Davis, BE Discussion paper No. 51, and Grilli (1989).

[10]"Fundamental disequilibrium" has never been formally defined, but is usually taken to mean a situation in which a sustainable current account position cannot be achieved without unacceptable consequences for domestic economic activity.

[11]Williamson.

[12]Walters, *op. cit.*

[13]Friedman, "The Case for Flexible Exchange Rates."

[14]"Exchange Rate Volatility and World Trade," IMF Occasional Paper No. 28, 1984.

[15]See Francesco Giavazzi and Alberto Giovannini, "Models of the EMS: Is Europe a Greater Deutsche Mark Area?" in Ralph C. and Richard Portes (eds.) *Global Macro-economics: Policy Conflict and Cooperation,* IEA and CEPR, 1987.

[16]Sir Leon Brittan: A speech to Bankers Association for Foreign Trade, June 5, 1989.

[17]See Wendy Dobson, "Economic Policy Coordination: Requiem or Prologue," IIE, April 1991, for a discussion of the strengths and weaknesses of G-7 coordination.

Commentary:
Financial Market Implications
of Trade and Currency Zones

John G. Heimann

In order to present my views on Andrew Crockett's excellent paper, I will divide my comments into two sections:

(1) How trade and currency zones affect regional economic integrations: monetary and other macroeconomic policies, and management of financial relations between major economic zones and

(2) how such zones affect the financial and institutional structure and the supervision and regulation of that structure.

Mr. Crockett argues that there is an inherent dynamic in regional economic integration, with increasing trade leading toward formal trade zones, pressure for capital liberalization, and closer cooperation on currency arrangements. His discussion of the forces pushing Europe toward monetary integration is persuasive in supporting his thesis.

Interestingly, the same forces that he describes in the European context have been visible in the global context of G-7 currency arrangements as well. As Mr. Crockett notes, the "tripolar" paradigm can be misleading by overlooking the importance of the trend toward global integration that has continued even as regional ties became closer. The development of closer trading links within the three main areas of the industrialized world over the last twenty years has spurred liberalization of international capital flows and rapid movement toward a unified global capital market.

But the move toward a unified global market also carried the drawback of promoting speculative capital flows and exchange rate instability, as witnessed in the spectacular rise and fall of the dollar in the 1980s. Concerns about the potentially damaging effects of exchange rate instability on trade and investment prompted closer cooperation on currency arrangements between the major nations, starting with the Baker-Miyazawa accord in 1986 and evolving into the Louvre Accord framework for currency management that has been (more or less) in place since February 1987. Although the commitment toward "target zone" management of dollar-yen and dollar-deutsche mark has been far less formalized than European currency arrangements, it illustrates the same set of forces at the global level that Mr. Crockett describes at the regional level.

That said, a key question that remains unanswered is whether the concern about currency stability that prompted the Louvre Accord is justified. According to research cited by Mr. Crockett, growth in world trade does not appear to have been unduly hampered by large currency movements among the main industrialized nations in the 1980s, nor is it clear that overall levels of capital investment suffered. In addition, it can be argued that the move to stabilize exchange rates carried the undesirable side effect of exporting higher inflation from the United States to Japan and Germany as their central banks, in effect, helped the United States monetize its deficits. Since considerable disagreement about the desired degree of global exchange rate stability remains, it can be expected that the same issues Mr. Crockett has raised about capital liberalization and exchange rate stability at the regional level will continue to be of great importance at the global level as well.

Mr. Crockett describes clearly the economic logic behind the proposition that movement toward fixed currency and free capital flows within a trading bloc will require the abandonment of national monetary autonomy. In the context of Europe's movement toward monetary integration, he describes the need to develop new instruments of control and new institutions to compensate for the loss of monetary autonomy involved in the move toward economic and monetary integration. Obstacles to establishing a Eurofed that is not simply an extension of the Bundesbank are discussed as well as the need to establish European Communitywide indicators as a guide to setting policy at the communitywide level.

This point strikes at the heart of the Brussels versus Westminster argument that causes so much consternation in the United Kingdom. A fixed currency zone in Europe has clearly removed (to differing degrees) the ability of national governments to implement monetary policy. This disenfranchisement has been greatest for those nations that have the tightest currency links within the exchange rate mechanism (ERM) (Netherlands, Belgium, and to a lesser degree, France and Denmark) and who have had to almost fully replicate German monetary policy changes in the past. Fiscal policy control has not been ceded so quickly but the ability of national governments to adopt contrasting fiscal stances is still limited by ERM constraints. However, in the future, it is expected that rules on fiscal policy may be imposed on aberrant national governments in order to safeguard Economic and Monetary Union.

What might be usefully added to the analysis is some discussion of the impact of a move toward monetary integration on domestic fiscal policy as well. Recent work by Giavazzi and Spaventa ("The New EMS," Center for Economic Policy Research, Discussion Paper No. 369) points out that, with the abandonment of the use of monetary policy for domestic stabilization, EC members may have to make more flexible and determined use of fiscal policy for that purpose. Unfortunately, the track record of state and local governments in the United States is not encouraging on this score. They are already in the position that EC member states will be in when they lose autonomy over monetary affairs, and appear to use state-level fiscal policy in a pro-cyclical manner—that is, raising spending when the economy is doing well and cutting it when the economy weakens.

Mr. Crockett's warning that trade zones can lead to trade diversion as well as trade creation is well-taken, as is his observation that the more political "capital" that is expended to promote regional trade and currency zones, the less there is left over for use in global negotiations. I concur that governments need to be aware of this danger and continue to work toward a successful conclusion of the multilateral discussions of the Uruguay Round.

His observation that there is no satisfactory model of international economic relationships underlying the G-7's coordination process may be accurate, but it is worth noting that there is a successful example of a large, geographically and economically diverse region that has maintained monetary unity and free internal capital movement. It is the United States. If Europe can provide a model of how nations with diverse political systems, cultures, and languages can achieve economic integration comparable to that in the United States—without resorting to a "Fortress Europe" approach toward its relations with the rest of the world—then broader visions of global free trade and closer economic integration will, in time, become possible.

Mr. Crockett then poses a series of questions as to the effect of zones on the financial and institutional structure:

(1) Does this mean that financial structures will tend to converge in the member countries of a single market area?

(2) Will large multinational conglomerates tend to absorb smaller institutions?

(3) Will a single major financial center exert a centripetal force on financial activity in the whole area?

I agree with his view that it is unlikely Europe will see rapid changes in the existing financial structures as a direct and immediate result of single market legislation. The longer term, however, depends on what happens in the rest of the world. There will be some changes which will be the result of further improvements in technology and the commercial logic arguing for consolidation. But, as he notes, the most likely area for change is the capital markets system which is rapidly becoming more integrated throughout Europe and throughout the world. Free competition will clearly act as a catalyst in the European capital markets and whereas it is true that the

European financial centers are in competition, they are clearly dominated by London. This will continue since London has the critical mass of people, technology, and the like unless the British authorities take actions which will drive market participants away. On the other hand, it is logical to conclude that considerable growth in capital markets will be outside London in centers such as Paris and Frankfurt which are making an attempt to attract capital market activities. Hence, the European capital markets will grow on an absolute basis, as will London, but on a relative basis, growth outside London should be greater.

With respect to diversification, I agree with Mr. Crockett on his fundamental points. Obviously, the repeal of Glass-Steagall and Article 65 will be accompanied by a considerable diversification activity on the part of banks in the United States and Japan. But these actions will be on the margin; they will not transform the financial institutions over the short run.

On a global basis over time, I believe that large multinational conglomerates will tend to absorb smaller institutions. Put another way, rationalization of the international financial structures will follow domestic restructuring which is now happening in the EC; ABN/AMRO, Hispano Americano/Central, bank mergers in Italy, and a multiplicity of cross-shareholding arrangements; in the United States, Bank of America/Security Pacific, Manufacturers Hanover/Chemical, C&S/Sovran; and in Japan, where we have already witnessed two major bank mergers.

Over the next decade, the financial structure will evolve into a two-tiered system, global institutions and global markets, plus discreet regional and national markets served by regional and national institutions. To some degree this has been going on for years, and as the journalists say, "more to come."

Financial scandals are this summer's songs. In the United States, Salomon has shocked the markets as it confessed to improper behavior in the U.S. Treasury market. The Japanese are awash in scandals involving large financial institutions where securities houses have been involved in customer paybacks and the ramping of

shares, fraudulent loans in the banking system, and assorted crimes
and misdemeanors. In Frankfurt, illegal insider trading activities
have been uncovered. And the shock waves of the criminal manipulation of BCCI continue to reverberate.

These scandals follow on the savings and loans mess in the United
States, the fall of Drexel Burnham, and the excesses of the junk bond
era; the Blue Arrow and Guinness affairs in London; and other
problems within the world's financial system.

In the case of Salomon, was the dispersal of supervisory responsibility between the Treasury, the New York Fed, and the Securities
and Exchange Commission a recipe for ineffective oversight? On an
international scale, is the lack of a consolidated supervisory overview of BCCI the reason why its condition went undetected? In
Japan, is the obverse true—namely, the concentration of basic
supervisory powers within the MOF which has viewed Japanese
financial institutions as an instrument of national policy, rather than
the object of policy?

As Mr. Crockett correctly notes, the basic rationale for supervision is

—to assure prudent management of financial institutions;

—to assure that the interests of depositors and investors are
protected; and

—to foster competitive efficiency.

He points out that the regulation of international banking, with all
its flaws, is more advanced than the regulation of international
securities markets. He further adds that in banking, institutions are
more important, whereas in the securities business, markets are
more important than institutions. Yet we live in an age where
banking and securities activities are coming closer together.

International banking regulation has come a long way since
Herstatt. The Bank for International Settlements Committee on

banking supervision—the Cooke Committee, now to be chaired by Jerry Corrigan of the New York Fed—has made meaningful progress on many fronts, such as capital adequacy. Yet much remains to be done. Mr. Crockett points out, as an example, the competitive complications of deposit insurance arrangements between host and home countries, unless the schemes are harmonized. Banking has become international; supervising it has not!

The key issues are:
(1) How is systemic risk best limited?

(2) Should branches of foreign banks be treated the same way as subsidiaries?

(3) Under whose rules should deposits be insured?

(4) Should there be an agreed way to resolve competing international claims on the assets of a failed bank (BCCI)?

These issues and more are discussed in the Group of Thirty's Occasional Paper—*International Trade in Banking Services: A Conceptual Framework*—authored by Sydney J. Key, an economist with the Board of Governors of the Federal Reserve System, and Hal S. Scott, a professor at Harvard, which lays out a framework for strengthening the regulatory system. They have provided a "Banking Matrix" using three sets of regulation—Home Country, Host Country, and Harmonized Rule—that underlie the often confusing principals of national treatment, mutual recognition, and effective market access.

What must be achieved over time is an international supervisory system of harmonized standards. This is easier to apply to credit institutions than to market practice. If the trend toward further integration of credit institutions with capital market activities continues and since markets are more difficult to harmonize than banks—then I believe that more and more market harmonization will be directed through the institutions that operate in those markets. In the final analysis, we need to pay more attention to capital market activities and the supervision thereof than we do at the present time.

Mexico's Macroeconomic Adjustment and Growth Perspectives

Pedro Aspe

Over the last decade, the world economy has changed dramatically. Almost every nation on the planet is gearing its economy toward a market economy. They want to be more flexible, they want to be more open, and they want to be more efficient. They have to be.

Back in the eighteenth and nineteenth centuries, the assumptions of comparative factor advantage were more persuasive than they are today. Many industries were fragmented, production was more labor intensive and less skill intensive, and international trade patterns reflected differences in natural resource endowments and capital.

Today, economies of scale are widespread. Products are highly differentiated. We have seen explosive technological change, especially in widely applicable technologies such as microelectronics.

Advanced materials and information systems have rendered the traditional distinction between high and low technology industries obsolete. And now, it's not only the manufacturing industries that are facing more international competition—so are the service industries.

Many firms now compete with truly global strategies. They sell their products and services worldwide, and they can take advantage of more attractive factor costs and institutional conditions.

It is painfully obvious that those few countries that still subscribe to protectionist policies are only walking further down that primrose path to self-sufficiency—and poverty. Today, we have a much broader notion of what constitutes the wealth of nations. A wealthy nation is one where any legitimate business, started by anyone, has a chance to be successful, and one where the authorities work to foster, rather than hinder, the conditions which allow their country's entrepreneurs to develop and to compete in the international marketplace.

Policy has had to look economic reality square in the face. And now that it has, policy is going back to address the fundamentals of economic welfare. Now we know that a healthy economy is based on a few simple, but very often difficult to attain principles.

On the one hand, macroeconomic stability and consistent policies are critical. Without that, a country suffers a chaotic inflationary environment, and therefore, speculation and capital flight. And all the talk about privatization, deregulation, and trade liberalization will be nothing more than that: Just talk.

Confidence is a prerequisite for economic recovery and sustained growth. But confidence is not a gift. It must be earned through the adjustment effort—or rather, confidence is rented because it is never yours and because it can be taken away at any time. This means the adjustment effort is never over. The adjustment effort has to go on each and every day.

On the other hand, although fiscal and monetary prudence are crucial, it must also be recognized that permanent economic growth can only be achieved when such prudence is accompanied by the modernization of the economic structure. It is then very important to combine the policies that foster a stable macroeconomic climate with actions leading to increases in productivity, a high national savings rate, a more progressive income distribution, and a more important role for the private sector.

The economic crisis of the 1980s showed us that stabilization and structural change must proceed together. That decade also taught us that, in a world where the globalization of markets is opening new frontiers, it is essential to have established the economic basis for each country's people to actively participate in the world economy.

The Salinas Administration, which began December 1, 1988, has worked together with the Mexican people to implement and follow through with a tough, wide-ranging program of economic adjustment and structural change, which started with the de la Madrid Administration. Our goal has been to consolidate the correction of monetary and fiscal imbalances, and to eliminate the distortions that inhibit economic growth. But this program is more than an attempt to "correct macroeconomic disequilibria." It also includes an ongoing social pact to attack price inertia, the systemic elimination of nontariff barriers to trade, the modernization of the financial sector, a sweeping fiscal reform, and a financially sound social spending program.

As for correcting the fiscal imbalance, Mexico's fiscal effort over the last eight years has no parallel in the postwar experience of the Western economies. The Mexican public sector's primary balance had been in deficit for several decades—and yet, since 1983, it has recorded a sizable surplus every year. The size of this adjustment from 1982 to 1990 amounts to 14 percent of gross domestic product (GDP). We're talking about the equivalent of almost three Gramm-Rudmans, fully enforced and with no waivers.

Over this period, in the face of both domestic and external financing constraints, public expenditures net of interest payments were reduced by 10 percent of GDP, while public revenues rose substantially as a result of the fiscal reform and public sector relative price corrections.

Nevertheless, the experience of one country after another proves that to achieve lower inflation and investor confidence, it is not enough to have spectacular, yet transitory, spending cuts. A successful adjustment program involves permanent adjustment, and it involves policies that address the expansion of the productive base. Thus, structural change must be an essential part of any successful strategy. In Mexico, we have tried to combine these two crucial aspects on

several fronts: the fiscal system, social spending, the financial
sector, our industrialization and development policies, privatization,
and trade liberalization.

Let's consider the fiscal system first. Almost eighteen months ago,
we launched a sweeping tax reform. Its main objectives: to promote
economic efficiency by establishing adequate incentives for investment; to enhance Mexico's international competitiveness by bringing our domestic tax system more into line with that of our major
trade partners, to promote domestic savings; and to improve income
distribution.

The basic idea has been to increase fiscal revenues through lower
tax rates, while at the same time broadening the tax base—both for
corporate and personal income. Specifically, we have brought down
the maximum tax rate for individuals from 52 percent in 1989 to 35
percent today, and we have brought down the corporate tax rate from
42 percent to 35 percent. In order to bring down tax rates and still
achieve fiscal balance and macroeconomic stability, we have been
fighting tax evasion and we have been treating formerly over-
protected interest groups like the rest of the taxpayers.

It's now been a little more than a year and a half, and the results
of this reform have been highly encouraging. In spite of the reduction
in tax rates, last year total revenues increased at a real rate of 8
percent—compared to a 3.9 percent growth in GDP. We had a 4.5
percent real increase in income tax collection and we had more than
16 percent real growth on our value added tax revenues. As for
enforcement, a few figures are revealing: Between 1930 and 1988—a
period of fifty-eight years—the Fiscal Jury prosecuted and convicted
only two cases for fiscal evasion. Now, in less than thirty months,
more than 200 cases have been indicted.

According to the Mexican Constitution, the state must provide
certain strategic and social services. But in the past, scarce resources
had been put to use in a wide variety of activities that benefited few
sectors, while essential services, such as education, infrastructure,
health care, and justice administration, were left wanting. Back in
1983, the Mexican government began a major divestiture program

as part of the structural reform of public enterprises. To give you an idea of the progress that is being made, in 1982, there were more than 1,100 state-owned companies. To date, 770 have been privatized, merged, or liquidated, and 165 are in process. That means that out of 1,155 originally state-owned firms, there are now only 120. Of course, this has helped improve the Mexican economy's overall productivity—but it has also been an important factor in improving the public finances on a permanent basis. This improvement has been key for increasing the state's effectiveness in providing strategic and social services.

Here I should stress that divestiture is not necessarily synonymous with privatization. It has been said that sometimes one bankruptcy is worth many sales. Not every government enterprise can be sold. Many of them simply are unviable—and recognizing this is an essential step. Many people think that the goal of the economic program should be to save it all—but often it is better to compensate the workers generously, once and for all, rather than to keep bleeding the public treasury. Besides, calling a bankruptcy by its name is a clear signal that the government knows what it is doing, and that it is committed to do what must be done to permanently correct structural imbalances.

So far the Salinas Administration has successfully concluded sales of a number of large enterprises. For example, we have privatized the two national airlines, Mexicana and Aeromexico, and one of the largest copper mines in the world, Compania Minera de Cananea. And in May of this year, we completed the privatization of Telefonos de Mexico.

With respect to social spending, our greatest challenge over the next year is to eradicate poverty and to correct the inequalities among different segments of the population. Poverty and glaring inequality threaten not only the economic modernization efforts, but they also threaten the democratic process and even national sovereignty.

The National Solidarity Program is our effort to use the resources that are now available after having made corrections in the public finances to strengthen social spending, but in such a way that we do not substitute or exclude citizen action. The National Solidarity Program convokes, aids, and coordinates the efforts of all of Mexican society. It recognizes the proposals of ethnic groups, of poor farmers, and of poor urban neighborhoods. These individuals and their interests are represented in decisionmaking.

The National Solidarity Program has made possible the electrification of 9,000 communities, which benefits 8 million people; it has also made possible the rehabilitation of 120,000 schools and the construction of 1,600 potable water and drainage systems in 224 cities. Furthermore, this program has also helped more than a million poor farmers improve their production. All of this has been achieved since 1989.

Our efforts in the financial sector have focused on making the domestic financial system more efficient. The most important step has been to initiate the reprivatization of the commercial banks.

We have introduced a number of new financial instruments to what was already a fairly advanced money market. Few people are aware that the foundations of a modern money market were laid down back in 1978 when the Mexican Treasury Bill, known as the "Cete," was introduced. In recent years we have created bonds indexed to the exchange rates and to the consumer price index, treasury bills with longer maturities and flexible interest rates, and a large market of bankers' acceptances and other instruments not subject to standard regulations and with flexible interest rates and maturities.

Also, in December 1989, Congress passed a legislative package which provides for the modernization of nonbank financial institutions such as brokerage houses and the stock exchange, insurance companies, leasing companies and warehouses, as well as the development of financial groups.

Another important part of the financial reform is that the central bank has cut back financing to the federal government. This is directly related to strengthening the public finances in that it means lower public sector borrowing requirements. But also, since it increases confidence, this directly translates into more attractive opportunities for noninflationary public sector borrowing. Specifically, during the first half of this year, the central bank slashed total net financing to the federal government by almost 30 percent in nominal terms. Meanwhile, nominal and real interest rates continue to drop.

Mexico has made another key effort with trade reform. Our sweeping trade liberalization has transformed a highly protected economy into an open economy. To give you an idea of how dramatic that transformation has been, in 1982, virtually all imports to Mexico were subject to nontariff barriers. Today, less than 20 percent of the value of our imports is subject to quantitative restrictions, in any form. And tariffs have plummeted. In 1982, they were at a maximum level of 100 percent. Today, maximum tariffs stand at only 20 percent.

As a result of these reforms, Mexico's trade structure is much more diversified. Back in 1982, crude oil exports accounted for 75 percent of Mexico's total exports. We have directly attacked that unhealthy dependence on crude oil. Manufactured exports now account for over half of all Mexican exports and oil exports account for less than 30 percent of total exports.

Another major element in our trade reform efforts is the Free Trade Agreement with the United States and Canada. The Salinas Administration has begun negotiations with its North American counterparts with the firm understanding that the agreement, which will grant a reciprocal and fair treatment to all parties, will make possible a better use of economies of scale and will generate new investment and employment opportunities.

When we look at the experiences of countries like Spain and Portugal, we see that a small and labor abundant country can join in a free trade area and reap enormous benefits, especially if it exploits the comparative advantages of its own and its larger and more industrialized counterparts.

But Mexico will not be the only winner in a Free Trade Agreement. The United States and Canada are both facing the challenge of the

European Economic Community's economic integration with the low labor cost countries of Eastern Europe, as well as less ballyhooed steps Japan is taking to integrate with Asia, and especially Southeast Asia. Together, the Mexican and the North American markets have enormous potential. To get an idea of how enormous that potential is, just look at the border area between Mexico and the United States. Although many people are surprised to hear this, it is a fact that, over the last ten years, the Mexico-U.S. border area has been the fastest growing region in the world.

For Mexico to join the world economy, we need foreign direct investment. We expect foreign direct investment to play an important role, complementing domestic direct investment, in promoting employment, in modernizing plant and equipment, and in opening new export markets. As per our new foreign investment rules, foreigners may now invest in sectors which used to be off-limits, only open to Mexican nationals. For example, foreign direct investment is now permitted in glass, cement, iron, steel, airlines, secondary petrochemicals, and cellulose. Also, via specially designed trusts, foreigners may now invest in the Mexican stock markets.

As the process of structural change advances, it has become increasingly clear that structural reform measures do indeed have a profound impact on macroeconomic performance—but they have also changed the way the public authorities should look at the aggregate data.

In economics, there is a more elegant way to say this: "The transmission mechanisms have changed." And this change in itself implies a change in the way fiscal and monetary policy should respond to external shocks.

Let me explain what this means for the case of Mexico: In the transition from a closed, overly regulated economy suffering from hyperinflation to an open, stable economy, the same current account deficit can have totally different implications for exchange rate stability, inflation, and growth. For instance, in a closed, inefficient economy, a balance of payments deficit is usually the result of excessive public spending, which, to be financed, requires public sector external borrowing. This usually ends in a devaluation, a recession, and a jump in the inflation rate. Thus, here the causality runs from public spending to current account deficit, to borrowing, to an exchange rate collapse, hyperinflation and then fiscal adjustment to restore equilibrium.

On the other hand, let's look at an economy with a more active private sector. Let's suppose there is an autonomous improvement in the investment climate, such as might come from the prospect of joining a free trade area. Here the causality is precisely the reverse. Here the current account and the capital account are more closely linked because the current account balance is the result of new private sector projects. These projects are directly financed with capital repatriation or foreign direct investment. Thus, when there is a private sector current account deficit, there is, at the same time, a private sector capital account surplus. The excess of imports over exports is automatically financed, so there is no reason to expect a devaluation, or a recession, or hyperinflation.

In summary, whereas before the structural change a current account deficit is bad news, after the structural change a current account deficit is good news. It is a signal that foreign and domestic capital have confidence in the now more modern economy.

Thus in the future, our notion of what constitutes macroeconomic "normality" will have to be very different from what it used to be in the sixties, the seventies, and eighties. We should expect to see substantial primary government budget surpluses as a result of the commitment to fiscal discipline and from higher domestic savings rates. And as the economy offers more and increasingly attractive opportunities, and as higher productivity results in improved standards of living, we should also expect to see lower inflation and a sustainable real exchange rate appreciation—and we should expect to see relatively persistent private capital inflows. Current account deficits will be reduced to the extent that capital imports translate into higher levels of exports.

In the last ten years, Mexico has come a very long way in reshaping its development strategy. Our experiences over the phases of economic expansion, crisis, and adjustment have taught us that in promoting economic growth, government budget deficits and inflationary finance have a very limited role. These experiences have also taught us that instability has very uneven effects on income distribution. And these experiences have also taught us that sound macroeconomic policy is less a matter of ideology than it is a pledge to work for social justice.

Under President Carlos Salinas, Mexico is making the transition from hyperinflation to stability. But as Mexico makes that transition, Mexico also faces the challenge of joining a world economy that is undergoing dynamic transformation. Deregulation and a technological revolution that has fundamentally changed the way we organize ourselves to trade, produce, and finance are fueling the emergence of economic blocs and free trade areas.

On the fruits of our own efforts, we Mexicans have regained our self-confidence. But as authorities, we are fully aware that for Mexico to make a successful transition to stability—and for Mexico to fully participate in the world economy—we must have the support of all Mexicans. And we must create, together with the international community, an environment of cooperation based not only on the recognition of the enormous potential gains from exchanging materials, financial and technological resources, but also from the cultural and political interaction of our societies.

The Macroeconomic Policy Implications of Trade and Currency Zones

Jacob A. Frenkel
Morris Goldstein

The motivation for a conference on trade and currency zones is not hard to find. Over the past five to six years, many of the initiatives for improving the design and functioning of the trade and exchange rate system have been advanced in a regional rather than in a global context.

The most dramatic developments have been in Europe—and this even putting aside both the historic events in Eastern Europe and German unification. After more than a decade of experience with the European Monetary System (EMS), the twelve member countries of the European Community (EC) are now actively engaged in discussions and negotiations on the path to Economic and Monetary Union (EMU); a sister Intergovernmental Conference is simultaneously discussing political union. Proposals for a European EMU have, of course, been made and discussed before—most notably in connection with the Werner Report (1971)—without bearing fruit. This time, however, prospects for the establishment of a central European monetary authority, a fully integrated financial area, and a single European currency (at least within the EC) have to be taken seriously. For one thing, some significant preparatory steps have already been taken, including the liberalization of capital flows within the EC as part of the broader based progress toward completion of the internal market, and the enlargement of the Exchange Rate Mechanism (ERM) of the EMS—buttressed in October

157

1990 with the entry of the United Kingdom. For another, the process of moving toward EMU has gotten down to concrete specifics. Thus, for example, considerable background work has been undertaken on both the draft statutes for a European Central Bank (ECB) and on the kinds of fiscal policy indicators that would be useful in discouraging excessive fiscal deficits of individual member countries. To be sure, a number of contentious issues remain that make hazardous any projections about the speed, membership, and perhaps, even the end result of the process. But the momentum toward EMU is difficult to deny.

There are no proposals in either North America or in Asia and the Pacific that are as ambitious in the contemplated scope and depth of regional economic integration as what is now being negotiated in Europe. In this sense, while one can speak of the possible evolution of a tripolar system, it is clear that the three poles are forming at very different speeds. Still, there are some important initiatives—mostly in the trade area—that merit attention. A free trade agreement (FTA) between Canada and the United States was signed in January 1988 and went into effect in January 1989. In March 1991, Argentina, Brazil, Paraguay, and Uruguay signed the Treaty of Asunción which envisages the formation of a tariff-free common market by the end of 1994. Then in April 1991, Mexico, Venezuela, and Colombia announced plans to create a free trade zone by July 1994. And in July 1991, negotiations began among Canada, Mexico, and the United States on the formation of a North American FTA. Looking yet farther down the road, President Bush's Enterprise for the Americas sets out the long-term goal of a free trade zone stretching all the way from Alaska to Tierra del Fuego.

Thus far, the countries of Asia and the Pacific have been the most cautious in putting forward any formal, regional trade or currency proposals. This may reflect, in part, the importance of North America, and to a lesser extent Europe, in that region's foreign trade. At the same time, it is relevant to note that Japan's exports to its regional neighbors are almost as large as its exports to North America, and that for the Asia and Pacific region as a whole, intraregional trade (averaging across exports and imports) now accounts for a larger share of total trade than it does in North

America.[1] Also, Japanese direct investment in the rest of Asia has expanded rapidly in recent years. Finally, there is some recent empirical evidence that financial policy, particularly interest rate policy, in a number of Asian countries is now more influenced by monetary policy developments in Japan than by developments in other financial centers outside the region.[2]

This paper discusses the macroeconomic policy implications of currency zones. By a currency zone, we mean an agreement by a group of countries to irrevocably fix their exchange rates to one another—including the option of a common currency—and to permit full integration of their financial and banking markets.[3] We have focused on currency zones because the implied loss of the nominal exchange rate as a policy instrument carries with it more extensive implications for the conduct of monetary and fiscal policies than are likely to result from say, trade zones alone (where no such exchange rate commitment exists); in any case, several other papers being prepared for this conference are slated to emphasize the implications of trade zones. We have also chosen to illustrate the policy issues involved by reference to European or American experience. We would submit, however, that many of these issues are also likely to be of relevance in other currency unions, ranging from the CFA franc zone in Africa to the USSR.

In the next section of this paper, we review a set of long-term developments in the world economy that help to place the emergence of currency and trade zones in broader perspective. Specifically, we highlight trends in relative economic size and in the international use of currencies, in relative inflation performance, in the behavior of key-currency exchange rates, in the geographical pattern of international trade, and in the integration of capital markets. Against this background, we next address the conduct of monetary and exchange rate policy in an emerging currency union. Here, we concentrate on the goals of monetary policy, on the consequences of giving up use of the nominal exchange rate, and on the choice between gradual and rapid transition to a monetary union or currency zone. In the final section, we investigate the implications of a currency zone for the conduct of fiscal policy. After discussing the incentives for fiscal adventurism in a currency union, we examine market discipline, fiscal rules, and peer group surveillance as possible mechanisms for achieving greater fiscal policy discipline.

Trends in the world economy

Exchange rate and trade policies, including the formation of currency and free trade zones, do not evolve in a vacuum. Instead, they typically reflect broader, long-term developments of both an economic and political nature. In this section, we review six economic trends that will condition the feasible evolution of the system in the period ahead.

Changes in relative economic size

A key development in the world economy over the past thirty years has been the trend toward *greater symmetry in economic size* among the industrialized countries of North America, Europe, and the Asia and Pacific region. In short, and as documented in Table 1, the relative economic size of North America—and of the United States in particular—has declined, while that of other regions—especially, the Asia and Pacific region led by Japan—has increased. The changes have been more marked for shares of world output than for shares of world trade. The industrial countries of Europe now account for about a third of the world's output, slightly more than the share generated by the United States and Canada combined, and more than twice the share attributable to Japan, Australia, and New Zealand. Europe's share of world trade—at near 50 percent—is also twice as large as that of any other region.

The main implication of these changes in relative economic size is that the future is likely to be characterized by a sharing of economic leadership. Attempts to recreate a Bretton Woods type system with a single hegemon are not apt to be viable. Instead, the system is likely to have a *multipolar* orientation.

The international use of currencies

A second notable development in the world economy has been the trend toward increasing international use of currencies other than the

Table 1*
Relative Economic Size[1]
(In percent)

	Shares of World Output[2]		Shares of World Trade[3]	
	1962	1988	1962	1990
Western Hemisphere				
United States	41.5	25.8	15.1	13.8
Canada	3.0	2.7	4.8	3.7
Developing Countries	5.0	6.5	6.4	3.5
Total	49.6	34.9	26.3	21.1
Asia and Pacific Region				
Japan	4.4	11.2	4.0	7.7
Australia	1.3	1.4	1.9	1.2
New Zealand	0.3	0.2	0.6	0.3
Developing Countries	7.7	9.0	7.2	13.6
Total	13.7	21.9	13.7	22.7
Europe				
Industrial Countries	28.6	32.1	46.2	48.3
Developing Countries	2.6	2.5	3.1	2.0
Total	31.2	34.6	49.3	50.3
Other Developing Countries				
Africa	2.6	2.8	4.6	2.4
Middle East	2.9	5.8	6.1	3.5
Total	5.5	8.6	10.7	5.9

[1]Country groupings are consistent with the classification in Fund publications, which divide the developing countries into five areas: Africa, Asia, Europe, Middle East, and Western Hemisphere. Excluded from the world total are the output and trade of the country group "U.S.S.R. and other nonmembers n.i.e." as defined in *Direction of Trade Statistics: Yearbook 1990.*

[2]GDP at market prices. Shares for 1962 are derived from data in IFS, *Supplement on Output Statistics,* Supplement Series No. 8, 1984. Shares for 1988 are based on 1980 GDP levels in U.S. dollars, from the same source, and 1981-88 growth rates of GDP at constant prices, from IFS *Yearbook,* 1990.

[3]Based on the sum of exports plus imports. Shares for 1962 are derived from data in IFS, *Supplement on Trade Statistics,* Supplement Series No. 15, 1988. Shares for 1990 are derived from the 1991 WEO data base.

*Taken from Goldstein and Isard, 1991.

U.S. dollar—particularly the deutsche mark and the Japanese yen. Selected indicators of the international use of currencies are shown in Table 2.

Data on the currency composition of official reserve holdings, of Eurocurrency deposits, of external bank loans, and of external bond issues confirm that the U.S. dollar remains the dominant international currency but also that its weight has been declining; meanwhile, the weights of the deutsche mark and yen have been rising. Estimates of currency turnover in foreign exchange markets, based on survey evidence collected by the Federal Reserve Bank of New York and the Bank of England, are not available over a long enough time period to identify reliably any underlying trends; they are, nevertheless, useful for illustrating the prominence of the deutsche mark, the yen, and the pound sterling among nondollar currencies.

Figures on the currency invoicing of international trade point in the same general direction as other indicators but are heavily influenced by large differences across the major countries in the shares of their own exports and imports that are denominated in national currency units. In this connection, the relatively low use of the yen as an invoicing currency for Japan's foreign trade is striking. On the export side, this has been attributed by Tavlas and Ozeki (1991) to: the relatively large share of Japanese exports that go to the United States, where a high share of imports is invoiced in the importer's currency; the relatively high transactions costs involved in obtaining trade finance through the bankers' acceptance market in Japan; and decisions by Japanese exporters to price in the importer's currency as part of a strategy aimed at preserving market share in the importing country. On the import side, more than half of Japan's imports consist of primary products, which are traditionally invoiced in dollars and sterling.

Table 3 provides two snapshots of the exchange rate practices of International Monetary Fund (IMF) member countries, one taken last year and one taken in 1975. While changes in the use of particular currencies are dwarfed by other trends—namely, the switch away from single-currency pegs toward currency-basket pegs, the forma-

Table 2
Selected Indicators of the International Use of Currencies

(In percent)

	U.S. dollar	Deutsche mark	Japanese yen	Pound sterling	Swiss franc	French franc
a. Identified official holdings of foreign exchange of Fund member countries						
1968[1]	54.1	1.3	—	13.4	—	1.9
1980[2]	68.6	14.9	4.4	2.9	3.2	1.7
1990[3]	49.6	18.7	8.6	3.1	1.5	2.0
b. Eurocurrency deposits						
1981-84	74.0	11.4	1.8	1.4	5.8	0.9
1989[4]	59.7	13.9	5.5	3.1	4.9	1.3
c. External bank loans						
1981-84	83.3	1.7	5.9	3.1	1.2	—
1985-89[4]	68.3	2.6	11.3	9.0	1.3	n.a.
d. External bond issues						
1981-84	63.2	6.3	5.7	3.4	14.7	—
1985-89[4]	48.0	8.2	10.0	6.5	10.7	1.5

Table 2 (continued)

Shares of currencies in foreign exchange transactions against the U.S. dollar

New York interbank market						
March 1980		32	10	23	10	7
April 1989[5]		33	25	15	12	3
London interbank market						
March 1986		28	14	30	9	4
April 1989[5]		22	15	27	10	4
Shares of currencies in invoicing of exports from the six largest industrial countries						
1980	59.2	17.5	3.4	8.7	—	8.2
1987[6]	46.2	23.1	6.5	9.3	n.a.	9.3
Shares of national exports and imports invoiced in national currency						
1980						
Exports	97.0	82.3	29.4	76.0	—	62.5
Imports	85.0	43.0	2.4	38.0	—	33.1
1988[7]						
Exports	96.0	81.5	34.3	57.0	n.a.	58.5
Imports	85.0	52.6	14.1	40.0	n.a.	48.9

[1] IMF Annual Report, 1975.
[2] IMF Annual Report, 1990.
[3] IMF, preliminary estimates for Annual Report 1991, Table I.3.
[4] Tavlas and Ozeki (1991), Table 17, WP/91/2.
[5] Tavlas (1991), Table 12, WP/90/3.
[6] Tavlas (1991), Table 10, WP/90/3.
[7] Tavlas and Ozeki (1991), Table 13, WP/91/2.

Table 3
Exchange Rate Practices of Fund Members, 1975 and 1990

Number of Fund member countries whose currencies:	As of			
	June 30, 1975	(percent)	March 31, 1990	(percent)
Are pegged to a single currency	81	66.4	53	35.1
Of which:				
U.S. dollar	54	44.3	34	22.5[2]
French franc	13	10.7	14	9.3
Pound sterling	10	8.2	0	0.0
Participate in the exchange rate mechanism of the EMS	0	0.0	9	6.0
Are pegged to a composite of other currencies	19	15.6	41	27.2
Of which:				
SDR	5	4.1	7	4.6
Other	14	11.5	34	22.5
Managed floating[1]	4	3.3	27	17.9
Float independently or jointly	18	14.8	21	13.9
Total	122	100.0	151	100.0

Source: IMF *Annual Report*, 1975 (Table 9) and IMF *Annual Report*, 1990 (Table II.17).

[1] In 1975, includes countries whose currencies are pegged to others but change the peg frequently in light of some formula; in 1990, includes countries whose currencies are adjusted according to a set of indicators.

[2] Includes Bahrain, Qatar, Saudi Arabia, and United Arab Emirates whose exchange rates showed limited flexibility against the U.S. dollar. Their exchange rates are determined on the basis of up to ±7.25 percent. However, because of the maintenance of a relatively stable relationship to the U.S. dollar, these margins are not always observed.

tion of the EMS, and the increased resort to managed floating based
on a set of indicators—here too, one notices the reduced—albeit still
dominant—use of the dollar. Interesting enough, while the yen
carries a relatively high weight in some currency baskets, not a single
Fund member country has yet opted for pegging (exclusively) to the
yen. Pegging to the deutsche mark is encompassed (de facto) within
EMS arrangements.

Again, we would regard the growing international use of currencies other than the dollar as suggesting that a sharing of leadership
responsibilities will be needed to promote international monetary
stability. A multicurrency system has both advantages and disadvantages. Because official reserves and private financial holdings are
diversified, it implies a reduced vulnerability of portfolio holders to
adverse shocks or weak policies in any particular anchor country.
Also, the presence of several competing monies may provide a
source of policy discipline. At the same time, the greater potential
for asset substitution implies that continued cooperation among the
major players will be desirable.

Relative inflation performance

Suffice to say that developments over the past several decades have
strengthened the case for emphasizing price stability among the objectives of macroeconomic policy. Tables 4 and 5 summarize the inflation
experience of industrial and developing countries, respectively.

Two conclusions stand out. First, the three largest countries have
been among the leaders in holding down inflation. As indicated in
Table 4, Germany's inflation performance has been consistently at
or near the top of the industrial-country league standings in each of
the last three decades; for the 1954-90 period as a whole, its inflation
performance has been unsurpassed. Japan has established strong
anti-inflationary credibility by turning in the best inflation performance of the 1980s; its inflation record over the longer period has
been less consistent than that of Germany but nevertheless still ranks
high, particularly if wholesale price inflation were substituted for
consumer price inflation in Table 4. (Indeed, on that former
measure, Japan emerges with the second-best inflation performance

Table 4*
Consumer Price Inflation Rates Among
Industrial Countries, 1954-90[1]

(In percent, with rank ordering in parenthesis)

	1954-90	1954-60	1961-70	1971-80	1981-90
United States	4.4(7)	1.5(4)	2.8(6)	7.9(7)	4.7(7)
Canada	4.8(8)	1.5(5)	2.7(5)	8.1(8)	6.1(9)
Japan	5.0(9)	1.9(8)	5.8	9.1	2.0(1)
Australia	6.2	2.6	2.5(2)	10.5	8.2
New Zealand	8.0	3.1	3.8	12.5	11.3
Germany	3.1(1)	1.6(6)	2.6(3)	5.1(2)	2.6(3)
France	6.3	4.3	4.0	9.7	6.7
Italy	7.9	2.1(9)	3.9	13.9	10.1
United Kingdom	7.0	2.3	4.1	13.8	6.3
Austria	4.1(4)	2.2	3.6(9)	6.3(3)	3.6(5)
Belgium	4.3(5)	1.4(3)	3.0(7)	7.4(6)	4.7(8)
Denmark	6.4	2.6	5.9	9.9	6.3
Finland	7.1	4.4	5.0	11.3	6.8
Greece	10.2	4.6	2.1(1)	14.5	18.9
Iceland	23.0	5.5	11.7	34.1	37.0
Ireland	7.7	2.3	4.8	13.8	8.3
Luxembourg	3.9(3)	1.1(1)	2.6(4)	6.7(4)	4.5(6)
Netherlands	4.4(6)	2.8	4.3	7.3(5)	2.5(2)
Norway	6.1	2.8	4.5	8.4(9)	8.1
Portugal	11.0	1.6(7)	4.2	18.3	17.7
Spain	9.6	6.3	6.2	15.1	9.7
Sweden	6.1	3.2	4.1	9.2	7.3
Switzerland	3.3(2)	1.1(2)	3.3(8)	5.0(1)	3.2(4)

Source: IMF, World Economic Outlook database.

[1] Average annual rates.

*Taken from Goldstein and Isard, 1991.

over the 1954-90 period). The United States, after doing relatively well in controlling inflation in the 1950s and 1960s, experienced an erosion of monetary policy credibility in the 1970s; the Federal Reserve then came a long way toward rebuilding that credibility by acting forcefully to bring down inflation during the 1980s.

The second conclusion is that the developing countries as a group have had much more difficulty in holding down inflation. By way of illustration, for the five regional country-groupings depicted in Table 5, median inflation rates have ranged from 8 to 13 percent during the 1970s, and from 7 to 13 percent during the 1980s; moreover, there have been quite a number of cases of acute or chronic inflation.

Table 5*
Consumer Price Inflation Among Developing Countries, by Region, 1971-90

	Average Inflation[1]		Median Inflation[1]		Number of High Inflation Episodes[2]		
	1971-80	1981-90	1971-80	1981-90	Chronic	Acute	Runaway
Africa	14.1	17.0	10.8	10.2	10	5	1
Asia	10.0	8.7	8.8	7.7	2	1	1
Europe	14.6	59.9	8.3	12.9	2	1	2
Middle East	13.6	14.2	11.2	7.1	2	1	1
Western Hemisphere	40.8	232.1	13.0	11.7	10	6	9

[1]Annual changes, in percent, from World Economic Outlook data bank. Average inflation rates represent arithmetic averages over each decade of weighted geometric averages for each year, where weights are proportionate to the U.S. dollar values of GDPs over the preceding three years.

[2]Based on individual country experiences reported in World Economic Outlook, May 1990, Table 13. Chronic inflation implies annual rates of 20-80 percent for five or more consecutive years. Acute inflation implies annual rates over 80 percent for two or more consecutive years. Runaway inflation implies annual rates over 200 percent for one year or more.

*Taken from Goldstein and Isard, 1991.

As is well known, one of the key motivations for fixing the exchange rate is to "tie one's hands" on monetary policy, so as to share in the superior anti-inflationary credibility of the anchor country. The classic case of this phenomenon, at least during the 1980s, has been the disinflation experience of the EMS countries, relying on the nominal anchor provided by the Bundesbank.

The main messages that ought to be taken away from Tables 4 and 5 are: (1) that the three largest industrial countries have a legitimate claim to serve as potential nominal anchors for regional currency areas, and (2) that many developing countries, and some industrial countries as well, have an incentive to find—be it via exchange rate targets or otherwise—a better nominal anchor than they have had in the past.

Behavior of key-currency exchange rates

Another significant feature of the global landscape has been the behavior of key-currency exchange rates. For our purposes, it is enough to note that: (1) the short-run variability of key-currency exchange rates has been much larger under the regime of generalized floating than under the previous exchange rate regime (see Chart 1); (2) there have also been large medium-term swings in real exchange rates for the three major currencies (see top panel of Chart 2); and (3) real exchange rate variability has primarily reflected the variability of nominal exchange rates under the present regime of managed floating (see bottom panel of Chart 2).

In papers prepared for earlier Jackson Hole symposia, we have discussed at some length the criteria that might be employed to evaluate whether this short-run variability of exchange rates is "excessive" and whether the longer-run swings of real exchange rates represent "misalignments."[4] We will not repeat that debate here. Instead, we will merely note that there are those who hold the view that exchange rate variability, on the order of what has been experienced over the past twenty years, is costly enough to warrant a change in the system in the direction of more fixity of nominal exchange rates.[5]

Chart 1
Volatility of Nominal Exchange Rates, 1961-90

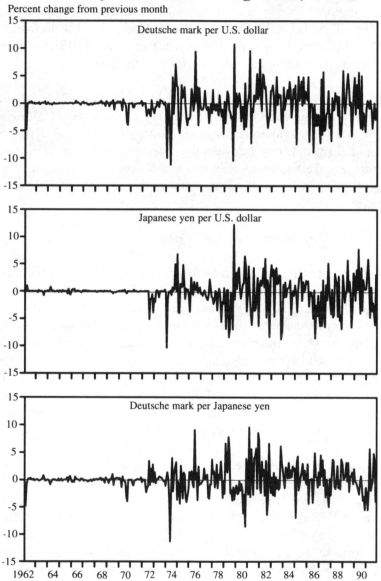

Source: IMF, International Financial Statistics

Chart 2
Cumulative Changes in Effective Exchange Rate Indices, 1975-90

Cumulative percent change since January 1975

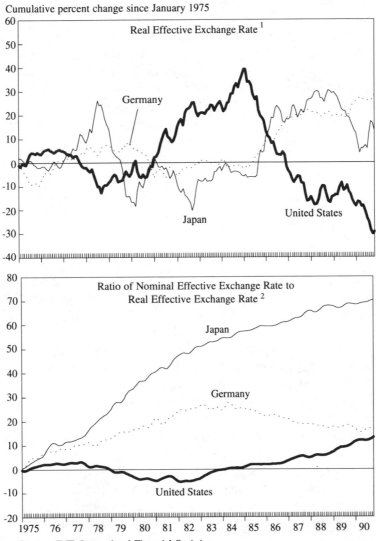

Source: IMF, International Financial Statistics
[1]Based on relative normalized unit labor costs in manufacturing for 17 industrial countries.
[2]Equivalent to the ratio of the foreign nominal normalized unit labor cost index to the domestic nominal normalized unit labor cost index.

Geographical patterns in international trade

Yet a fifth development in the global economy worth mentioning is that intraregional trade has progressed to such an extent that countries could potentially shield a significant portion of their total foreign trade from (nominal) exchange rate variability and/or from trade barriers by joining common currency and/or free trade areas with their major regional trading partners. Tables 6 and 7, in fact, set out the results of a calculation that speaks to this possibility. In those tables, it is assumed that the world is divided into three blocs, each of which contains one of the three largest industrial countries. Other countries are assigned to the bloc with which they have the most bilateral trade. Not surprisingly, this leads to the developing countries of the Western Hemisphere being included in the American or dollar bloc, and to the developing countries of the Pacific being assigned to the yen bloc; the developing countries of Africa and the Middle East wind up in the European or ECU bloc.

In this hypothetical, tripolar world, about 40 percent of the dollar bloc's trade would be internal; the corresponding percentages for the yen bloc and the ECU bloc would be higher—roughly 50 and 80 percent, respectively.

If it is thought to be excessive, there are two ways to reduce the amount of exchange rate variability. One way is to reduce the degree of variability of a given number of exchange rates; the other way is to reduce the number of exchange rates. We would not want to pretend that the hypothetical blocs outlined above are either optimal currency areas or optimal trade blocs. Surely, they are not—especially on the trade side where we remain to be convinced that anything short of a global free trade area makes sense as a long-run goal. Our point instead is merely to demonstrate that calls for more exchange rate stability do not necessarily imply that this must come from reduced variability across the three major currencies.

Integration and globalization of capital markets

The sixth and final development on our list is the growing integration and globalization of capital markets. Chart 3 portrays but one shorthand measure of this increased integration. It assesses the integration of domestic and offshore markets by the interest differential between the cost of interbank funds denominated in the same currency in the two markets. As is evident, these differentials were reduced dramatically during the 1980s, especially for countries like France which relaxed their capital controls. The behavior of covered interest rate parity tells a very similar story. Admittedly, evidence of capital market integration is less compelling when one moves from shorter to longer-term instruments and when one looks at correlations of national saving and investment (of the Feldstein-Horioka variety). [6] But the main qualitative conclusion that capital market integration has increased is robust. There is likewise little doubt that the "foreign" presence in major domestic financial markets has been on a rising trend. Two indicators for the United States are representative: whereas foreign and international entities held approximately 7 percent of the federal government's outstanding securities at the end of 1970, the proportion had risen to more than 16 percent by 1988; also, between 1970 and 1985, the number of foreign banking offices in the United States rose from about 50 to more than 780.

In our view, the main implication of this increased integration of capital markets—aside from the traditional efficiency gains—is that policy authorities in the industrial countries will find it harder to insulate themselves from interest rate or regulatory developments abroad—and this no matter what the exchange rate regime.

Monetary and exchange rate policies in a currency union

So much for the global environment. In this section, we consider the implications of a currency zone for the conduct of monetary and exchange rate policy. We treat the two together because the nature of exchange rate commitments has an important bearing on the way in which monetary policy can be implemented. No country can simultaneously expect to maintain free trade, open capital markets, a fixed exchange rate, and independent monetary policy; this is what Padoa-Schioppa (1988a) has called " the inconsistent quartet." Indeed, if a country chooses the polar case of a binding exchange rate commitment, namely, a common currency, it is natural to regard it

Table 6*
Distribution of Exports by Destination, 1989[1]

(In percent)

Exporting Region	Destination of Shipments (Columns represent countries or groups in corresponding rows)														
	1	2	3	4	5	6	7	8	9	10	11	12	13	14	15
Western Hemisphere															
1. United States	...	22	14	35	12	2	—	16	31	27	1	1	1	3	34
2. Canada	74	...	2	75	6	1	—	5	12	10	—	1	1	1	12
3. Developing countries	36	2	15	53	6	—	—	5	12	27	1	3	1	2	35
4. Regional total	21	14	11	46	10	2	—	12	23	24	1	1	1	3	30
Asia and Pacific Region															
5. Japan	34	2	3	40	...	3	—	30	33	20	—	1	1	3	27
6. Australia	11	1	1	13	27	...	5	30	62	16	1	3	1	5	25
7. New Zealand	13	2	3	18	18	19	...	19	56	18	2	2	1	3	26
8. Developing countries	25	2	1	28	15	2	—	31	49	16	1	2	2	3	23
9. Regional total	27	2	2	31	10	2	1	31	44	18	1	2	1	3	25

Table 6 (continued)

Europe, Africa, Middle East

10. Industrial Europe[2]	8	1	2	11	2	1	—	5	8	71	2	2	3	3	82
11. Developing Europe	4	—	1	5	1	—	—	4	5	40	6	30	2	10	89
12. U.S.S.R. et al.[3]	2	—	1	3	6	—	—	11	18	46	28	...	2	2	79
13. Africa	20	1	4	25	5	—	—	5	11	52	2	1	7	2	63
14. Middle East	14	—	4	18	18	1	—	16	35	30	5	2	2	7	46
15. Regional total	8	1	2	11	3	1	—	6	10	65	4	3	3	4	79

[1] Based on IMF, *Direction of Trade Statistics: Yearbook 1990.* Sums of individual shares may differ from subtotals and totals due to rounding error. —indicates less than 0.5. ... indicates identically zero or not measured.

[2] Based on totals for all industrial countries less amounts for United States, Canada, Japan, Australia, and New Zealand.

[3] Albania, Bulgaria, Czechoslovakia, the German Democratic Republic, and the U.S.S.R., plus three countries—Cuba, the Democratic People's Republic of Korea, and Mongolia—from outside the region. Hungary, Poland, and Romania, which were members of the Fund in 1989, are included in developing Europe, and Viet Nam is among the developing countries of Asia.

*Taken from Goldstein and Isard, 1991.

Table 7*
Distribution of Imports by Origin, 1989[1]

(In percent)

Importing Region	Origin of Shipments														
	(Columns represent countries or groups in corresponding rows)														
	1	2	3	4	5	6	7	8	9	10	11	12	13	14	15
Western Hemisphere															
1. United States	...	19	9	28	21	1	—	22	43	22	1	—	3	3	29
2. Canada	71	...	2	73	6	—	—	6	13	13	—	—	1	—	14
3. Developing countries	43	2	15	59	8	—	—	5	13	21	—	1	2	3	28
4. Regional total	19	13	9	40	16	1	—	16	33	20	1	—	2	3	26
Asia and Pacific Region															
5. Japan	24	4	4	32	...	5	1	33	39	15	—	2	2	10	29
6. Australia	22	2	1	25	20	...	4	20	44	27	—	—	1	3	31
7. New Zealand	15	2	1	18	18	25	...	13	57	22	—	—	—	3	25
8. Developing countries	15	1	2	18	22	3	—	33	58	16	1	2	1	5	24
9. Regional total	18	2	2	23	15	4	1	32	51	16	1	2	1	6	26

Table 7 (continued)

Europe, Africa, Middle East

10. Industrial Europe	7	1	2	11	4	—	5	10	71	2	2	3	2	80
11. Developing Europe	5	—	2	7	2	1	4	7	46	6	24	2	8	86
12. U.S.S.R. et al.	6	1	4	12	5	1	11	17	40	27	...	1	3	71
13. Africa	8	1	2	11	7	—	9	16	59	2	2	7	3	73
14. Middle East	14	1	3	17	8	2	12	22	45	6	1	1	8	61
15. Regional total	8	1	2	11	5	1	6	11	66	3	3	3	3	78

[1] See notes to Table 6. For consistency with Table 6, imports (in dollar amounts) are measured as the sum of exports from all countries of origin.

*Taken from Goldstein and Isard, 1991.

Chart 3
Domestic and Offshore Interest Rates:
United States and France, June 1973-December 1989

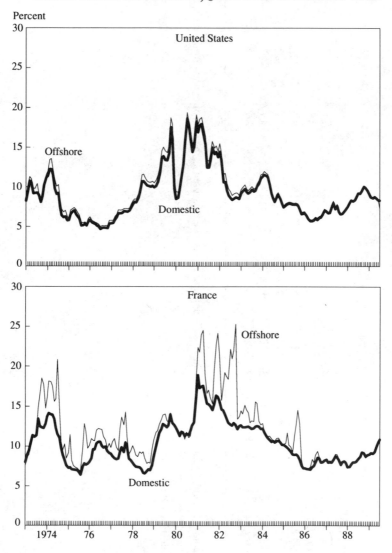

Sources: Data Resources, Incorporated; Organization for Economic Cooperation and
Development (OECD)

Chart 3 (Continued)
Domestic and Offshore Interest Rates:
United States and France, June 1973-December 1989

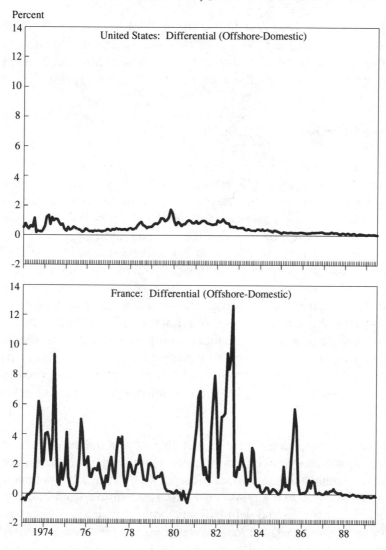

Sources: Data Resources, Incorporated; Organization for Economic Cooperation and Development (OECD)

as having implicitly also chosen the polar case of coordinated monetary policy, namely, a central monetary authority carrying out a common monetary policy.

In what follows, we first discuss the goals of monetary policy. We then go on to consider the factors that will determine the costs of abandoning the nominal exchange rate as a policy instrument. After that, we tackle the contentious issue of slow versus rapid transition to monetary union.

The goals of monetary policy

For any currency union—or even a quasi-fixed exchange rate regime—to be viable, it is essential that the participants reach a consensus on the goals of monetary policy. In our view, prospects for achieving such a consensus are much better now than they were ten years ago. The reason is that there is now more support for the proposition that *price stability* should be elevated above other goals.[7] It is not that price stability is intrinsically more important than say, high employment or economic growth; rather, it is the recognition that these other goals are unlikely to be achieved on a sustainable basis in the absence of low rates of inflation. In line with this theme, there is apparently agreement that a European Central Bank should have an explicit mandate to pursue price stability; also, to give some teeth to this mandate, it is proposed to give the ECB a significant degree of independence and to prohibit it from granting credit to the public sector.

It cannot, of course, be ruled out that any initial consensus on orienting monetary policy toward price stability in a currency union would be subject to strains once it comes time to actually implement that policy. The two strains most discussed (aside from country-specific real shocks and debt bailouts, both of which are addressed later on in this paper) are losses of seigniorage revenues associated with moving to lower inflation rates, and longer-term intercountry differences in income and employment.

The worry about seigniorage revenues is that some members of the currency union may rely on them more than others for helping to finance government expenditure. For the formerly high-inflation members of the union, loss of these revenues in the process of disinflation, particularly when it is difficult to increase revenue from more conventional forms of taxation, may therefore exacerbate an already weak fiscal situation. In this connection, it has been estimated by Dornbusch (1988) that some members of the EMS obtained as much as 3 percent of their GNP from seigniorage over the 1976-84 period.

While the seigniorage issue can be a transitional problem of some consequence, it should not, in our view, be regarded as a longer-term obstacle to a currency union. To begin with, high rates of inflation also produce distortions and ones that are likely to be more pervasive and costly for the future development of an economy than those associated with reduced reliance on the inflation tax. In addition, it should not be taken for granted that there is no scope for improving the structure of the tax and expenditure system to offset the loss of revenue from seigniorage; in some cases, in fact, the decline in seigniorage revenues could provide the impetus for improvements in fiscal management that likewise have longer-term benefits. Once the transition to a common monetary policy is made, it is also relevant to think of distributing whatever seigniorage revenues of the ECB are consistent with low inflation to participants in the union. We find it instructive that seigniorage concerns have not prevented the convergence to lower inflation in the EMS from continuing— with the result that reliance on seigniorage revenues in recent years (in Italy, Greece, Portugal, and Spain) has been considerably less than in earlier periods.[8]

The concern about intercountry differences in income and employment is that they could lead to a tug of war on the stance of monetary policy between more and less prosperous participants, with the less advantaged ones seeking a common monetary policy that was not consistent with low inflation. Certainly, monetary history is full of examples of these types of regional conflicts. Again, however, we do not see longer-term differences in say, per capita income levels, as a prohibitive factor. After all, sizable income differences continue to exist among regions of the United States; yet we are told that there is no consistent pattern in meetings of the

Federal Open Market Committee for participants from lower-in-
come (or even cyclically-depressed) districts to press for a looser
stance of (the common) monetary policy than those from more
prosperous districts. True, regional income differences in the United
States are much smaller than those in some other potential common
currency areas (the EC), the United States is a political union
whereas other areas may not be, and the United States has by now
had a long time to become familiar with the collective benefits
associated with belonging to a common currency area. Still, we
would argue that less prosperous regions too have much to gain from
moving closer to price stability, and that there is little evidence that
participation in a currency union, by itself, is inconsistent with a
gradual convergence of regional or intercountry income and employment differences.

Another question pertinent to the goals of monetary policy in a
currency area is what attitude to adopt toward *current account
imbalances*. Here, it is interesting to note that historically, not all
potential members of a European EMU have given the same weight
to current account balance relative to other goals. Masson and Melitz
(1990) highlight the comparison between France and Germany.
Over the 1963-88 period, the average current account imbalance
relative to GNP was -0.4 percent for France versus 1.2 percent for
Germany; the corresponding figures for average inflation performance were 7.2 percent for France and 3.6 percent for Germany.
Since 1987, the inflation performances of the two countries have
been very similar whereas current account positions have diverged
sharply (at least prior to German unification). There is also the
phenomenon during the 1987-90 period of capital flowing within the
EMS from low-inflation countries to countries whose inflation and
nominal interest rates are higher (Italy and Spain).[9] While the latter
countries have experienced declines in competitiveness and current
account deficits over this period, these deficits have been over-
financed by capital inflows. There is also the matter of a currency
union's aggregate current account position which could be a factor
influencing its exchange rate vis-à-vis nonunion currencies. In the
case of the EC, the aggregate current account position (relative to
GNP) has been close to balance over the past decade or so, but it
need not necessarily be so in the future.

Our view is that one needs to know the origin of a current account imbalance before it can be decided if it needs correction, and if so, how to correct it. Nonzero current account positions arise from a variety of sources, some of which are "good" and require no intervention, and some of which are "bad" and do require adjustment. An imbalance that arises, for example, from reversible inter-country differences in the age distribution of the population—which in turn generate different life-cycle private saving patterns—is likely to be benign. In contrast, an imbalance that reflects unsustainable foreign borrowing to finance a consumption spree surely falls in the malign category. More generally, in evaluating external imbalances, it will be useful to look at: whether the government's fiscal position is appropriate, whether any increased investment associated with the external imbalance is likely to earn a rate of return that exceeds the cost of borrowing, and whether any increased consumption is temporary and desirable for purposes of consumption smoothing. In an integrated financial area, the default premia that public and private borrowers have to pay will provide a signal of the market's evaluation of the underlying economic conditions. Still, monetary policy in a currency union is apt to operate more smoothly if participating governments themselves reach a consensus on how they will regard current account imbalances.

We turn next to the role that *exchange rate stability* should play in the design of monetary policy. It is convenient if we first deal with exchange rate management vis-à-vis countries outside the currency zone. Clearly, the firmer are exchange rate obligations with respect to nonunion currencies, the more constrained will be the common monetary policy within the currency zone. On other occasions, see Frenkel, Goldstein, and Masson (1989a), we have argued that it would be desirable for the international monetary system to evolve in the direction of a " two-tier" exchange rate policy, where exchange rate commitments were "looser" and "quieter" across the three major currencies than within budding regional currency areas. This would mean that monetary policy in the anchor countries would give the highest priority to price stability, except in those unusual cases when there is evidence of large exchange rate misalignments.

We base our view for this kind of evolution of the system on the following points. (1) The largest anchor countries have found it possible to achieve relatively good inflation performance without tying their hands on monetary policy to exchange rate targets. Also, while exchange rate targets may have reduced the costs of disinflation for countries with lackluster earlier inflation records, the available empirical evidence indicates that this is not the case for the anchor country itself. In fact, Giavazzi and Giovannini (1989) find that the relation between output and inflation has actually worsened in Germany during the EMS period. (2) The inflation performance of the anchor countries could well suffer if exchange rate commitments intruded unduly into the orientation of monetary policy, with unfavorable repercussions for countries that count on the anchor countries to export stability. (3) So long as the anchor countries do give the highest priority to price stability, tight and ambitious exchange rate commitments will lack the credibility they need to be effective, since market participants will learn that when push comes to shove, interest rate adjustments necessary to defend exchange rate targets are not forthcoming. (4) Real exchange rates across the poles need to change over time to reflect changes in real economic conditions. (5) A currency area that contained the three major currencies is likely to be too large; for example, stochastic simulations of empirically-based macroeconomic models (see Frenkel, Goldstein, and Masson [1989b] and Taylor [1986]) generally find that fixing exchange rates among the United States, Japan, and Germany implies larger variances for key macroeconomic variables than more flexible exchange arrangements. (6) Better disciplined monetary and fiscal policies in the anchor countries, which admittedly would need to be induced by mechanisms outside the exchange rate regime, would contribute to better behaved exchange markets for the anchor currencies.

This is *not* a call for a return to "benign neglect" in the management of major-currency exchange rates. We view a reasonable degree of stability of key-currency exchange rates as a public good for the system. For that reason, we think the larger industrial countries should continue to develop their own quiet estimates of equilibrium real exchange rates. These estimates of equilibrium exchange rates would be subject to considerable margins of error but there is little alternative to undertaking this exercise unless one is willing to accept the proposition that "the market rate is always the right rate." In those unusual cases where there is large difference between the estimated equilibrium rate and the market rate, the larger industrial countries would need to consider intervening. The intervention could take a variety of forms—ranging from concerted, sterilized exchange market intervention to, if necessary, coordinated adjustments in monetary policies. We stress that these would be *contingent* responsibilities—contingent upon strong evidence of large misalignments. While such an exchange rate commitment would clearly be less ambitious than those inherent in most target zone schemes, it may well be more effective because it is more credible (that is, more consistent with monetary authorities' revealed preference among occasionally competing policy goals).

Consequences of loss of the nominal exchange rate

Choosing a strategy for exchange rate management vis-à-vis currencies outside the currency zone is, of course, only part of the picture. The more pressing task is apt to be how to manage exchange rates *within* an emerging currency area. Suppose that potential participants in the currency zone have concluded that more fixity in their internal exchange rate relationships could yield sizable benefits (in terms of lower uncertainty facing trade and investment decisions, lower transactions costs, reduced costs of disinflation, better inflation performance, and so on). Prudence would still demand that they also weigh the consequences of having less resort to—or losing altogether—the nominal exchange rate as a policy instrument.

This is precisely where the traditional literature on the criteria for an optimal currency area demonstrates its continuing relevance. Here, we review briefly six of these criteria, namely, factor mobility, openness, diversification, wage-price flexibility, the structure of shocks, and the availability of other cushioning mechanisms. Also, we summarize some of the empirical evidence reviewed in Masson and Taylor (1991) and in Eichengreen (1990) to infer how those criteria might apply to a European EMU.

As Mundell (1961) pointed out thirty years ago, the higher is the degree of factor mobility within an area, the more likely it is that country-specific shifts in demand can be accommodated without increasing unemployment. As regards labor mobility, Europe would seem to be disadvantaged—at least relative to the United States.[10] A ballpark estimate would be that labor mobility in the EC—as measured say, by the proportion of the population that changes residence—is perhaps only a third or a half as high as within the United States. The higher dispersion of unemployment rates in Europe is also consistent with a lower labor mobility there.[11] Now it could be that labor mobility would rise somewhat as exchange rate uncertainty falls in an EMU[12]—but one can doubt that the inhibiting influences of language and cultural differences would still not carry the day.

Europe comes out much better on the criteria of openness and regional interdependence. If an area is very open to foreign trade, large changes in the nominal exchange rate may generate disruptive movements in the cost of living (see McKinnon [1963]). Also, the greater the share of intraregional trade, the greater the area which will benefit from the reduction in transactions costs associated with use of a common currency. Seen as a currency area, the EC countries have an openness ratio that is very similar to that of both Japan and the United States.[13] Moreover, as suggested in this paper, the degree of intraregional trade is higher in Europe than it is either in North America or in the Asia and Pacific region.

The more diversified is an economy's production structure, the less likely is it that a demand or supply shock to an individual industry will lead to an economywide disruption. For the most part, the EC countries do have such a well diversified production structure, with relatively low reliance on agriculture (Greece, and to a lesser extent Portugal, are the exceptions) and with manufacturing accounting for somewhere between one-fifth and one-third of total production; see Table 8. It is relevant to note that even though the EC countries differ nontrivially in their exposure to oil price fluctuations, the latest oil price shock has apparently not been associated with any exchange rate pressure within the EMS—contrary to the predictions of some observers.

The degree of wage-price flexibility also counts. If a country has

Table 8*
Selected Industrial Countries: Shares of Production by Category in 1986[1]

(In percent)

	Agriculture[2]	Construction	Energy and Mining[3]	Manufacturing	Services
Canada	4.0	7.6	9.0	23.4	56.0
United States	2.3	5.5	5.8	22.2	64.2
Japan	3.1	8.1	4.2	31.4	53.3
France	4.7	6.6	3.8	27.8	57.0
Germany	2.1	6.1	4.2	38.3	49.4
Italy	5.0	6.7	5.7	27.2	55.5
United Kingdom	2.1	6.7	7.8	27.6	55.9
Belgium	2.5	5.8	4.1	25.4	62.2
Denmark	6.6	8.3	3.0	24.6	57.5
Greece	17.3	7.4	5.1	21.1	49.1
Netherlands	5.2	6.3	9.1	23.4	56.0
Portugal	8.6	6.4	3.6	33.8	47.5
Spain	6.1	7.5	3.4	31.2	51.8

Source: OECD National Accounts

[1]GDP at current prices. Shares are scaled to sum to 100.

[2]Including hunting, fishing, and forestry.

[3]Mining and quarrying (including petroleum and natural gas production), plus electricity generation and gas and water distribution.

[4]Excluding government services.

*Taken from Goldstein and Masson, 1991.

a high degree of real wage rigidity, then nominal exchange rate changes will be of little use in attempting to alter employment and net exports. Similarly, if nominal wages are already flexible, then the freedom to alter the nominal exchange rate may not add much. Empirical work suggests that wage behavior in Europe is closer to the real wage-rigidity pole, while that in the United States is closer to the nominal wage-rigidity one (Bruno and Sachs [1985]). This would be consistent with more active use of the nominal exchange rate in the United States than in Europe. On a broader level, however, it raises the question of how to increase the flexibility of real wages in Europe. It remains to be seen whether increased competition in goods and factor markets associated with completion of the internal market (1992) will increase the flexibility of wages and prices, as some have suggested (Viñals [1990]), or alternatively, whether European unions and business associations will be able to consolidate market power across a wider area.

Criterion number five is the structure of shocks hitting the zone. *Ceteris paribus*, the more asymmetric or country-specific are these shocks, the greater the costs of abandoning the nominal exchange rate. One finding of recent empirical research is that the shocks hitting Europe are likely to be more symmetric than would those buffeting a larger currency zone, say, one composed of Europe and the United States combined. There is also the related issue of the policy response to shocks which, if implemented in a beggar-thy-neighbor fashion, could, itself, be a source of instability. Indeed, a recent EC Commission study, *One Market, One Money* (1990), employs the assumption that further progress toward monetary union would, *inter alia*, reduce the incidence of beggar-thy-neighbor policy responses to shocks, and in so doing, improve macroeconomic performance. Maybe.

Last but not least, one needs to consider the availability of other policy instruments that could be used to counter country-specific, real shocks, given that monetary and exchange rate policies will be already spoken for. The obvious candidates are automatic fiscal stabilizers and private capital markets.

Sachs and Sala-i-Martin (1989) argue that the system of fiscal federalism in the United States provides a significant, shock-absorbing function by altering federal tax payments and transfers to states and regions experiencing asymmetric income fluctuations. They estimate, in fact, that federal taxes and transfers cushion roughly one-third of the effects of region-specific shocks on disposable income. Similar estimates, carried out by Masson and Taylor (1991), suggest that in Canada, the corresponding figure for federal taxes and transfers is about one-quarter. In both countries, it is the alteration in federal tax payments—rather than that in transfers—that provides most of the cushioning effect.

In contrast, it has been estimated that at present (unionwide) taxes in the EC compensate for no more than one percent of country-specific income shocks. On first reaction, this would seem to suggest that Europe needs a unionwide fiscal authority on the scale of that in the United States. Such a conclusion would be too hasty. The principal reason is that the allocation of responsibilities for carrying out fiscal policy, as well as the structure and cyclical sensitivity of revenues and expenditures, are very different between the two areas. For starters, whereas the EC budget is presently about 1 percent of EC GNP and is not expected to exceed 3 percent even after completion of the single market, the federal budget in the United States accounts for roughly one-quarter of U.S. GNP. Again relative to GNP, the budgets of national governments in Europe are larger than that of the U.S. federal government. A second difference—emphasized by Mussa (1991)—is that while U.S. states generally show relatively low counter-cyclical movement in their budget positions and have revenue sources (for example, the property tax) and expenditure patterns quite distinct from those of the federal government, national European governments emerge in this regard as quite similar to the U.S. federal government. The upshot of all this is that much of what is done by the federal government in the United States is done by *national* governments in Europe. As such, a more limited role for a federal fiscal authority in Europe is by itself no indictment. What is important is that there be some cushioning mechanism in a currency zone to deal with region-specific shocks—not *who* does the cushioning. A second reason to be cautious about the need for a larger, federal fiscal authority in Europe is that estimates of the greater cushioning effect of region-specific shocks in the United States seem to be quite sensitive to how such shocks are measured. For example, von Hagen (1991) finds that if income transfers attributable to long-run differences in prosperity are separated from short-run cyclical disturbances, then the cushioning effect of the U.S. federal fiscal system is much smaller. In a similar vein, Atkeson and Bayoumi (1991), after distinguishing labor income from capital income and large U.S. states from smaller ones, find a cushioning effect on labor income from taxes and transfers that is similar as between large U.S. states and EC countries.

In principle, it is possible for region-specific income fluctuations to be smoothed without any assistance from the public sector. Specifically, if individuals used financial markets to geographically diversify their sources of income, then they would not be as vulnerable to region-specific fluctuations. Atkeson and Bayoumi (1991) have, in fact, just subjected this conjecture to empirical testing. They report two main findings. The first one is that individuals in the United States who derive most of their income from capital are able to insulate their incomes from fluctuations in the regional economy. In contrast, fluctuations in capital income in Europe are far more idiosyncratic—a result that provides further corroboration that capital markets in Europe have been less integrated than those in the United States. The second finding is that, in both the United States and Europe, regional labor incomes are closely tied to regional labor products and are *not* insured by significant countercyclical income from capital. The modest insurance against regional labor income shocks that does exist comes from government transfers and taxes. Thus, while, in theory, private capital flows can be a substitute for publicly-provided insurance mechanisms, in practice, this has not been the case.

To sum up, the literature on optimal currency areas provides a direct answer to the question of whether a group of countries seeking to form a currency zone can afford to give up the nominal exchange rate as a policy instrument. That answer is "it all depends." Further, the criteria that the answer depends on—being linked to structural and institutional characteristics of economies—imply that some country groupings will be more viable than others, and even that the same grouping will be more viable at one point in time than at another. Applying these criteria to the EC, for example, produces the conclusion that the EC is closer to an optimal currency area than would be a larger and more heterogeneous grouping which also included Japan and the United States. At the same time, there are clearly some operating characteristics (for example, labor mobility, real wage flexibility, capital market integration) on which the EC presently stands at a disadvantage relative to some existing currency areas (the United States), and others (for example, degree of divergence of real economic variables, of debt positions, and of fiscal policy behavior) that raise questions about whether it is yet "ready" to go further in that direction. It is to some of the relevant transition issues that we turn next.

Transition to a monetary union or currency zone

Even after a group of countries have decided that it is in their interest to move to irrevocably fixed exchange rates and to a single monetary authority, there is still the question of how rapidly to proceed from here to there. There are three options: go fast, go slow, go fast and slow (that is, split the group into two parts, with one sub-group going on a fast track and the other on a slower one). In Europe, this debate about the speed of transition has centered around the "gradualist" recommendations of the Delors Report (1989) which proposed a three-stage transition to monetary union in order to give the participating countries and the new institutions time to adjust.

The case for a *rapid transition* to monetary union rests primarily on three grounds:[14] (1) that it gives maximum credibility to exchange rate stability by eliminating exchange rates within the union; (2) that it minimizes the period of instabilities and vulnerabilities associated with the coexistence of full capital mobility, adjustable exchange rates, and multiple monetary authorities; and (3) that it captures more of the efficiency gains associated with moving closer to one money.

In our view, the most important argument for a rapid transition to a common currency is that a common currency will give maximum credibility to the authorities' commitment to fixed exchange rates. This is because market participants realize that a common currency is harder to "undo" than other kinds of fixed exchange rate arrangements. So long as separate exchange rates exist, markets may reason that authorities have not really given up their option to change them in exceptional circumstances—and this even in the face of both a long period since the last realignment and official statements galore pledging allegiance to the goals of monetary union. In this connection, Giovannini (1990) notes that even with extremely close monetary policy coordination with Germany and no realignments of their exchange rates vis-à-vis the deutsche mark for a long time, both Austria and the Netherlands continue to pay a premium on their short-term interest rates relative to Germany; similarly, while the interest rate premium paid by France has declined markedly with the convergence of French inflation rates to the German level and with the absence of franc devaluations since 1987, it has not totally gone away. Taking a longer-term perspective, Giovannini also argues that the most plausible explanation for the persistent pattern of average, ex-post excess returns on lira and franc deposits relative to deposits on deutsche marks is continuing, expected exchange rate changes that never took place. The main point is that it may be very difficult to eliminate exchange rate uncertainty and to achieve complete convergence of inflation and interest rates in the presence of separate exchange rates. The more one worries about the adverse effect of exchange rate uncertainty on trade, investment, and resource allocation in general, the more significant is such a distortion. Because adoption of a common currency minimizes the probability of further changes in exchange rates, it also offers the opportunity to make a final adjustment in exchange rates to deal with drifts in competitiveness and accompanying current account imbalances.

The second case for a rapid transition is really the case against the alternatives. More specifically, the concern here is that with the disappearance of capital controls, increased opportunities for the diversification of currency portfolios, and the continuation of current account imbalances, debt refinancings, and the like, both currency substitution and speculative attacks against fixed rates will increase. This, in turn, could render national monetary policies less effective and make defense of fixed rates more difficult (if not infeasible). These potential vulnerabilities are why some participants in the European EMU debate have argued that stage two should be short.

It is also why Padoa-Schioppa (1988b) has emphasized that if this stage of the transition is to be viable, participating countries will need to enhance their monetary policy coordination, including a readiness to engage in large-scale exchange market intervention and in coordinated adjustments in interest rates; establishment of a recycling mechanism to temporarily accommodate demands for currency diversification; and greater recourse to joint decisionmaking. Even then, some would argue that these are only band-aids and that the only real solution is to attack the problem at its source by making indivisible the responsibility for key monetary policy decisions and by eliminating exchanges within the zone. If that were done, the question arises whether the demand for money within the currency zone would be stable. In this connection, Kremers and Lane (1990), using a two-step error correction model, report that a stable, aggregate demand for narrow money can be identified for a group of countries participating in the ERM; in fact, they find that this aggregate function is more satisfactory than comparable money demand functions in individual countries. The intuitive explanation they offer for this finding is that the improved performance that comes about from capturing currency substitution and portfolio effects in the aggregate equation more than makes up for the reduced performance associated with imposing the same money-demand parameters on all countries in the sample.

The third argument for a rapid transition is that a common currency is the only way to eliminate all exchange-rate-related transactions costs within the zone. Most of these transactions costs are associated with bid-ask spreads and other commissions on foreign exchange-rate transactions. It has been estimated (Gros and Thygesen [1990] and EC Commission [1990b]) that the direct savings in transactions linked to adoption of a common currency could amount to about one-quarter to one-half of 1 percent of EC GDP; for small, open economies with "small" currencies (for example, Belgium-Luxembourg, Denmark, Ireland) and for countries with as yet relatively unsophisticated financial markets (for example, Greece, Portugal, and Spain), the estimated savings are larger—perhaps on the order of one-half to nine-tenths of 1 percent of their GDPs. This is obviously not a make-it-or-break-it rationale for a common currency but it is not peanuts either (0.25 percent of EC GDP amounts to roughly 13 billion ECU).

The case for *gradualism* in the transition to a currency zone is predicated essentially on two propositions: (1) that lack of convergence among members of the zone—encompassing both nominal and real variables—will undermine prospects for sustaining a common monetary policy aimed at price stability; and (2) that a transfer of responsibility for monetary policy from national central banks to a unionwide central bank—without adequate safeguards, or currency competition, or a track record of strong performance—would be premature and could result in only average—rather than best—inflation performance. Again, it is instructive to illustrate these points by drawing on the European EMU example.

As is well known, the period since 1982 has been marked by an impressive convergence toward lower inflation rates among members of the EMS; nevertheless, among the twelve member countries of the EC, there are still at least three member countries who in 1990 had inflation rates 3 to 14 percent above the EC average and 6 to 17 percent above the best performance in the EC. Divergences among member countries with respect to debt burdens and budget deficits are also large; so, too, with real per capita output and unemployment rates.

One concern about remaining differences in inflation rates is that the high-inflation countries may find the output costs of disinflation—associated with a rapid transition to monetary union—too costly to justify their continued participation (see Crockett [1990]). Over the past four years when nominal exchange rates have been stable in the EMS, France, for example, has been able to keep its growth of unit labor costs roughly in line with those in Germany but Italy has recorded a rather significant loss of competitiveness;[15] the worry is that the Italian example could be more the rule than the exception for other relatively high-inflation member countries. Implicit here, too, is the notion that the output costs of disinflation could be subject to hysteresis effects that make them closer to permanent than to temporary losses.[16] Yet if the low-inflation countries give in to these concerns, the result could be a compromise, common monetary stance that is too easy on inflation.

Chart 4
Dispersion of Real Per Capita Output[1]

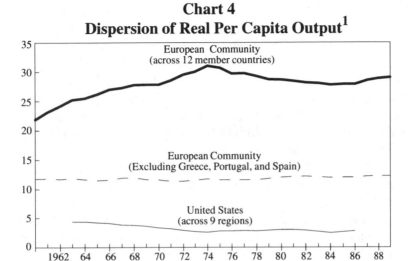

[1]Coefficients of variation, i.e. standard deviations of real per capita output, scaled by the mean (components are weighted by population).

Chart 4, taken from Masson and Taylor (1991), summarizes the behavior over the past thirty years of the dispersion of per capita output—both among EC countries and among regions of the United States. As noted by Masson and Taylor, three conclusions stand out. First, the dispersion of real per capita output is much larger (on the order of 10 times as large, as measured by the coefficient of variation) in Europe than in the United States. Second, much of the difference in dispersion between the two areas is reduced when the southern tier of the EC (Greece, Portugal, and Spain) is removed from the EC aggregate. And third, there is evidence of a steady (albeit slow) convergence of real per capita income across regions of the United States—a finding that casts doubt on the view that real convergence is impeded by participation in a monetary union.

Uneasiness about handing over the reins for monetary policy to a new and untried institution is partly a reflection of what is being given up in the process. While the Bundesbank is a national rather than a European Community institution, its performance as the nominal anchor of the EMS is by now well established. Moreover, it is well recognized that the output costs of any further disinflation will be conditioned by the credibility of the monetary authority. While some safeguards can be built into the charter of a new ECB—by giving it a good measure of independence and an explicit mandate to pursue price stability, and by prohibiting it from granting credit to the public sector—it is inevitable that the new institution will take time to establish its own credibility as an inflation fighter; as Mark Twain put it succinctly, "You can build a reputation on what you're going to do."Also, since responsibility for the key decisions on monetary policy would rest solely with the ECB, it would not be subject to discipline from currency competition within Europe (although it would still compete with central banks outside the currency zone); indeed, one rationale of the United Kingdom's "hard ECU" proposal is to keep the battle of competing monies going during the transition to EMU, so that the winner can be chosen in the marketplace rather than created by administrative decree and so that a fledgling common monetary institution has a track record before it is given command of the ship.[17]

The *two-speed* or two-track approach to the transition tries to capture the best of both worlds. By restricting the fast track to a smaller, more homogeneous group of countries, it seeks both to minimize convergence problems and to provide proof positive of the benefits of monetary union (including the ability to deliver a low rate of inflation). At the same time, it attempts to keep the momentum toward monetary union going for countries on the slower track, without pressuring them to converge faster than they themselves regard as desirable. The approach has been criticized primarily for the adverse effects it might have on "the countries left behind," and on union solidarity more broadly. More specifically, there are concerns that countries on the slower track would find their credibility impaired, and that even when they were ready to join the others, relationships would have already been formed within the early arrivals that newcomers would find hard to penetrate.

Our own (personal) view is that the two-track approach has a lot to recommend it. While there is no unique level of nominal or real convergence that is necessary for a monetary union or currency zone to be viable, a greater degree of convergence among members surely facilitates operations—especially during the initial phase when the new monetary institution is just establishing its anti-inflationary credibility and becoming familiar with its new environment. The fast track will likewise permit those countries whose currencies are likely to be the closest substitutes to move quickly through the vulnerable stage (two) where their separate currencies are still subject to speculative attack. We also believe that the only way to test the performance of a new central monetary institution is to give it the mandate to make the key decisions over the conduct of monetary policy, while simultaneously allowing it to face the pressures from sometimes conflicting goals. In contrast, if the new institution has to share responsibility for key aspects of monetary policy with other central banks, or if its mandate is restricted say, to just managing a parallel currency, then the lessons that can be drawn for its fitness to be the single monetary authority over a wider union will be limited. In this sense, the performance of the fast-track central bank is probably the best "dry run" that can be obtained under the circumstances. Finally, we suspect that the incentives for the weaker countries to improve their economic performance (so as to qualify for the fast track) would be stronger under the two-track approach— particularly if the fast-track monetary union shows good results and if the sanctions that can be applied to members (for poor policies) once they are already in the union are relatively mild. But much of this gets us into the subject of the next section, namely, fiscal policy discipline in a currency zone.

Fiscal policy in a currency zone

An underlying theme of the previous section was that monetary policy independence is inconsistent with participation in a currency zone. Much less settled at this stage is what constraints, if any, should be placed on national fiscal policies in a currency union. The debate on this issue, particularly in the European context, is heavily influenced by two observations.

The first one is that the exchange rate regime, itself, has not proven thus far to be sufficient to force a convergence around sound fiscal policies. Summarizing more than a decade's experience with the EMS—during which exchange rate commitments became progressively harder—the Delors Report (1989, paragraph 3) concludes:

" the EMS has not fulfilled its full potential . . . the lack of sufficient convergence of fiscal policies as reflected in large and persistent budget deficits in certain countries has remained a source of tensions and has put a disproportionate burden on monetary policy."

Table 9 illustrates (for 1990) the large differences among EC countries in ratios of debt-to-GNP. Estimates of the so-called "sustainability gap," defined as the difference between the actual primary budget surplus and the primary surplus that would be needed to stabilize the debt-to-GNP ratio (assuming average values for both the country's real growth rate and the real interest rate) likewise point to significant differences across EC countries.[18]

Table 9*
Debt Ratios in the European Community

	Debt Ratio 1989
	(In percent of GNP)
Belgium	128.4
Denmark	63.5
Germany	43.0
Greece	86.2
Spain	43.8
France	35.5
Ireland	104.9
Italy	98.9
Luxembourg	9.0
Netherlands	78.4
Portugal	73.1
United Kingdom	44.3
EC	58.4

*Taken from EC Commission (1990).

The second observation is that *if* fiscal policy discipline were not forthcoming in a currency zone, then the key objectives of the zone could well be threatened. For example, if a member of the union accumulated so much debt that it eventually became unable (or unwilling) to service it, there would be (de facto) pressure either on the central monetary institution to monetize the debt or on other members to bail out the errant borrower; alternatively, if that pressure were resisted—and the borrower was not willing to declare default—the country might even threaten to withdraw from the union so as to have the freedom to either monetize the debt or devalue its exchange rate. None of these scenarios is a comfortable one: either the anti-inflationary credibility of the union's central bank would be damaged, or the bailout would impair the future disciplining effect of market forces, or the cohesion of the union would be questioned. Reflecting these concerns, there has, for example, been support for including in any EMU agreement, explicit provisions prohibiting monetary financing and bailing out of budget deficits, as well as an injunction against " excessive deficits" themselves.

In this section, we first review the ways in which formation of a currency zone may affect the incentives to run a disciplined fiscal policy. After that, we discuss three mechanisms for encouraging greater fiscal policy discipline in a currency zone, namely, market forces, fiscal policy rules, and peer-group surveillance.

Incentive effects of a currency zone on fiscal policy

Suppose we characterize the process of moving toward a currency zone as having the following five elements: (1) national control of monetary policy is replaced by a central monetary authority; (2) goods and labor market integration increases (either because measures to promote economic union accompany those to promote monetary union—as in Europe—or because lower exchange rate uncertainty has positive feedback effects); (3) exchange rates become irrevocably fixed; (4) capital markets are liberalized; and (5) solidarity and mutual assistance among union members increases. We can then ask how each of those elements would affect the incentive to engage in errant, discretionary fiscal policy.

Perhaps the main implication of ceding control of monetary policy to a central authority is that each member of the currency zone will then have less assurance that the stance of (the common) monetary policy will support its intended fiscal policy action.[19] *Ceteris paribus*, this decreases the probability that go-it-alone fiscal policy action will be effective. For countries which already have relatively independent central banks, the change from the status quo may be minimal; but for others where monetary policy is under some obligation to support the national government's fiscal policy stance, the change could be one of substance. From the lender's point of view, he has to balance the likely lower probability (with a conservative common central bank) of a surprise inflation or devaluation eroding the real value of his claim, against the higher default probability associated with the borrower's inability to now print money to meet his obligation. In the end, we agree with Mussa (1991) that, on net, the switch to a central monetary authority should discourage fiscal adventurism.

Greater integration of goods and labor markets should also exercise a restraining effect. This is because greater goods market integration implies that more of the effect of a national fiscal stimulus will spill over abroad, and greater labor mobility implies that national authorities who spend and tax more than their neighbors (without providing an offsetting public service in return) risk losing the more mobile elements of their tax base to other jurisdictions. Of course, if some members enter the union with a large debt problem, the reduced scope to raise revenue from taxes, cum the revenue losses associated with reduced seigniorage, could also imply either greater recourse to borrowing or more pressure on the common monetary authority to monetize.

Fixity of exchange rates cuts the other way. More specifically, in a standard, Mundell-Fleming macroeconomic model with full capital mobility, fiscal policy is very effective (at home) under fixed rates and completely ineffective (at home) with flexible exchange rates. Moreover, under the same assumptions, a fiscal expansion with fixed rates has negative transmission effects abroad, while it has positive transmission effects under flexible rates. Put in other words, as we move closer to totally fixed exchange rates, the tendency is for fiscal policy actions to be more bottled up at home, that is, to be more effective. The negative transmission effects abroad come from the depressing effects of higher interest rates and of appreciation of the common currency against nonunion currencies (which dominate the expansionary effect of higher exports to the initiating country). In this connection, it is relevant to note that simulation studies of the increase in government expenditure in Germany associated with German unification generally find negative transmission effects to other EMS countries.[20] This conclusion about the greater (own) effects of fiscal policy action under fixed rates would be muted if private saving moved so as to offset public savings, or if goods market linkages were strong relative to capital market ones; it would be reinforced if the negative transmission effects abroad induced the common monetary authority to ease the stance of monetary policy. In any case, we would regard greater exchange rate fixity, *ceteris paribus*, as encouraging more active use of discretionary, expansionary fiscal policy.

The effect of capital market liberalization is Janus-faced. On the one side, access to a larger pool of saving generally means that a (large) country's fiscal policy expansion will be more effective since it can export some of its "crowding out" to its neighbors. On the other, if a country has privileged access to funds in its own market due to restrictions that are lifted upon entry into the currency zone, it could well find that its cost of borrowing has increased.

Last but hardly least, there is the matter of increased solidarity and mutual assistance—especially during episodes of potential financial crisis. Since the operation of a currency zone or monetary union is in a sense the polar case of economic cooperation and coordination, it cannot be ruled out that some members would regard the (potential) availability of financial assistance from other members as permitting a less disciplined fiscal policy course than otherwise—and this notwithstanding any existing "no bailout" pledge. The greater the holding by other members of the debtor's liabilities and the less costly are the conditions perceived by the borrower for a bailout, the more serious is this moral hazard likely to be.

Frankly, it is hard to know what the aggregate effect of these five incentives would be—particularly without reference to a specific group of countries. Nevertheless, if pressed, our gut feeling would be that so long as the central monetary authority is itself disciplined, the first two incentive effects outlined above would dominate the last three—thus, yielding the conclusion that a currency zone would encourage greater fiscal policy discipline. Even though more fixity of exchange rates makes larger the own effects of fiscal expansion, the negative transmission effects are likely to raise beggar-thy-neighbor criticisms from other members of the zone. In addition, the more often an errant borrower goes to the well for a bailout, the more onerous are the conditions for future assistance likely to become. And if, in the end, it is the residents of the errant country that foot the bill, they may take their revenge at the polls.

Mechanisms for enforcing greater fiscal policy discipline

Even if, on balance, the incentives associated with participation in a currency zone were judged as helpful to the cause of fiscal discipline, this is not to say that they would be sufficient to do the job; as noted earlier, this has not been the case so far in the EMS. It is therefore worthwhile to consider somewhat more generally what mechanisms exist for achieving that often elusive objective.

One route would be to entrust private financial markets with that role. Such *market-based financial discipline* would take the form of an initially rising default premium on the debt of a member country running excessive deficits. If those deficits persisted, the default premium would increase at an increasing rate, and eventually the country would be denied access to additional credit. This increase in the cost of borrowing, along with the threat of reduced availability of credit, would then provide the incentive for the country to correct its fiscal situation.

Advocates of the market approach (for example, Bishop and others [1989]) recognize that it will work only if certain conditions are satisfied, namely: (1) capital must be able to move freely, (2) full information must be available on the sovereign borrower, (3) the market must be convinced both that there are no implicit or explicit outside guarantees on sovereign debt and that the borrower's debt will not be monetized, and (4) the financial system must be strong enough to stand the failure of a "large" borrower.

Until very recently, most of the empirical evidence on market discipline has been anecdotal. Skeptics of the market-based approach point, for example, to the developing-country debt crisis of the early 1980s as demonstrating its inadequacy. But a plausible explanation for the slow rise in interest rate spreads on commercial bank loans to indebted developing countries is the perception of a bailout—either of the lending banks or of the countries themselves (see Folkerts-Landau [1985])—thus, violating one of the necessary conditions cited above. Similarly, the observation that sovereign borrowers pay different promised interest rates in the market does not establish that these interest rate spreads are closely linked to differences in fiscal-policy behavior rather than to other factors.

Recent empirical work has tended to concentrate on the experience of federal states. The experience of the United States is of particular interest for at least five reasons. First, the viability of the United States as a common currency area is long since firmly established; in operational terms, this means that one can legitimately disregard exchange rate expectations as contributing to differences in borrowing costs across say, U.S. states. Second, state governments do not have access to central bank financing. Third, with regard to creditors, U.S. states enjoy immunity from bankruptcy courts, much like a sovereign country does. Fourth, while many U.S. states have voluntarily imposed their own statutory limits on their deficit spending and/or borrowing, there are no federally imposed borrowing limits. Fifth, the U.S. capital market is presumably closest to the kind of deep, efficient financial area that some other aspiring currency areas hope to have in the future.

The fly in the ointment for empirical work has been the lack of a reliable data set on market yields for comparable, state, general-obligation (GO) bonds.[21] Recently, however, Goldstein and Woglom (1991) have drawn attention to the Chubb Relative Value Study. The Chubb Corporation, an insurance company, has conducted since 1973 a semiannual survey of twenty to twenty-five (sell-side) municipal bond traders. The traders are asked to give the yields on 5-, 10-, and 20-year maturity GO bonds for thirty-nine U.S. states and Puerto Rico, relative to the yield on a comparable New Jersey GO. The survey results for December 1989 are reproduced in Table 10. The results imply that, on average, traders felt that a comparable California 20-year GO should have a market yield 14.04 basis points below New Jersey's market yield, while a comparable Louisiana 20-year GO should bear a yield 70 basis points higher than that of New Jersey. The spread between comparable California and Louisiana GOs is more than 84 basis points in December 1989. As one would expect, these yield spreads also vary over the course of the business cycle: over time, the spread for a particular state can vary considerably. For example, during the recession year of 1982, the spread between the highest and lowest rated states of Oklahoma and Michigan was more than 170 basis points; in contrast, by 1989, the high-low spread had fallen by a factor of two and Michigan turned out to be a higher-rated state than Oklahoma.

Goldstein and Woglom (1991) employ the Chubb survey data to test the market discipline hypothesis. Specifically, using a pooled sample over the 1982-1990 period, they relate these (state) yield spreads to four measures of fiscal policy behavior that should be related to default risk, as well as to state-specific risk factors (not related to fiscal policy) that are captured in bond ratings. The fiscal policy indicators used as explanatory variables are the existing stock of debt relative to income, the difference between the trade rate of growth of real debt and the trend growth in income, the current year's budget deficit, and an index of the stringency of the state's constitutional debt limitations. Procedures are also undertaken to account for changes in default risk over time, for possible simultaneity between market yields and the volume of state borrowing, and for a possible nonlinearity in the effect of the debt variables on market yields.

Goldstein and Woglom's (1991) main finding is that U.S. states which have followed more prudent fiscal policies are perceived by market participants as having lower default risk and are therefore able to reap the benefit of lower borrowing costs. In this context, more prudent fiscal policies encompass not only a lower stock and trend rate of growth of debt relative to income, but also relatively stringent (albeit, self-imposed) constitutional limitations on the state's borrowing authority. According to Goldstein and Woglom's

Table 10*
Chubb Relative Value Study, December 1989
(Basis point spread for 20 yr. state GO,
relative to a New Jersey 20 yr. GO)

Ranking:	Moody's Rating	Avg. Response	Std. Dev.
1 California	Aaa	-14.04	3.84
2 North Carolina	Aaa	-11.91	4.32
3 Virginia	Aaa	-10.65	4.76
4 Connecticut	Aa1	-9.96	5.09
5 Missouri	Aaa	-8.30	5.28
6 South Carolina	Aaa	-6.74	5.58
7 Georgia	Aaa	-6.39	2.58
8 Maryland	Aaa	-4.65	3.51
9 Tennessee	Aaa	-4.09	5.80
10 New Jersey	Aaa	0.00	0.00
11 Ohio	Aa	1.39	3.41
12 Utah	Aaa	5.57	4.84
13 Maine	Aa1	7.00	4.95
14 Minnesota	Aa	8.13	3.79
15 Montana	Aa	8.39	5.25
16 Delaware	Aa	8.61	4.51
17 Kentucky	Aa	8.70	5.31
18 New Hampshire	Aa1	9.52	3.84
19 Rhode Island	Aa	10.26	3.58
20 Vermont	Aa	11.17	3.56
21 Alabama	Aa	12.09	3.83
22 Wisconsin	Aa	12.13	3.93
23 Pennsylvania	A1	12.91	4.83
24 Mississippi	Aa	13.39	4.49
25 Hawaii	Aa	13.87	3.83
26 Michigan	A1	14.04	4.84
27 New Mexico	Aa	14.48	3.59
28 Illinois	Aaa	14.48	4.67
29 Oregon	A1	16.57	3.59
30 Florida	Aa	17.26	4.11
31 Nevada	Aa	18.74	4.00
32 New York	A1	20.39	4.75
33 Oklahoma	Aa	21.61	7.29
34 Texas	Aa	22.74	5.93
35 North Dakota	Aa	22.83	10.11
36 Washington	A1	24.48	3.05
37 Alaska	Aa	27.39	7.49
38 West Virginia	A1	28.22	5.34
39 Puerto Rico	Baa1	48.09	6.99
40 Massachusetts	Baa1	62.39	11.50
41 Louisiana	Baa1	70.00	12.07

*Taken from Goldstein and Woglom, 1991.

estimates, a (hypothetical) state with fiscal policy characteristics that were one standard deviation "looser" than the mean of the sample would pay roughly 15-20 basis points more on its general obligation debt than another state with fiscal policy characteristics that were one standard deviation "tighter" than the sample mean. In evaluating the size of this fiscal policy-related default premium, one should keep in mind: that there have been *no* defaults on state general obligation bonds in the postwar period—a factor which suggests a low probability of default; and that a default premium of say, 20 basis points is not a trivial expense in relation to a real borrowing cost of say, 2 or 3 percent (or even to a nominal promised yield of say, 6 percent).

Showing that misbehaved fiscal policies raise a country's cost of borrowing is one thing. Showing that an increase in borrowing costs leads, in turn, to a corrective adjustment in fiscal policy is quite another—especially in situations in which high public debts reflect political polarization or distributional conflicts over the sharing of the fiscal burden. On that second half of the market discipline hypothesis, empirical work has unfortunately thus far been silent.

A second possible mechanism for encouraging greater fiscal discipline is binding *fiscal policy rules*. This is, for example, the mechanism favored in the Delors Report (1989). These rules would impose upper limits (relative to GNP) on budget deficits and on debt stocks of individual member countries, as well as limit recourse to public borrowing for purposes of investment. Rules can, in general, reduce negotiation costs and burdensharing conflicts; also, they can enhance the predictability of policy actions. The chief criticism of them in the present context is that rigid fiscal rules would be incapable of taking adequate account of differences in the circumstances of members. For example, the same budget deficit is apt to be less cause for concern in a country with a high private saving rate, a low stock of debt, and a good track record on inflation than in one with the opposite characteristics. Much as with our previous discussion of current account imbalances, there can be good deficits and bad ones. For example, rigid fiscal rules on say, budget deficits, could prevent automatic stabilizers in individual countries in a currency zone from cushioning country-specific shocks. There are likewise difficult measurement questions. How should "government" be defined, what should be included in the deficit, and on and on. To take a specific example, Delaware looks on the surface to have a relatively high debt burden; yet it carries quite a high credit rating. The reason is that because of its relatively small size, many of the functions that in other states are carried out by local municipalities, are carried out in Delaware by the state government, that is, what is counted as state debt in Delaware is really municipal plus state debt. Markets know this and take it into account in pricing Delaware's debt; but a rigid rule might not be able to accommodate this idiosyncracy. Enforcement is also a consideration. While some fiscal policy rates will be adhered to, others may not. In this connection, von Hagen (1991) reports a greater tendency for states with debt limits and stringent balanced budget requirements to substitute unrestricted for restricted debt (by delegating functions and debt-raising power to off-budget entities and to local governments).

Yet a third mechanism, which finds expression in some recent EC Commission reports (1990a, 1990b), also calls for constraints on national fiscal policies but adopts a more discretionary format. Specifically, it proposes that *peer-group, multilateral surveillance* be reinforced so as to discourage errant fiscal policies of individual member countries. Suffice to say that this tack too is open to criticism. Multilateral surveillance exercises typically employ a broad set of economic indicators. This sets up the risk that different indicators will send conflicting signals for policy adjustment, thereby allowing an errant fiscal policy to continue for too long. Without previously agreed guidelines,[22] there is also the danger that negotiations, cum pressures for solidarity within the union, could delay unduly the needed fiscal adjustment. Moreover, even though there can clearly be cases when fiscal policy actions create negative externalities for other member countries that are not fully captured in the price mechanism, fiscal policy is much tougher to coordinate than say, monetary policy because of the long lags and sometimes different jurisdictional issues involved.[23]

What then to do? Our own view is that efforts would pay the largest dividends if focused in two areas. First, try to move closer to the necessary conditions for market discipline to work effectively. This means, *inter alia*: improving information flows on sovereign borrowers; removing as far as possible implicit and explicit guarantees or bailouts; strengthening the financial system so that even a large borrower can occasionally fail; and ensuring that if there is a failure, costs be imposed on both borrowers and lenders so that such behavior is less likely to be repeated in the future. Second, use peer-group surveillance to encourage countries who already have potentially unsustainable fiscal situations to make adjustments—if possible, before they enter currency unions. Once in the union, such peer-group surveillance can continue to play a helpful, supplementary role in discouraging obvious, large fiscal policy excesses. If countries see "tying their own hands" on fiscal policy as useful to bolster their credibility in the marketplace—much as many states in the United States have concluded—then they will voluntarily adopt such rules; also, the rules themselves are to differ from country to country to reflect each country's own institutional and structural characteristcs. What counts is effectiveness—not symmetry.

   The views expressed are the authors' alone and do not necessarily represent the views of either the Bank of Israel or the International Monetary Fund. This paper was written while Jacob Frenkel was economic counselor and director of research at the IMF. We are grateful to Peter Isard and Paul Masson who have worked closely with us over the past few years on many of the issues discussed in this paper. Thanks are also due to Alberto Giovannini for helpful comments on an earlier draft.

Endnotes

[1]See Tables 6 and 7 in the second section of this paper.

[2]Frankel (1991)

[3]This is basically the same definition given for a monetary union in the Delors Report (1989). Throughout this paper, we often use the terms currency zone and monetary union interchangeably.

[4]Frenkel and Goldstein (1988) and Frenkel, Goldstein, and Masson (1989).

[5]Cooper (1991).

[6]Goldstein, Mathieson, and Lane (1991).

[7]Polak (1988).

[8]EC Commission (1990b).

[9]Giavazzi and Spaventa (1990).

[10]Masson and Taylor (1991).

[11]Eichengreen (1990).

[12]Bertola (1989).

[13]Giavazzi and Giovannini (1990).

[14]Frenkel and Goldstein (1991).

[15]Giovannini (1990)

[16]Masson and Taylor (1991).

[17]United Kingdom (1989, 1990).

[18]EC Commission (1990b).

[19]Mussa (1991).

[20]Masson and Meredith (1990).

[21]General obligation bonds are "full faith and credit" obligations of the state, whereas revenue bonds are only backed by the revenue of the specific project financed by the bond.

[22]Frenkel (1990).

[23]Tanzi (1989) and Frenkel, Goldstein, and Masson (1990).

References

Atkeson, Andrew, and Tamim Bayoumi. " Do Private Capital Markets Insure Against Risk in a Common Currency Area?" IMF, July 1991, unpublished.

Bertola, Giuseppi. " Factor Mobility, Uncertainty, and Exchange Rate Regimes," in M. de Cecco and A. Giovannini, eds., *A European Central Bank?* Cambridge: Cambridge University Press, 1989.

Bishop, Graham, Dirk Damrau, and Michelle Miller. " 1992 and Beyond: Market Discipline CAN Work in the EC Monetary Union." London: Salomon Brothers, November 1989.

Bruno, Michael, and Jeffrey Sachs. *Economics of Worldwide Stagflation,* Cambridge, Mass.: National Bureau of Economic Research, 1985.

Cooper, Richard. " What Future for the International Monetary System?" in Jacob Frenkel and Morris Goldstein (eds.), *International Financial Policy: Essays in Honor of Jacques Polak,* IMF, 1991, forthcoming.

Crockett, Andrew. " Monetary Integration in Europe," in Jacob Frenkel and Morris Goldstein (eds), *International Financial Policy: Essays in Honor of Jacques Polak,* IMF, 1991, forthcoming.

Delors Report. *Report on Economic and Monetary Union in the European Community,* Committee for the Study of Economic and Monetary Union, June 1989.

Dornbusch, Rudi. " The European Monetary System, the Dollar, and the Yen," in Francesco Giavazzi, Stefano Micossi, and Marcus Miller (eds), *The European Monetary System.* Cambridge: Cambridge University Press, 1988.

EC Commission. " Economic and Monetary Union: The Economic Rationale and Design of the System." Brussels: March 1990a.

_____. *One Market, One Money.* Brussels: October 1990.

Eichengreen, Barry. " One Money for Europe? Lessons from the U.S. Currency Union," *Economic Policy,* (April 1990), pp. 118-187.

Folkerts-Landau, David. " The Changing Role of International Bank Lending in Development Finance," IMF *Staff Papers,* (June 1985), pp. 317-363.

Frankel, Jeffrey. " Is There a Yen Bloc Forming in Pacific Asia?" Washington: Institute for International Economics, 1991, unpublished.

Frenkel, Jacob A., and Morris Goldstein. "Exchange Rate Volatility and Misalignment: Evaluating Some Proposals for Reform," in *Financial Market Volatility.* Kansas City: Federal Reserve Bank of Kansas City, 1988, pp. 195-220.

_____ and _____. " Monetary Policy in an Emerging European Economic and Monetary Union," IMF *Staff Papers,* (June 1991), pp. 356-373.

Frenkel, Jacob, Morris Goldstein, and Paul Masson. " The Rationale for, and Effects of International Economic Policy Coordination," in William Branson, Jacob A. Frenkel, and Morris Goldstein, (eds.) *International Policy Coordination and Exchange Rate Fluctuations.* Chicago: University of Chicago Press and National Bureau of Economic Research, 1990, pp. 9-55.

_____, _____, and _____. " International Dimensions of Monetary Policy: Coordination versus Autonomy," in *Monetary Policy Issues in the 1990s.* Kansas City: Federal Reserve Bank of Kansas City, 1989a, pp. 183-232.

_____, _____, and _____. " Simulating the Effects of Some Simple Coordinated Versus Uncoordinated Policy Rules," in Ralph Bryant and others, (eds.) *Macroeconomic Policies in an Interdependent World.* Washington: The Brookings Institution, 1989b, pp. 202-259.

Goldstein, Morris and Geoffrey Woglom. " Market-Based Fiscal Discipline in Monetary Unions: Evidence from the U.S. Municipal Bond Market," in M. Canzoneri and others, (eds.), *Establishing A Central Bank.* Cambridge: Cambridge University Press, 1991, forthcoming.

Goldstein, Morris, Donald Mathieson, and Tim Lane. *The Determinants and Systemic Consequences of International Capital Flows,* IMF Occasional Paper No. 77, March 1991.

Goldstein, Morris, and Peter Isard. " Issues in the Evolving Multipolar International Monetary System," IMF, July 1991, unpublished.

Giavazzi, Francesco, and Alberto Giovannini. *Limiting Exchange Rate Flexibility: The European Monetary System,* Cambridge, Mass.: M.I.T. Press, 1989.
_____, and Luigi Spaventa. " The 'New' EMS," CEPR Discussion Paper No. 369. London: Centre for Economic Policy Research, January 1990.
Giovannini, Alberto. " European Monetary Reform: Progress and Prospects," *Brookings Papers on Economic Activity,* 1990:2, pp. 217-274.
Gros, Daniel, and Niels Thygesen. " Toward Monetary Union in the European Community: Why and How." Brussels: Center for European Policy Studies, May 1990, unpublished.
Kremers, J. M., and Timothy Lane. " Economic and Monetary Integration and the Aggregate Demand for Money in the EMS," IMF *Staff Papers,* December 1990, pp. 777-805.
Masson, Paul, and Jacques Melitz. " Fiscal Policy Interdependence in a European Monetary Union," IMF Working Paper No. 90/24, IMF, March 1990.
_____, and Guy Meredith. " Domestic and International Macroeconomic Consequences of German Unification," in Leslie Lipschitz and Donough McDonald, (eds.) *German Unification: Economic Issues,* IMF Occasional Paper No. 75, December 1990, pp. 93-114.
_____, and Mark Taylor. " Common Currency Areas and Currency Unions: An Analysis of the Issues," IMF Research Department, August 1991, unpublished.
Mussa, Michael. " Monetary and Fiscal Policy in an Economically Unified Europe." Paper presented at Carnegie-Rochester Conference on Public Policy, Revised, January 1991.
Mundell, Robert. " A Theory of Optimum Currency Areas," *American Economic Review,* (September 1961), pp. 657-65.
McKinnon, Ronald. " Optimum Currency Areas," *American Economic Review,* (September 1963), pp. 717-25.
Padoa-Schioppa, Tommaso. " Toward a New Adjustable Peg?" in C. Fred Bergsten and others, (eds.) *The International Monetary System: The Next 25 Years.* Symposium at Basel University, June 1988a.
_____. " The European Monetary System: A Long-Term View," in Francesco Giavazzi, Stefano Micosi, and Marcus Miller (eds.), T*he European Monetary System.* Cambridge: Cambridge University Press, 1988b.
Polak, Jacques. " Economic Policy Objectives in the Major Industrial Countries and their Effects on Policymaking," in Wilfried Guth (ed.) *Economic Policy Coordination.* Washtingon: IMF and HWWA, 1988.
Sachs, Jeffrey, and X. Sala-i-Martin. " Federal Fiscal Policy and Optimum Currency Areas." Harvard University, 1989, unpublished.
Tanzi, Vito. " Fiscal Policy and International Coordination: Current and Future Issues." A Conference on Fiscal Policy, Economic Adjustment, and Financial Markets at Boconni University, January 1988.
Tavlas, George, and Yuzuru Ozeki. " The Japanese Yen as an International Currency," IMF Working Paper 91/2, January 1991.
Taylor, John. " An Econometric Evaluation of International Monetary Policy Rules: Fixed Versus Flexible Exchange Rates." Stanford University, October 1986, mimeo, .
United Kingdom, H.M. Treasury, " An Evolutionary Approach to EMU," 1989.
_____. *Treasury Bulletin,* HMSO, 1990.
Viñ als, Jose. " The EMS, Spain, and Macroeconomic Policy," CEPR Discussion Paper No. 389. London: Centre for Economic Policy Research, March 1990.

Commentary: Macroeconomic Policy Implications of Currency Zones

It is a great pleasure to return, once again, to Jackson Lake Lodge where the visage of the craggy peaks of the Grand Tetons across the gleaming surface of Jackson Lake always seems to provide such appropriate inspiration for discussions of the international monetary and financial system. It is especially a pleasure to comment on the thoughtful and stimulating paper of Jacob Frenkel and Morris Goldstein.

Few here will be surprised—and perhaps some may even be reassured—that I share most of the views that Jacob and Morris express in their fine paper. There is, after all, a certain element of incest associated with my commentary on their paper.

Before assuming his responsibilities as governor of the Bank of Israel and before his five-year tour of duty as economic counselor and director of research at the International Monetary Fund (IMF), Jacob was, for many years, my close colleague and frequent coauthor at the University of Chicago. I have also known Morris for many years. While we have not yet had the opportunity to work as colleagues and coauthors, who knows what the future may hold? (For the present, at least it may be said that I did not suggest that Morris draft the comments on his own paper.)

Rather than remark on the wide range of important issues discussed by Frenkel and Goldstein, I should like to focus my brief comments

213

on three central issues: (1) the essential relationship between exchange rate policy and monetary policy, (2) the critical political element in the choice of exchange rate regime and (3) the nature and functioning of market mechanisms for enforcing fiscal discipline on national governments.

First, as Frenkel and Goldstein emphasize, especially in an environment of open trade and capital mobility, there is a tight relationship between the choice of national monetary policies and the choice of exchange rate regimes. Specifically, the decision to fix the nominal exchange rate between national currencies is necessarily and simultaneously the decision to limit very severely the range for independent national monetary policies—it is almost (if not quite) the decision to adopt a single, unified monetary policy. From this vitally important principle, there follow critical implications both for the circumstances under which a currency bloc will be appropriate and viable and for the operation of a currency bloc if one is established.

For the question of the appropriate size and makeup of currency blocs, the key issue is the willingness and desirability of subordinating national monetary policies to the constraints implied by fixed nominal exchange rates. Here, I would emphasize the basic conclusions of Frenkel and Goldstein. For a variety of reasons, on economic grounds, a stronger case can be made for greater exchange rate fixity *within* the European, American, and Asian blocs than *between* these major blocs. Also, I heartily endorse the following key point of Frenkel and Goldstein concerning the viability of arrangements to fixed exchange rates between these blocs.

"So long as the anchor countries (of the blocs) do give the highest priority to price stability (as the objective of monetary policy), tight and ambitious exchange rate commitments will lack the credibility they need to be effective (since market participants will learn that when push comes to shove, interest rate adjustments necessary to defend exchange rate targets are not forthcoming."

Within a currency bloc, there are essentially two alternatives:

either there will be a leading national monetary authority that determines its own policy, with other countries adjusting to that policy; or there will need to be some more symmetric mechanism for determining the overall monetary policy of the bloc. To an important extent, this is the key issue to be resolved in discussions about a European central bank for the European Monetary System (EMS). It is generally agreed among members of the EMS that there should be a high degree of nominal exchange rate stability (perhaps evolving into a common currency). Up to this point, the Bundesbank, which has consistently pursued a low-inflation monetary policy, has provided the nominal anchor for the EMS. Rather, the key question concerning the establishment of a European central bank is whether to replace Bundesbank leadership with a more politically symmetric mechanism for determining monetary policy in the EMS.

This question leads naturally to my second main point—the general importance of political considerations in determining monetary and exchange rate arrangements. Nothing in the economic concept of an "optimal currency area" automatically implies that sovereign nations would naturally and inevitably constitute the geographic domains of monetary units. Nevertheless, at least in modern times, there are few examples of national governments that have not sought to enforce a single monetary standard within their domain of political authority. As a scientific matter, the hypothesis that political considerations dominate over economic factors in determining the domains of operation of different currencies is extremely powerfully supported by the empirical evidence. No other hypothesis can conceivably explain the close correlation between currency areas and domains of political authority both over time and across the surface of the globe.

Political considerations also importantly influence monetary and exchange rate arrangements among nations. As Frenkel and Goldstein conclude—and as I would agree—creation of a currency bloc and ultimately of a single currency in the European Community (EC) has both potentially important economic benefits and potentially important economic costs. Concerning the relative balance of benefits and costs, economic analysis indicates forcefully that "it all depends." Political considerations, however, suggest tighter exchange rate arrangements and closer monetary coordination among members of the EC as an expression of increasing political solidarity. In the end, whether the EC creates a powerful European central bank (that effectively takes control of EC monetary policy) and ultimately moves to a single currency depends, in my judgment, more on the strength of European political identity than on narrow calculations of economic benefits and costs.

My third main point concerns mechanisms for imposing fiscal discipline on national governments. As Frenkel and Goldstein note, little has been settled at this stage concerning the implications of currency zones for the issue of fiscal discipline. I would add that inadequate fiscal discipline can be a problem regardless of a country's monetary and exchange rate arrangements, although the nature of those arrangements may affect manifestations and consequences of inadequate fiscal discipline.

Under a floating exchange rate regime or under an adjustable peg system, when a country gets into fiscal difficulties, the adjustment to deal with these difficulties often involves a change in the exchange rate. In contrast, under a single unified currency system, a national government or a sub-national governmental unit loses the capacity to alter the exchange rate as part of the mechanism for dealing with a fiscal crisis. After a detailed discussion of the pluses and minuses of the alternative exchange rate and monetary systems, Morris and Jacob conclude that fiscal discipline tends to be a little stronger under a fixed exchange rate or unified currency regime than under a floating exchange rate regime.

Perhaps recent experience in the United States provides further useful evidence on this point. We observe that many state governments have recently faced large fiscal deficits and have been taking dramatic, some might even say draconian, measures to correct their fiscal imbalances. In contrast, the federal government of the United States has cruised happily along for nearly a decade with a budget deficit of more than 3 percent of GNP, and is currently running a deficit of nearly double that size. Even though the federal government has not relied on money creation to finance its deficit, the fact that the U.S. government issues its own money appears somehow to provide greater fiscal flexibility than is typically enjoyed by state governments that do not have separate monies.

The last issue that I want to discuss in the Frenkel/Goldstein paper is how fiscal discipline is imposed in a system with a single currency or with rigidly fixed exchange rates. The mechanism for imposing discipline is not only, and probably not primarily, the tendency for borrowing costs to rise as an individual debtor's activities appear to become less and less fiscally prudent. Instead, the most important mechanism for imposing discipline is what happens when the crunch comes—when actual and potential creditors come to believe that a borrower may be unable or unwilling to service his obligations. That is when fiscal discipline is most actively and effectively enforced.

It is important to understand that this critical part of the mechanism of fiscal discipline functions for private debtors as well as for governmental borrowers. For example, as a number of practitioners of leveraged buyouts have learned during the past two years, fiscal discipline is imposed when your creditors decide not to advance new loans or to roll over existing loans. Similarly, for virtually all businesses that get into financial difficulty, the sternest discipline is imposed when the crunch comes—when creditors come to doubt that they will be repaid.

This same mechanism operates for governmental borrowers. Fiscal discipline was finally imposed on New York City in the crisis of the mid-1970s when the city could no longer roll over its short-term debt. For national governments (borrowing in foreign currencies), the same point is illustrated by the recent debt crisis. As several developing countries discovered in the early 1980s, fiscal discipline is sometimes imposed not by a gradual rise in their borrowing costs, but rather, by a sudden shutdown of credit availability. Thus the key issue for fiscal discipline is how the system functions in a crisis and what circumstances provoke a crisis.

On this point, it is important to re-emphasize something that Morris said in his presentation—for the system of fiscal discipline to work effectively, both debtors and creditors need to recognize that they will bear part of the costs of a financial crisis. Debtors must bear an important part of the costs so that they will have appropriate incentives to avoid the indiscretions that generate fiscal crises. Thus, in the case of New York City, it was important that subway fares and bridge tolls needed to be increased and municipal payrolls needed to be reduced as conditions for financial assistance. Similarly, as Pedro Aspe emphasized yesterday, the Mexican government had to make tough decisions about massive cuts in its budget deficit as an essential condition for resolving its financial crisis.

Creditors also need to feel the pain of financial crises. After all, as a moral matter, excessive and imprudent borrowing is possible only if there is excessive and imprudent lending. Perhaps more important, as a practical matter, excessive and imprudent borrowing is effectively stopped when fiscal discipline is imposed by the termination of excessive and imprudent lending. The incentive to terminate such lending comes from the desire of creditors to avoid the pain of being caught in a financial crisis. The creditors who prudently withdraw before the crisis, get out whole; those who delay, take their lumps. If creditors know that they will suffer no losses, they have no incentive to pull the plug on excessive borrowing. This, of course, is an important part of the great savings and loan debacle. Insured depositors knew that they had nothing to lose by lending to institutions that offered particularly attractive interest rates, even if those institutions were deeply insolvent. For creditors to be provided with the essential incentive to impose effective discipline on borrowers, creditors must know that they are likely to suffer losses, along with borrowers, if lending is excessive and imprudent.

To conclude these remarks, I require an appropriate transition which I borrow shamelessly from Monty Python—"And now for something completely different."

Much of the discussion at this conference has focused on the growth of trade blocs and the demise of the General Agreement on Tariffs and Trade (GATT). Personally, I take a more optimistic view of the development of the world trading system. At the beginning of this century the world was divided into trading blocs, as it has been for much of history. Those trade blocs were called "empires" and they were often exclusive, protectionist, and antagonistic. During the period of the GATT—the period since World War II—we have moved dramatically away from the old imperial systems and toward a much more open system of world trade. Recent developments in the European Community and in North America are not reversals of this broad trend of development of the world trading system.

Indeed, the most important developments of the past five years have clearly been in the direction of broadening the principles of open trade. One of the most important exceptions to the general rules of the GATT for most of the postwar era has been the special exemption granted to developing countries from abiding by the rules of open trade. Somehow, the combination of mercantilist illogic, nationalist bravado, and Marxist nonsense placed the knife of protectionism into the hands of developing countries and invited them to slit their own throats. During recent years, an ever growing group of developing countries have recognized the stupidity of inward looking economic policies and have moved unilaterally to remove their self-constructed barriers to participation in the world trading system. This is a very positive development, most especially for these countries, but also for the GATT system. In the Uruguay Round of trade negotiations, many developing countries are no longer protectionist pleaders for special privileges. Quite rightly, they demand that the industrial countries live up to their rhetoric, saying, in effect, "Look, you stinkers, why aren't you abiding by the rules of open trade?"

Another great exception to the general application of GATT principles has been the world's last great empire—the Soviet Union and its former satellites in Central Europe. The past two years have seen the demise of that empire, and many of the subject states of that empire are now banging at the door of GATT and of the European Community, demanding entry into the system of open world trade.

Thus, there is legitimate concern about the delay in concluding the Uruguay Round and the threat that it may ultimately fail. There is also reason to worry that regional trading arrangements may incorporate some protectionist elements. Nevertheless, the main trend of development is still toward a more open system of international trade. "The force is with us."

Commentary:
Macroeconomic Policy Implications
of Trade and Currency Zones

Tommaso Padoa-Schioppa

In recent years there has been a significant increase in the number and size of country groupings being formed and leading to formal and informal trading agreements. Today, most industrialized nations are involved in such groupings. The European Community (EC) embarked on the 1992 Internal Market Program in 1986 and is now heading toward Economic and Monetary Union (EMU). Other landmarks in the process are the U.S.-Canada Free Trade Agreement and the Australia-New Zealand Closer Economic Relations Agreement.

The movement continues. Discussions are under way in Europe, between the EC and the member countries of the European Free Trade Agreement (EFTA) with a view to creating a European Economic Space; the transition of Central and Eastern Europe toward a market system is stimulating interest in a reorganization of trade relationships between them to replace the now obsolete Comecon; and proposals have been put forward to negotiate free trade agreements between the EC and EFTA countries on the one hand and the Eastern European countries on the other. Outside Europe, an extension of the U.S.-Canada free trade agreement to include Mexico is being discussed; the U.S. "Enterprise for the Americas Initiative," launched last year, envisages other free trade areas in the hemisphere; a common market agreement was recently signed by the Southern Cone countries of Latin America; and, finally, the informal Asian Pacific Economic Cooperation Process could evolve into a more formal regional arrangement.

These developments pose a number of problems for both economists and policymakers. Economists discover that traditional trade theory was based on an excessively simplistic picture of both the world and the structure of a modern economy. Policymakers have to make concrete choices in the bilateral, regional, and global fora of trade negotiations.

In this paper I will touch on only a few of the many issues raised by trade and currency zones. I shall focus on their internal and external macroeconomic policy implications, but shall first spend some words on definitions and concepts as I think that much of the current debate on these issues is obfuscated by terminological confusion. I shall conclude with a general point on reconciling a "zone" approach with a "global" approach.

My remarks will be considerably influenced by the EC example, which is undoubtedly the most significant experience in this century of the progressive deepening of the organization of a multicountry economy. Right now, the EC is deeply involved in negotiating a treaty that would transform its own zone into an Economic and Monetary Union, so that some of the points made today and yesterday seem to be slightly out of date in the light of the important political—though not yet legal—commitments that have been entered into on the EC level.

Definitions and concepts

A certain vagueness in defining the subject of the debate may contribute to the success of the debate itself—some vagueness, but not too much. Different persons express different views, but these views may refer to different subjects rather than to the same subject. In our case the vagueness concerns the very topic of the conference, namely what we mean by trade zones and currency zones.

In yesterday's discussion the only element defining a zone was considered to be geographical extension (number of countries involved), possibly corrected by the proximity factor mentioned by Paul Krugman. I think that at least two other elements are crucial: the economic content of the zone's arrangements and the legal and institutional structure of the zone. As to the economic content, it makes a great difference whether trade is simply in manufactured goods or in services as well, whether the protection considered consists only of tariffs, or also of norms, regulations, tax regimes, and so on. As to the legal and institutional structure, the issue is, in broad terms, how the classic—legislative, executive, and judiciary—functions of government are exercised in the stipulation and management of the agreements. How much discretion is allowed in implementing and interpreting the agreed provisions? To whom is it entrusted? Are there law-enforcement mechanisms? More generally, how much " supranationality" is involved in the arrangements?

For each of the three elements (geographical extension, economic content, and institutional structure), arrangements can range from "limited" to "comprehensive," in an almost continuous spectrum, forming a three-dimensional space in which individual countries, groups of countries, and the world can be mapped. Thus a nation state with no internal decentralization and no economic relationships with the outside is very local on the first account and very comprehensive on the other two, lying in one corner of the box, whereas the United Nations is close to the opposite corner.

If we disregard these complexities and use the term trade and currency zone to designate arrangements that are completely different with respect to these three elements, then disagreement is due more to terminological confusion than to diverging analyses and policy judgments.

Consider trade zones: the European Community, which is certainly limited in geographical extension, notwithstanding three successive enlargements, has an economic content that extends to movements of goods, services, capital, and persons, and it is taking liberalization to the point of literally eliminating borders. In addition, the European Community has far-reaching legislative, executive, and judiciary powers applying to such areas as external relations, competition policy, industrial concentration, public procurement,

health and safety regulations, and state monopolies in public services, and so on. As regards its structure, the EC has a complete set
of institutions that is much closer to the legal and institutional
apparatus of a nation than to any of the other existing regional
arrangements.

Turning to the content of a currency zone, we can use the classification of the possible ways of organizing a currency zone
proposed yesterday by Andrew Crockett and David Laidler: floating
rates, crawling pegs, adjustable pegs, and monetary union. I shall
not return to this theme, except to note that here, too, the institutional
structure has to be considered along with the two other elements.
Take the notion of monetary union, which is interchangeably identified with a regime of irrevocably fixed exchange rates or with a
single monetary authority. Analytically, there is not much difference
between the two: a system with permanently fixed exchange rates is
a system in which effectively only one monetary policy exists for the
whole area, "as if" there was only one central bank. But this means
disregarding the institutional element. In practice, it would make an
enormous difference, for both the economics and the politics of a
monetary union, if the union were based on an exchange rate rule or
the replacement of a plurality of monetary authorities with a single
authority.

When the simplistic one-dimensional approach is replaced by the
more accurate three-dimensional approach, the two main issues
discussed so far—are trade and currency zones "good" or "bad?"
and does a trade zone imply a currency zone?—become clearer and
probably less controversial. Without dwelling on them, I shall make
two points.

First, on the "good or bad" issue, the nontrivial question is how
to assess a regional agreement that in terms of economic content and
institutional structure goes further than a global arrangement could
conceivably go. Determining whether there is a tradeoff between
progress on different axes and, if so, what is the best mix, is a matter
for political judgment. I doubt whether economists have much to say.
For my part, I think that, while the preservation and strengthening
of the global system is a most important objective, economically and

institutionally "deep" regional systems are desirable both because they may lead the way to a similar evolution of the global system and as useful intermediate layers in an otherwise unmanageable world of 190 sovereign countries. I also think that the global and the regional approaches may well be mutually reinforcing.

Second, on currency zones, there is a need for consistency between trade and currency arrangements. This is hard to deny. Indeed, what economist would affirm that all monetary regimes are alike for the economy? The issue can only be discussed with reference to a refined classification of trade and currency zones, by asking what currency arrangement is consistent with what trade arrangement and accepting that, as trade arrangements evolve, currency arrangements have to adapt. It is not my task here to explain why and how the EC has decided to move to Economic and Monetary Union. I shall only recall that the EC has largely passed the stage of pondering the pros and cons of EMU and is well advanced in the process of drafting a treaty to move to a single central bank and a single currency.

Internal implications

In the EC, where "trade zone" means the single market and "currency zone" means a monetary union with a single monetary authority, the main issue concerning the macroeconomic policy implications of trade and currency zones is: what are the implications of such a zone from a fiscal point of view? In other words: does a trade and currency zone require a fiscal policy zone? By "fiscal policy zone" I mean an arrangement whereby member states' budgetary policies are not completely independent and possibly the "zone" can conduct a fiscal policy of its own. At the outset, a distinction should be made between two aspects of the problem. They could be called the discipline aspect and the policy mix aspect respectively.

On the discipline aspect, the question is whether a fiscal policy zone is to be considered a prerequisite, or a necessary component, of a monetary union; or, more precisely, whether a fiscal union is necessary for a monetary union to be viable, that is, for price stability to be effectively pursued by the central monetary authority. In the

EC debate, opinions are divided. Those who claim that a fiscal zone
is not necessary, argue that creating a strong monetary authority, a
central bank that is equipped and willing to pursue price stability
inflexibly, would be sufficient to achieve price stability, regardless
of the fiscal behavior of member states. After all, they observe, this
proposition is valid at the level of a single country. What is crucial
is that a strong monetary constitution be designed to ensure a clear
separation between monetary policy and fiscal policy. Compared
with a sovereign nation, the separation in the European Community
would be sharper and, in addition, national governments would be
subject to more stringent fiscal discipline on two accounts. First,
they would have no authority to regulate and even less to manipulate
the capital market to which they would turn to finance themselves.
The availability and the cost of funds would depend only on their
creditworthiness. Second, they would not be able to monetize their
debt (see Padoa-Schioppa, 1988b) as neither their governments nor
their parliaments would have control of the printing press. Hence,
problems of fiscal indiscipline would, at least in the medium run, be
less likely to arise in a monetary union, though they would not be
completely eliminated.[1] They also point out that there is no federation in the world in which there are federal rules concerning the
budget; not the United States, not Canada, not the Federal Republic
of Germany, not Switzerland, nor Belgium.

Those who claim that a fiscal zone is necessary observe that
considerations applicable to other federal systems are not valid for
the EC. The member states are large in relation to the EC as a whole,
so that their budgets are potentially more destabilizing than state
budgets in most federations; and the EC's central budget is too small
to have a macroeconomic impact of its own. It should be noted,
however, that while these propositions may be true now, the U.S.
federation once resembled the EC much more closely, in terms of
the relative size of both individual states and the federal budget.

On the whole, the economic argument claiming that a fiscal union
is a necessary precondition of a monetary union on monetary stability
grounds is weak. While adding a fiscal constitution to EMU does not
seem indispensable, there have to be rules to prevent fiscal imbalances from interfering with the conduct of monetary policy. They

include the ban on direct central bank financing of government budgets and the so called "no bailout" provision, whereby neither the EC, nor other member states will take financial responsibility for any fiscally imprudent member state.

The above does not imply that fiscal rules are not desirable. My own view is that they ought to be regarded as an important ingredient of a sound economic constitution. Indeed, in this field, as in other areas such as the organization of the single market, the constitution-making process now under way in the EC is an opportunity that should not be missed to exploit the lessons of the last few decades by adopting economic laws that improve the existing ones. According to this view, fiscal rules would not be simply a corollary of the Economic and Monetary Union, but an additional element of the organization of the EMU.

But how are we to formulate budget rules that would impose discipline? The main difficulty is that no rule can completely eliminate the need for interpretation. The same budget deficit may be "bad" or "good" depending on a number of factors (cyclical conditions, size of the budget, structure and composition of expenditures and revenues, balance-of-payment situation, and so forth) that are almost impossible to pin down in a rule. The question then is who should exercise the discretion that is necessary to decide whether or not a rule has been complied with in a particular case. This leads to the further question of the level of government. Should fiscal rules be embodied in the constitution of the federation, that is, in the EMU Treaty, or, as in the case of the United States, at the level of state constitutions? The Intergovernmental Conference preparing the EMU Treaty is discussing these issues. In the solution that is emerging, the treaty will forbid "excessive deficits" and lay down some criteria for determining what is "excessive." The future will tell how operational these provisions will be.

Let me now turn to the second main aspect of the macroeconomic policy implications of an EC-like trade and currency zone. This has to do with policy-mix considerations. The question is whether the EC should have the (constitutional) means of determining its overall fiscal stance. Two reasons are given by those who suggest a positive answer: the desire to avoid overburdening monetary policy as the sole EC macroeconomic policy tool and the need to define an EC-wide monetary and fiscal policy mix within the larger context of international (G-7) policy coordination procedures. For both these reasons, it is argued, a fiscal macropolicy capacity should be established at the EC level. However, support for a fiscal policy capacity is much weaker than for rules of budgetary discipline, reflecting the current aversion to forms of fiscal activism.

Here again, if such a capacity were to be established at all, its design should incorporate appropriate safeguards against the excesses of fiscal activism we have witnessed in the recent past. An EC fiscal policy could operate through national budgets or through the EC budget. For a number of reasons,[2] the first solution seems preferable. Indeed, empowering the EC to control national budget balances would require member states to relinquish too large a measure of sovereignty. It would imply that the European Community was empowered to determine the size and structure of public expenditure and the taxation of otherwise sovereign nations and to devise sanctions for noncompliance. Budgetary power is inextricably linked to the exercise of an allocative function which is a strict prerogative of elected national assemblies. On the other hand, as experience has repeatedly shown, relying on a voluntary coordination of national budgetary policies would be too weak a procedure to produce meaningful decisions. If scope for fiscal activism at the EC level had to be provided one day for the purpose of stabilization, the natural policy tool would be the EC budget. Although small, today's EC budget of about 1.5 percent of the EC's GDP is already sufficient to conduct a more than purely symbolic fiscal policy, and it seems reasonable to expect that its size will grow in the future. Needless to say, the balanced-budget constraint that presently characterizes the EC budget would have to be relaxed. A budget balanced over the cycle would suffice. Mechanisms would have to be devised whereby the EC would have the instruments to shift over time the collection of the revenues that finance its expenditures. The double constraint of balancing the budget over multiyear periods and weaving revenues instead of expenditures would clearly tie EC fiscal activism to a much sounder constitution than the ones we have seen so far.

In conclusion, neither economic theory nor the constitutional experience of other federal systems provide compelling arguments to conclude that European monetary union will be viable only if it is coupled with a transfer of fiscal authority from national to EC authorities. What is important is that a strong monetary constitution be in place. However, fiscal rules should be regarded as desirable per se to reduce governments' budgetary discretion. As for the determination of a fiscal policy stance for the EC area as a whole, the arguments in favor of giving the EC such a capacity are valid. The way to establish such a capacity, however, should not be to grant the EC the power to impose decisions on national budgets, but rather to allow more flexible use of the European Community budget.

External implications

While the internal macroeconomic policy implications are mainly fiscal, the external ones are mainly monetary. As a matter of fact, macroeconomic policy cooperation between countries has historically taken the form of an exchange rate regime. Although both fiscal and monetary domestic policies produce significant spillover effects, in these two areas coordination procedures have generally not gone beyond soft exercises of mutual information. The question then is to identify the significance and implications of EMU for the international monetary system, a task that is not facilitated by the fact that such a "system" is rather ill-defined today, perhaps nonexistent.

If the European Community becomes a single market cum single currency entity, its role in the international monetary and financial world can be expected to increase significantly compared with those of the member states today. It will have an integrated banking system and capital market, several important financial centers and considerable financial strength, based on an aggregate current account surplus and a large stock of foreign exchange reserves. Its financial structures are likely to play a strategic role in accompanying the transformation and, hopefully, the eventual takeoff of the economies of Central and Eastern Europe. All these are natural premises for significant changes in the present shape of international monetary relationships, characterized by a plurality of reserve currencies with floating rates and a soft management of them.

In an EMU that adopts the ECU as its single currency, private and public investors' portfolios will most likely undergo important shifts in composition to give ECU-denominated assets a share closer to that of the EC economy than the present aggregate of EC countries. This process will require careful management and effective cooperation by central banks to avoid exchange rate shocks.

With EC currencies merging into EMU and the ECU, what is today the main determinant of the demand for deutsche mark-denominated official reserves will vanish.[3] While this will presumably cause an increase in the dollar share in world reserves, the United States, Japan, and other non-EC monetary authorities will probably have to build up considerable ECU balances in their official reserves. On the whole, I do not think, however, that these portfolio adjustments are likely to dethrone the dollar as the main international currency. It will take more than EMU and a sizable external U.S. debt to eradicate deep-seated habits in the pricing of primary commodities, in the invoicing of many internationally traded goods and services, and in the selection of transaction and intervention currencies. The trend may well be toward aligning the dollar's monetary role with its economic and financial ones, but it is likely to be a slow one. Historical experience of the rise and decline of international currencies supports this view.

Compared to the present dollar-yen-deutsche mark tripolar system, a dollar-ECU system would, I think, have the advantage of greater uniformity in the relative size of the component economies. More importantly, perhaps, it would imply a simplification of the present threefold role of the deutsche mark, as a national, EC, and international currency. The potential conflicts between the national and international roles of a currency have long been known, both in theory and practice. Besides not being politically viable, a de facto or de jure EC monetary union based on the deutsche mark in the role played by the dollar in the early Bretton Woods years is technically unthinkable. Too many of the conditions that made that role possible for the dollar in the 1950s are lacking for the deutsche mark in the 1990s. And it is perhaps not by accident that there are now more restrictions on the use of the deutsche mark by nonresidents in financial transactions than for the other main EC currencies.

International monetary coordination in a multicurrency reserve system is a blend of competition and cooperation. There are reasons to believe that in a tripolar dollar-ECU system, both elements of the exercise would improve. With three currencies of comparable importance, the incentive to be competitive in terms of quality (price stability, efficiency of clearing and settlement procedures, attractiveness of financial centers, and so on) would be equally powerful for all the members. At the same time, bargaining power would be more evenly distributed in the negotiations on cooperative measures.

Another implication concerns the institutional framework for international monetary cooperation. Today this reflects the stratification over time of different fora and Parkinson's well-known law that committees can be created, never destroyed. It also reflects the weakness of the role of international institutions, not only as a negotiating partner speaking for the "common good" but also as providers of fully independent technical support. The significance of the middle letter of the International Monetary Fund's acronym paled long ago. It should be acknowledged that not all the 155 countries affiliated to it have the same role and responsibilities in managing the international monetary system. In a dollar-yen-ECU system a G-3 should replace the present plethora of Gx, Gy, and so on. This would obviously make the cooperative exercise more efficient, but would run the risk of further strengthening the "ad hoc" nature of such cooperation. It would be therefore desirable to enhance the political and technical role played by the IMF in support of international cooperation. Whether this will be achieved, however, is quite uncertain, not only because of traditional reluctance to strengthen supranational institutions, but also because the latter may seem less, not more, necessary in a game of very few players.

Last but not least, there is the issue of the exchange rate regime of a dollar-yen-ECU tripolar world. Some years ago proposals were put forward for the creation of a "world EMS," that is, a new and formalized adjustable peg regime that would differ from Bretton Woods but not having a formal leader and by opposing less resistance to parity adjustments. I continue to believe[4] that the EMS owes too much to EC-specific factors to be easily replicated worldwide: the homogeneousness of its economic structures, the high level of trade integration, the existence of a solid and comprehensive institutional edifice, and continuous occasions for meeting and consultations, and so on. Moreover, the EMS itself has proven to be subject to system erosion, like any policy regime. It seems more likely that the cautious experiment of exchange rate cooperation inaugurated at the Plaza and the Louvre will evolve at a slow pace, without dramatic accelerations.

In conclusion, the external macroeconomic policy implication of an EC-type trade and currency zone could be to establish, much more than has been the case so far, a genuine multicurrency reserve system based on a tripolar relationship. The monetary regime could, at least initially, remain one of mildly managed floating and soft coordination among the main reserve centers. This can be seen as no more than a simplification and rationalization of a state of affairs in which we have been for about five or six years now. The importance of such a simplification and rationalization, however, should not be underestimated. Since the problems and potential instability posed by a global financial system, whether in the form of private or public cross-border, cross-currency, debts or in that of crises and tensions in banking or capital markets, are likely to remain with us, any improvement in the existing system is to be welcomed.

Conclusion

The macroeconomic aspects, important as they are, only represent one of the problems posed by trade and currency zones, perhaps not the most important one. They are sufficient, however, to highlight two important features. First, regional arrangements have an internal dynamic involving all the three elements (geographical extension, economic content, and institutional structure) that combine to define a zone. Free trade arrangements tend to evolve into a single market, the institutional requirements increase, the financial integration of a single market calls for some form of agreed monetary regime. Second, there is a need to fit regional arrangements into the global system, to stimulate positive interactions between the two, or at least to prevent conflicts.

Today, the European Community is mainly concerned with the

former feature; the world with the latter. The not forgotten concerns about Fortress Europe and the debate developing in the United States on whether efforts should be directed to regional rather than to global trade negotiations point to the growing danger that an antagonistic view of the relationship between the two will develop. However, since the same economic, and political, and ethical, rationale is at the origin of both regional and global arrangements, it is crucially important that there should be a general philosophy applicable to both and consistent with their common rationale.

One element of such a philosophy deserves special attention: global arrangements—be they the GATT, the U.N., or the Bretton Woods institutions—should, in their very design, allow for regional arrangements by establishing ground rules for their features and behavior in the global sphere, very much as they do for nations. Any deepening of regional integration, up to the creation of new fully-fledged federal entities, should be welcomed, provided it complies with those ground rules. After all, why should Canada or Belgium be free to loosen their centralized constitutional structure and a group of sovereign states not be free to tighten their links as the thirteen North American newly independent states did 200 years ago? And why should the existing number of 190 sovereign nations be considered optimal?

This opens a vast ground for improving and revising the existing global arrangements, with Article XXIV of GATT[5] representing a significant precedent. It also opens a vast ground to intellectual work, because we lack a satisfactory economic theory of a multi-tier "government" of the economy; and even our constitutional theory in this field is far from adequate. Thus, this final remark is more a starting point than a concluding one.

Endnotes

[1]Frenkel and Goldstein in their paper on EMU (Frenkel and Goldstein, 1991) cite evidence that in federal fiscal systems, such as the United States and Canada, states that pursued a more prudent fiscal policy had lower borrowing costs than others and states that had voluntarily "tied their hands" by enacting constitutional limitations on borrowing also reduced their borrowing costs by comparison with others. But—they remind us pointedly—there is no evidence that higher borrowing costs induce governments to correct fiscal policy excesses.

[2]For a detailed argumentation, see Padoa-Schioppa (1990).

[3]Deutsche mark-denominated reserves are about 20 percent of the world total; these deutsche mark reserves are largely held by EC countries.

[4]See Padoa-Schioppa (1988a).

[5]The article permits customs unions and free trade areas to be formed provided that tariff or nontariff barriers imposed by the participant countries are not higher or more restrictive vis-à-vis nonparticipants than thoser prevailing prior to the formation of the union or free trade area.

References

Cecchini, P. "The European Challenge, 1992. The Benefits of a Single Market," *Gower*, London, 1988.

Frenkel, J. and Morris Goldstein. " Monetary Policy in an Emerging European Economic and Monetary Union: Key Issues," IMF *Staff Papers,* No. 2 (June, 1991).

Gomel G., F. Saccomanni and S. Vona. " The Experience with Economic Policy Coordination: the Tripolar and the European Dimensions," *Temi di Discussione*, Banca d'Italia, n. 140 (July 1990).

Hufbauer, G.C. Background paper for " The Free Trade Debate," Reports of the Twentieth Century Fund Task Force on the Future of American Trade Policy. New York: Priority Press Publications. 1989.

Keohane, R.O. " After Hegemony: Cooperation and Discord in the World Political Economy." Princeton: Princeton University Press. 1984.

Lawrence, R.Z. "Comments during a 'Symposium on Europe 1992'," *Brookings Papers on Economic Activity,* No. 2, 1989.

Meade, J. " The Theory of Customs Unions." Amsterdam: North Holland, 1956.

OECD. " Regional Integration: A Review of Macroeconomic Trends and Possible Implications," 1989, unpublished.

_____. " Trade Implications for Non-Participants of Recent Regional Arrangements Among OECD Countries," 1990, unpublished.

Olson, M. " The Logic of Collective Action." Cambridge: Harvard University Press, 1965.

Padoa-Schioppa, T. "Toward a New Adjustable Peg?" Per Jacobsson Lecture on The International Monetary System: the Next Twenty-Five Years. Basle, June 12, 1988, (1988a).

_____. "The European Monetary System: A Long-Term View," in F. Giavazzi, S. Micossi and M. Miller (eds.), *The European Monetary System,* Cambridge: Cambridge University Press. (1988b).

_____. " Toward a European Central Bank: Fiscal Compatibility and Monetary Constitution." A paper presented at the Bank of Israel Conference on *Aspects of Central Bank Policymaking*. Tel Aviv, January 1990.

Viner, J. " The Customs Union Issue." New York: Carnegie Endowment for International Peace, 1950.

Vona, S. " Il commercio mondiale verso il 2000: libero scambio o protezionismo?" Milano: Franco Angeli.

U.S. Leadership and Postwar Progress

Allan H. Meltzer

Twenty years after World War I, the major industrial countries were on the eve of another great war. Recovery from the Great Depression was incomplete in many of these countries. In the United States and some other democracies, per capita income was below the level reached in 1929. Abroad, the spread of totalitarian government appeared to be both an unstoppable trend and, given the economic performance of Germany and Italy, a possible solution to stagnation and depression.

At home, New Deal experimentation with economic planning and government direction of economic life had become popular with many voters and seemed likely to continue and to spread. Many believed or professed that capitalism was an eighteenth or nineteenth century idea whose time had passed. And, since comprehensive planning and democratic government lead to conflict, democracy, too, was often seen as an impediment to economic progress rather than an essential feature of a free and progressive society. This message, or something similar, was heard in large parts of Africa and Asia.

More than forty years after the end of World War II, the outlook for democratic government, private ownership, and market direction of economic activity is very different. The postwar generations look ahead guided by a different experience. There have been wars, but no major war. There have been recessions, but no major depression. And, there has been remarkable progress in living standards in the democratic market economies and in the spread of democratic government.

Looking back, we can see that more people in more countries have experienced larger increases in standards of living or income than at any time in recorded history. Life expectancy has increased. Infant mortality has declined, and health standards have improved in many parts of the world. Japan has become a stable, democratic, and wealthy country. Japan's output and its people's incomes have increased at a rate that permits children to enter the labor force at incomes, after adjusting for inflation, that are three to four times the incomes received by their parents a generation earlier. Western Europe turned away from false totalitarian promises to embrace the democratic, market system. They, too, enjoyed large increases in standards of living. Countries like Spain and Portugal eventually rejected authoritarian government, joined the market system, and embraced Western European institutions based on political and economic freedom. Per capita incomes in Taiwan, Hong Kong, and Singapore advanced so rapidly that standards of living in these countries now exceed the levels in Portugal, Spain, or Ireland and are approaching the level of long established developed countries such as Australia, New Zealand, or the United Kingdom. Even in countries like Brazil or Mexico, where the decade of the 1980s has been burdened by debt and mistaken policies, postwar growth has raised standards of living markedly. For example, Brazil experienced real growth of per capita income of more than 3 1/2 percent a year from 1965 to 1988 despite the continuing problems that reduced the growth rate for the 1980s.

The postwar decades constitute a great experiment in the properties of economic systems. The results of the experiment are as clear as is likely to be found in the social sciences. Where the market system has operated, the typical experience is that countries have developed, standards of living have increased, education and health have improved, and democracy has been encouraged. Where some form of socialist planning has been tried, the typical experience has been economic stagnation and political repression. There is less sustained progress than in the market economies and less freedom also. Indeed, if this were not so, we would not have witnessed the rejection of socialist planning once an alternative became attainable. Communist parties that at times stood on the edge of power now change their names and even their programs.

Of course, exceptions to these generalizations can be found. Not all market economies have progressed, and not all have become democratic. Some socialist countries have raised living standards, as in China, but often the most dramatic improvements have come when state direction and planning have been reduced. Hungary's experience with reduced state control and China's with loosening its agricultural controls are two examples.

The clearest comparisons, and the most useful experimental evidence, come from those countries where we can hold constant factors such as history and culture that may affect the pace of economic development. Taiwan, Hong Kong, and Singapore together can be compared to the People's Republic of China in the same way that West Germany can be compared to East Germany or North Korea to South Korea. In these comparisons, differences in history and culture are insignificant, while social and economic arrangements have diverged widely. After forty years, there can be little doubt about the outcome. Hong Kong and China are of particular interest since Hong Kong's population includes large numbers of migrants who fled from China in the years after 1949. Average income of those who left is now 15 to 20 times the average for those who remained behind.

Yet, not all market economies prosper. Argentina and Bolivia are examples of countries that have not shared in the postwar prosperity. Many historical periods have produced poorer results than the postwar years. The interwar period is an example cited earlier. These differences between periods and countries call for an explanation.

The superior postwar performance of many countries owes much, I believe, to the institutions and policy arrangements put in place at the end of World War II. These provided for the defense of common interests, rules for trade and payments, and a general disposition—often challenged and not always followed—to rely on markets and market processes to allocate resources.

During the postwar years, in contrast to the interwar period, the United States took the lead in fostering and sustaining a framework that encouraged political stability, economic growth, and reliance on markets. U.S. decisions were not always wise or well thought out. At times, and sometimes unavoidably, mistakes were made, and there was much room for improvement. Looking back, however, we cannot fail to note the substantial progress in living standards and in the spread of democratic government and to inquire about the relation between postwar policies and these developments.

The first task is to develop the linkage between progress and postwar arrangements for political stability, trade rules, monetary policy, and reliance on markets. The second task is to inquire whether, or to what extent, new or revamped arrangements are now required if progress is to continue.

Political stability

Comparison of interwar and postwar political arrangements for defense and their achievements is a study of differences. Collective security in the interwar period was to be the responsibility of the League of Nations. The United States did not join, but even if that vote had been reversed, it seems unlikely that the United States would have been willing or able to organize a coalition against the totalitarian countries. In the 1920s, U.S. defense spending was 15 to 20 percent of the budget but less than 1 percent of GNP. Domestic concerns were dominant in the United States, as in most countries, and the relative position of the United States was much less imposing after World War I than a generation later.

For better or worse, the failure of the League of Nations as a peace-keeping institution was matched to a degree in the postwar. Political divisions between the totalitarian and democratic countries prevented the United Nations (UN) from developing its authorized peace-keeping role. Although agreement was possible in a few instances, generally the UN was a relatively ineffective organization. The major difference in postwar defense or political developments was the organization of defense outside the UN.

There are two aspects. One is the development of regional agreements, of which the North Atlantic Treaty Organization (NATO) was most successful. The other was the commitment by the United States to use force or threat of force in Korea, Vietnam, and Kuwait, but also in Greece, Turkey, and Iran in the 1940s, Iran and Lebanon in the 1950s, Cuba and the Dominican Republic in the 1960s, Libya and Panama in the 1980s and at other times and places. Even where the United Nations was the nominal organizer of the policing activities, as in Korea or Kuwait, the United States took the lead in organizing, directing, and carrying out the operations. The United States was not alone, or solely responsible. Other countries joined in some of the operations and worked alone, as Britain did in Malaysia and the Falklands and France in Chad.

All of these operations were not planned or executed wisely or well. Nevertheless, these efforts and the continued relatively large expenditures for defense made the commitment to maintain political stability credible. The costs of ensuring the peace and serving as policeman were high, but the costs of aggression were usually seen by would-be aggressors as higher still. Thus, a public good—political stability—was created and sustained, again not always perfectly. No less important, the Soviet Union and its allies in the Warsaw Pact eventually found the competition too costly to continue, perhaps establishing either that open, democratic societies have a comparative advantage in the development of the new technologies on which modern war is now based or that democracies' advantage lies in the relative economic strength of their economies and their ability to add to that strength. In either case, the result is far different from those early postwar conjectures (or Henry Kissinger's pessimism in the 1970s) that had military strength and the projection of power as an advantage of the totalitarians.

Scholars will debate for years about the relative importance of three factors leading to the end of Communism as a world force: the failure of the Soviet Union and other centrally planned economies to develop, President Reagan's commitment to U.S. rearmament in the 1980s which required a commitment of additional Soviet resources larger than the Soviets were willing to squeeze out of their economy, and President Gorbachev's personality or personal objectives. What matters for present purposes is that U.S. defense spending, service as policeman, and organizer of collective security contributed importantly to the outcome. Absent that spending and preparedness, the outcome would have been different, perhaps the gradual extension of Soviet power and U.S. withdrawal that Henry Kissinger feared in the 1970s, perhaps the Euro-communism or "Finlandization" that were prominent concerns at that time.

A public good is created when all the benefits that the good or service provides are not captured by the producer. By serving as a policeman, the United States provided two distinct types of public goods. First, it mobilized support for political stability and encouraged others to join in enforcing or maintaining peace and stability. Second, it raised the cost of aggression, thereby encouraging many (by no means all) countries to devote their talents to peaceful pursuits.

Spending on armaments absorbs resources. Iran and Iraq, for example, spent heavily on arms and now find much of their arsenals destroyed. More generally, spending for arms by countries in the Middle East lowered living standards in these countries and in neighboring countries that rearm for aggressive or defensive purposes. Resources, including skilled managers, were directed to the military instead of to trade and development. Control of resources was concentrated in a few hands instead of being broadly dispersed by the market. Opportunities for specialization, trade, and exchange were not developed. The Middle East is a region where the efforts by the United States to serve as policeman have not been successful. The region illustrates some of the costs of political instability, just as Western Europe or the trading arrangements among East Asian countries illustrate the benefits of political stability.

With the provision of a public good, there are opportunities for free riding, which occurs if a country acts on the assumption that the benefit will be supplied whether or not it contributes its share of the costs. A small country—even one of the larger European countries—could anticipate that U.S. decisions to defend Europe or spend for defense were independent of the amounts any single European country would spend for this purpose. Each European member of the alliance had an incentive to shirk on its military spending, thereby shifting the costs to others without commensurately reducing the benefits received. Similarly, European countries had incentives to take a free ride by restricting the use of their troops to European defense, leaving to the United States to bear the main costs of maintaining political stability elsewhere. Some took advantage of these opportunities to free ride.

The total costs to be shared include much more than the expenditures to support troops in the field, as in the recent war in Kuwait and Iraq or the earlier war in Korea. Large sums are spent to develop weapons systems useful in different types of encounters. These costs are part of the successful performance of the police function. Most of these costs have been paid by the United States. Granted, weapons development has some auxiliary benefits for the developer. Some of the technology may be transferred to nondefense industries. It is unlikely that the benefits compensate for the costs, however. Much of the work is specifically military, with little opportunity for transfer. Some is secret and cannot be transferred. Without denying that there have been successful technology transfers, it seems likely that investment in civilian technologies would have provided higher nondefense returns.

Under U.S. leadership, the postwar political order provided a relatively stable political system under which countries were able to develop and achieve the benefits that come from trade and exchange. Countries could concentrate on peaceful pursuits. Many seized the opportunity. Trade expanded, encouraging the rise in living standards, often at rates that were higher and persisted longer than in any previous period.

The political order was sustained by concerns about the intentions and actions of the Soviet Union and by the willingness of the United States to both tolerate free riding and bear a considerable part of the total cost of maintaining stability. Both factors are no longer present to the same degree.

If nations are to be subject to the rule of law and accept peaceful settlement of disputes, there must be enforcement. Enforcement is costly, but failure to enforce can be more costly. Someone must pay the enforcement costs.

If there is no enforcement, stability and trade will decline or grow more slowly. Petty tyrants aggravate their neighbors; bigger tyrants threaten the entire system. Without agreement on collective action, either the system based on freedom and political stability is weakened or countries bear the enforcement costs individually. Part of these costs could be avoided by everyone if there is an agreement to share the (smaller) costs of maintaining political stability.

The United States seems no longer willing to bear the preponderant share of the costs of enforcing political stability. There has been much discussion of burdensharing—redistribution of the costs. The decision to shift part of the decisionmaking about Iraq and Kuwait to the UN may have helped to get some of the costs of that operation more widely shared. But if others bear more of the costs, they will want more influence over the decisions. The UN Security Council could agree about Kuwait and Iraq, but the UN is not noted for its ability to make decisions quickly or agree about ends and means of settling disputes. Other multinational bodies would face similar problems of agreeing on political objectives. The European Commission is an example.

Failure to agree on the ends to be pursued and the means to accomplish them risks the loss of the political stability and economic progress. Yet some nation or group of nations must decide which disputes are threats to stability that require collective action and which have costs that are borne mainly by the parties to the dispute. The former require action to enforce stability; the latter do not. Someone must decide, also, how the total costs, including costs of weapons development and policing are to be shared. The solution of these problems requires not only new institutions or arrangements but agreement on objectives and the means of achieving them.

Trade rules

The interwar period was characterized by rising tariffs and protection that hindered the expansion of trade. A crude measure of the degree of protection in the United States, duties as a percentage of U.S. imports, rose from 16 percent in 1920 to 59 percent in 1932. Increases in U.S. tariffs, in 1922 and 1929, reduced U.S. imports and led to retaliation that reduced U.S. exports, particularly after 1929. During the 1930s, many countries chose policies to increase domestic demand for domestic goods and reduce demands for imports, so-called "beggar-thy-neighbor" policies, to increase domestic employment.

In the postwar years, rules for trade and agreements to reduce tariffs lowered tariff barriers, particularly between developed countries. The principal agreement is the General Agreement on Tariffs and Trade (GATT). GATT rules prohibit discrimination against particular countries, require "national treatment" of imports with respect to taxes and regulation, and provide for dispute settlement.

By 1987, when all the reductions agreed to in the Tokyo Round of trade agreements (1973-79) had been made, the United States, the European Community (EC), and Japan had reduced tariffs on industrial products to less than 5 percent on average. Although tariffs have declined substantially, the 5 percent number is not fully informative. There are four reasons.

First, there is considerable dispersion within the group of industrial products and between industrial products and other goods. Countries typically have lower tariffs on goods that they export than on goods they import. For example, Japan has a 1.5 percent tariff on transportation equipment but a 25.4 percent tariff on food and tobacco. The United States has a 0.2 percent tariff on paper and paper products but a 22.7 percent tariff on wearing apparel.

Second, countries have developed nontariff barriers to trade, and these barriers have increased as tariff barriers have declined. So-called voluntary quotas now cover a wide range of goods, including industrial products. Health, safety, and other regulations are sometimes genuine efforts to exclude undesirable products, but they are used also to protect domestic producers.

Third, many goods and services are excepted from the full force of GATT rules. Protection and subsidies for agricultural products are a familiar example. Intellectual property, including movies, books, and computer software, are not subject to GATT rules but are covered by much weaker agreements.

Fourth, many developing countries, though members of GATT, are not subject to the same rules as developed countries. The General System of Preference allows developing countries to maintain higher duties on imports. These preferences are intended to compensate for lower levels of development, but they also hamper development by raising costs of production in the developing countries and encouraging inefficiency.

Despite these restrictions on open trading arrangements, world trade has spurred economic development and the growth of world output in the postwar years. Between 1950 and 1972, world trade increased at an average rate of 5.9 percent per year after adjusting for inflation. From 1960 to 1972, world output, as measured by the International Monetary Fund (IMF), rose 4.7 percent per year. Notwithstanding oil shocks, disinflation, and the much discussed variability of fluctuating exchange rates, world trade (adjusted for inflation) grew 4.7 percent a year from 1972 to 1990 while world output (as measured by the IMF) rose by 3.2 percent.

Trade encourages development by permitting developing countries to specialize in the production of products and services in which they have comparative advantage, build plants of optimum size, shift labor and materials into world-class industries, finance economic development from the export surplus, and increase their population's skills and opportunities. Many of the same advantages accrue to developed countries. Developed countries have been pushed by the growth of trade and by competitive pressures to invest in technology and education, improve products and production processes, and increase productivity and standards of living.

The postwar years found many countries pursuing development strategies based on export-led growth. These strategies required other countries to accept import-led consumption. The importing countries gained by shifting resources into more productive uses, by specializing, and by exporting the goods and services for which they had comparative advantage. Thus, exporters and importers contributed to each other's development and to the development of the world economy.

The system of GATT rules is still in place but enforcement is ineffective. Dispute settlement procedures are slow and uncertain. Increasingly, large countries have chosen to operate outside the GATT rules, subsidizing production and exports and imposing quotas and other restrictions on imports. Many of these measures seek, or achieve, cartel arrangements that divide markets among producers and reduce competition.

Proponents of "fair" or managed trade have encouraged the development of cartel agreements for steel, automobiles, apparel, textiles, semiconductors, machine tools, and many agricultural products. These agreements, and subsidies for agricultural output and exports, reduce competition, raise prices for consumers, damage low cost producers, and divert trade, thereby reducing previous gains to living standards.

Rules for trade are a public good. The rules provide benefits to all participants in the open trading system, but rules must be enforced against free riders who benefit from the rules imposed on others and try to benefit also by preventing the same rules for open access from applying to their suppliers. Quotas, subsidies, and many nontariff barriers must be seen as attempts to gain special advantage—to free ride on the system. The more such actions succeed, the smaller are the gains achieved by the system of rules. This is the crux of current trade disputes. The rules are not comprehensive, and they have not changed sufficiently to reflect the changing composition of trade. Existing rules are not enforced uniformly. Enforcement mechanisms are weak or nonexistent.

Three types of response reflect the lack of enforcement. One is the movement to managed or "fair" trade. This has produced a number of cartels to divide markets for a growing list of products. There is nothing "fair" about these arrangements. Cartels, or market sharing agreements, stifle competition, discriminate against nonmembers, raise prices to consumers and, until they break down, reduce innovation and growth.

A second response has been unilateral action by individual countries and groups or bilateral negotiation. Bilateral negotiation, often using threats and counterthreats, has not been a very effective means of reducing subsidies, prohibitions, and other barriers to trade. These negotiations typically require one country to incur short-term, visible costs to receive some less visible long-term benefits.

The third response is multilateral negotiation, which permits all parties to achieve some visible short-term gains to offset losses. The Kennedy, Tokyo, and intermediate rounds successfully reduced barriers in all countries. The current Uruguay Round attempts to do more—to remove nontariff barriers, improve dispute settlement procedures, and bring agriculture, services, and investment under GATT rules. It now seems unlikely that the bold measures initially proposed will be adopted. Even if agreement is reached, the increase in efficiency and standards of living is likely to be small. If this conjecture is correct, it seems likely that protectionist actions will increase and more of the mutual benefits of an open trading system will erode.

One much discussed alternative to an open trading system is a system of rival trading blocs that permits relatively free trade within the blocs, under enforced rules, but restricts trade with countries outside the bloc. Reduction of trade barriers within the European Community, approval of the U.S.-Canada agreement, possible negotiation of an agreement with Mexico creating a North American trading bloc, with possible extension to include parts of Central and South America, are taken as evidence of this development. Extrapolation gives rise to a conjecture that there will be three trading blocs—Western Europe, East Asia, and most of North and South America—with relatively free or open trade within the blocs and trade restrictions between blocs.

To see what this implies, I have grouped countries into three blocs.

The conjectures do not clearly define membership in the blocs. The European Community is well defined at present but could expand to include countries remaining in the European Free Trade Association or in Central and Eastern Europe. The Americas bloc now contains only the United States and Canada but in the future might include Mexico and parts of Central and South America. The Asian bloc is the least clearly defined. I have chosen to include in the EC only the twelve current members. The presumed membership of the three blocs is:

*EC:*Belgium, Denmark, France, Germany, Greece, Ireland, Italy, Luxembourg, Netherlands, Portugal, Spain, and United Kingdom;

*Asia:*Australia, Hong Kong, India, Japan, Korea, Malaysia, Philippines, Singapore, Taiwan, and Thailand;

*Americas:*Argentina, Brazil, Canada, Chile, Mexico, United States, and Venezuela.

These countries were parties to about two-thirds of the world's trade in the four years 1986 to 1989. The assignments are arbitrary, of course, and several possible bloc members are omitted. Oil exporting countries, China, and Eastern Europe have not been assigned to any of the three blocs. I believe that changes would not alter main conclusions about the desirability of trading blocs as an alternative to more open trading arrangements.

Table 1 shows average trade data for the years 1986 to 1989 inclusive. The numbers in the table are half the value of exports plus imports within and between blocs during these years, in billions of dollars.

The table shows that two of the three blocs have more trade outside than within the bloc. The exception is the EC, with $289 billion average trade between members of the bloc, far more than the EC's trade with the other blocs combined. Intra-Asian trade has increased markedly during the period, partly as a result of slow growth in the Americas and partly as a result of substantial Japanese investment in other Asian countries. But, as the table shows, Asia and the Americas are each other's largest trading partners; Asian trade with the Americas is almost twice the volume of intrabloc Asian trade.

Table 1
Volume of Trade Within and Between Supposed Trading Blocs, 1986—1989 (in billions)

	Americas	Asia	EC
Americas	$108		
Asia	$144	$78	
European Community	$102	$70	$289

These data suggest the importance of trade among blocs. For the United States or Japan, a bloc within Asia or the Americas is an inferior substitute for interbloc trade. The detail reinforces the conclusion from the aggregates; Canadian-U.S. trade is more than $70 billion of the $108 billion average inter-American trade; Japan-U.S. trade is $63 billion, 80 percent of total intra-Asian trade and 125 percent of Japan's average trade with its Asian partners. It would not be in the interests of either Japan or the United States to develop intrabloc trade as a substitute for open, international trade. Even for the EC, trade with the Americas—particularly the United States—is 7 to 8 percent of total trade and nearly 20 percent of trade outside the bloc. A significant reduction in interbloc trade would be costly to the world economy and to the major trading countries.

Costs would not be limited to the loss of trade and income. There would be less competition, reducing pressure to improve products and processes. The mix of products traded, hence the composition of output, would be altered. Western Europe and Japan buy and sell a different mix of goods and services to the United States than Latin America. Latin America cannot supply consumer durables and autos to the U.S. market competitively, and the United States does not have a comparative advantage in producing and supplying many of the goods that Latin Americans buy from Europe or Asia. The same would be true of an Asia bloc substituting for the trade that Japan does with the United States and the EC. A shift in trade from the global market to a system of regional blocs would change demands in a direction unfavorable to the exploitation of countries' comparative advantages.

Further, the United States and most of the countries in the Americas as a group are net debtors while Germany and Japan are net creditors. The debtors cannot service their debts, and the creditors cannot be paid, unless the debtors have net current account surpluses. This requires net exports from the debtor countries to the creditors, not in a single year but on average over time. A movement toward trading blocs would make debt service more difficult.

The high cost for major countries of a system of trading blocs suggests that countries will be slow to move in that direction. A more likely alternative is continued growth of trade restrictions. This would erode the open trading system and reduce opportunities for more efficient production, specialization, and increases in standards of living.

Rules requiring more open, competitive trade contributed importantly to making the postwar experience significantly better than the interwar experience. These rules are no longer adequate, and they are poorly enforced or not enforced at all. Failure to develop and enforce new standards for open trade has eroded one of the main forces raising postwar living standards in the market economies. Unilateral action, including action by the United States in response to perceived and actual restrictions abroad, has further weakened the international system. Improvement of the trading system and more rapid expansion of world trade depend upon the development of enforceable rules, improved enforcement, and therefore, on the sacrifice of some national sovereignty.

Monetary stability

The postwar years, particularly the 1970s, were years of widespread, persistent inflation. Although disinflation in the 1980s lowered the rate of inflation in the developed countries, inflation continued in most of these countries. High inflation became the norm in several developing countries, including Argentina, Brazil, Peru, and Yugoslavia, while countries such as Israel and Mexico restrained their high rates of inflation but did not achieve price stability.

Although the postwar record is far from the desirable goal of price stability, major countries have fared substantially better than they had in the interwar years. Market economies avoided both the 1920s' hyperinflations in Germany and Austria and the 1930s' severe deflation and unemployment.

In the early postwar years, low inflation in the market economies reflected the low inflation in the United States and the operation of the Bretton Woods system. The latter provided that members of this international system would maintain fixed exchange rates against the dollar, so their rates of inflation depended on U.S. inflation. U.S. inflation rose after the middle 1960s, until the Bretton Woods system ended in 1973. The Bretton Woods system transmitted the inflation to the rest of the world.

In the years since 1973, the major currencies—the dollar, deutsche mark and yen—have fluctuated against each other. Many countries have chosen to fix their exchange rates to one or more of the major currencies. The principal countries of Western Europe have adopted a system of fixed but adjustable rates—the Exchange Rate Mechanism of the European Monetary System. More recently, this European system has moved toward a system of fixed and unchanging parities, and controls on capital movements have been removed by all of the principal members as a first step toward introduction of a common currency. Other countries have tied their currencies to the dollar, the French franc, or to a basket of currencies.

Experience with inflation since 1973 permits no clear conclusion about inflation under fixed or fluctuating exchange rates. Several countries in Europe have lowered inflation by fixing their exchange rates to the German deutsche mark and, to avoid repeated devaluation, have brought their rates of inflation close to the German rate. But countries with fluctuating rates, such as Japan in the 1970s and the United States and the United Kingdom in the early 1980s, lowered their rates of inflation also.

Fluctuating exchange rates can reduce domestic costs of production and selling prices of exports during recessions without forcing steep reductions in money wage payments and other contractual agreements. Evidence shows that during periods of disinflation unemployment has increased less on average in the principal fluctuating rate countries. Also, unemployment has declined more rapidly in countries with fluctuating exchange rates following periods of sustained disinflation. This evidence is consistent with the claim that costs of disinflation are lower under fluctuating exchange rates.

A common conjecture suggests that the world economy is moving toward three currency blocs. The conjecture gains some plausibility from the proposed development of a single currency for the European Monetary System by the end of the decade. The demand for the new currency, the ECU, if it comes into use, would lower the demand for other reserve currencies, principally deutsche marks and dollars. If the Europeans fail to agree on a common currency, the deutsche mark will be more widely held as a reserve currency and used as a unit of account.

At the end of the 1980s, the dollar remained the principal reserve currency; about 60 percent of official reserves were in dollars; the deutsche mark was second with 15 to 19 percent of official holdings. The yen was in third place, but the yen's percentage of official reserves never exceeded 8 percent.[1] Perhaps more relevant for the idea of currency blocs is the yen's share of the reserves held by principal Asian countries—20 to 30 percent. The Asian countries continued to hold most of their reserves in dollars.

If the years 1988 and 1989 are representative, based on data gathered by the Bank of England, one-third of all straight bond issues on the Euromarkets were denominated in U.S. dollars; more than ten other countries shared the remainder. For equity-related bonds, the dominance of the dollar as a unit of account was more striking; more than 70 percent of the issues were dollar denominated. The major competitors were not the deutsche mark and ECU but the Swiss franc and yen for straight debt and the Swiss franc for equity-related bonds.

Whether the dollar is displaced as the principal world currency will depend on relative rates of inflation, on trade patterns, and on the relative freedom of asset transactions in the United States and other markets. If the United States continues as a principal trading partner for many countries in Asia, Latin America, Europe, and North America, the dollar will remain as a medium of exchange,[2] and dollar assets will continue to serve as reserves for these countries. If the United States achieves and maintains domestic price stability, dollar assets will remain a store of value for many foreigners and the dollar will remain a principal reserve currency, most likely *the* principal reserve currency, for many years into the future. Most commodity prices would continue to be denominated in dollars, and payments for these commodities would be made in dollars.

The monetary system now differs from the earlier postwar years. There are now viable alternatives to the dollar. A return to an inflationary policy that produces higher average inflation for the dollar than for other currencies would devalue the dollar, erode the position of the dollar as a reserve currency, and expand the use of less inflationary reserve currencies. Variable rates of inflation for the principal currencies would contribute to instability in currency markets, and possibly in economic activity, by inducing more frequent shifts in asset portfolios, interest rates, and exchange rates.

Price stability for principal currencies provides a public good for other reserve currency countries and for small countries. No country, acting alone, can achieve price and exchange rate stability. Small countries have a particular problem; they are too small to affect world prices. Their efforts to achieve domestic price stability in an inflationary world can be realized only, if at all, by allowing exchange rates to change enough to buffer price movements on world markets. This is costly for small countries that depend on world trade.

If each of the major developed economies maintains domestic price stability, this source of variability in fluctuating rates between the dollar, deutsche mark, and yen will be removed. Countries on fluctuating rates will achieve greater price and exchange rate stability. Smaller countries would be able to avoid inflation and deflation by fixing their exchange rates to the currency of one (or more) of the major developed countries. Their price levels would remain relatively stable, reflecting the price stability of the major economies. Since their exchange rates are fixed, they would achieve both price and exchange rate stability.

In defense of the hegemon

Criticism of the United States as "hegemon" of the postwar, market economies neglects the importance of rules and institutions that sustain stability and provide opportunities to increase standards of living in a peaceful (or more peaceful) world. I have argued that the postwar rise of living standards, in comparison with living standards in the interwar and other periods, owes much to the political, trade, and monetary stability achieved under U.S. leadership.

The rules for political, trade, and monetary stability were not ideal. Nor was the implementation ideal. There was much room for improvement. A clearer sense of political objectives and the cost and benefits of achieving them might have avoided the use of force in some cases or invoked greater use of force in others. The rules for trade and monetary stability were often circumvented, ignored, or sacrificed to other objectives.

Rules alone did not make economies grow and prosper. Falling transport and communication costs contributed to the growth of trade and living standards. New technologies increased opportunities for investment and growth. Improvements in education and particularly the spread of higher education in many parts of the world broadened horizons and increased opportunities. No doubt, other factors can be added. One must remember, however, that falling transport costs and new technologies did not produce comparable results in the interwar period or, in the postwar era, within the socialist countries operating under a different hegemon and very different rules.

What matters for current purposes is that the rules worked so well that the relative positions of the United States and other countries have changed markedly. The United States has become wealthier, but others have gained in relative wealth. The United States is now less willing to enforce rules for trade and political stability and less able to impose the rules of the trade and monetary system on others.

Fortunately, Japan and Germany have been more committed to monetary stability than has the United States. Unfortunately, they seem less committed to extending, strengthening, and enforcing rules for trade and political stability when such actions would impose costs on them.

Rules for trade, defense or police, and price stability are required, I believe, if living standards are to rise in the future at the rates of the past 40 (or even 20) years. Each will affect resource use and economic efficiency. All affect the distance people look ahead and their perceptions of opportunities that are worth undertaking.

The United States, as hegemon, provided a framework of rules that worked better than the rules of the interwar years. Enforcement has been beneficial, but it is also costly. The United States has shared the benefits more fully than it has shared the costs. This distribution of costs and benefits is not likely to continue. Indeed, it has begun to change.

A problem for the market economies is to maintain and enhance stability. This requires new or revised rules and a system for sharing costs and responsibilities more fully. Without new rules and new commitments to enforce them, the exceptional progress of the postwar years will not be sustained.

Endnotes

[1]The three currencies have approximately the same shares of Euro-currency market deposits. See G. Tavlas, *On the International Use of Currencies: The Case of the Deutsche Mark*. Essays in International Finance 181. Princeton: March, 1991.

[2]Tavlas and Ozeki compared the currencies used for exports and imports of major countries in 1980 and 1987 or 1988. The use of the dollar for U.S. exports and imports and the deutsche mark for German exports is dominant. About half of Germany's imports are denominated in other currencies. The yen lags behind, used for less than 30 percent of Japanese exports and 14 percent of Japanese imports in 1989. See G. Tavlas and Yuzuru Ozeki, "The Japanese Yen as an International Currency," International Monetary Fund, January 1991, Table 13. Tavlas and Ozeki show that the yen denominated share of the debt of five principal Asian borrowers rose from 20 percent in 1980 to 38 percent in 1988, while the dollar share fell from 47 percent to 27 percent. The yen replaced the dollar in these transactions as Japan became a major creditor country and the United States became a major debtor.

Commentary: Global Implications of Trade and Currency Zones

Leonhard Gleske

Allan Meltzer's paper on "U.S. Leadership and Postwar Progress" is a comprehensive description and comparison of interwar and postwar political and economic developments in the Western world. At the same time, it is a lucid analysis of the factors that were, and were not, at work in both periods. His paper is both interesting and informative.

I find myself in broad agreement with most of what Professor Meltzer says about political stability, trade rules, and monetary stability. I also share Professor Meltzer's conclusion that in a world where the relative positions of the United States and other countries have changed markedly—not least as a result of the beneficial, somewhat hegemonic role which the United States played over many years in the postwar period—the maintenance and enhancement of stability may require new or revised rules and a system of sharing costs and responsibilities more fully.

The time available to me can perhaps be used best by focusing largely on one matter. Is the world moving toward a more balanced tripolar monetary system involving the dollar, the yen, and the deutsche mark or a future single European Community (EC) currency? What are the monetary policy and financial implications of the trend toward currency zones?

Politically and economically, the United States is still the strongest power in the world today, but the days of its solitary dominance, which characterized the world economy until the second half of the 1960s, are gone. This development is by no means surprising. In the long postwar period of peace and security, the formation of further centers of dynamic economic power was to be expected, after the reconstruction of the Western world economy had been accomplished.

However, the end of the period of reconstruction coincided with a distinct rise in the U.S. rates of inflation after the mid-1960s, thus bringing to an end the long period in which a domestically stable dollar had served very usefully as an anchor of stability for the whole international monetary system. Without the prerequisite of a stable dollar, the Bretton Woods system had to come to an end.

In all probability, the change in the economic positions within the world economy was sure to have some impact on the role the dollar had gained as a reserve and investment currency. But inflation in the United States has caused the international role of the dollar to be impaired more than would otherwise have been the case. The international position of the dollar was, of course, never really in danger—in contrast to what happened to the pound sterling in the sixties when it largely lost its quality as a reserve currency. Given its share of close to 60 percent in international reserves, the dollar is still by far the most important reserve currency, and continues to be the key investment currency in the international financial markets. In both functions, however, the dollar now has to compete with other currencies. Monetary authorities and investors, in general, now have attractive alternatives to choose from.

Although expectations of interest rate movements and political developments play a role in this competition, domestic price stability is the most decisive factor here—in the long run, at any rate.

I fully agree with Professor Meltzer when he predicts that the dollar will remain a principal reserve currency, and most likely *the* principal reserve currency, provided the United States achieves and maintains domestic price stability, so that dollar assets continue to be a store of value.

Domestic price stability is even more important in the case of the other, smaller reserve currencies. Let us take a look at Germany in this respect: Monetary authorities throughout the world are now holding about 20 percent of their reserves in deutsche marks. At the end of 1990, total deutsche mark reserves equalled $160 billion. Quantitatively even more important are the other deutsche mark investments by non-residents. Including deutsche mark investment in the Euromarket, and excluding double counting, assets denominated in deutsche marks totalled just under DM 900 billion at the end of 1990, with the major proportion being invested in the short term or in liquid form.

German authorities have at times attempted—unsuccessfully—to curb the development of the deutsche mark into an international currency. The deutsche mark's current role in the international sphere can be viewed as proof of the confidence market participants have in the conduct of a non-inflationary economic policy. The consequences of any loss of this confidence could be very serious for a medium-sized economy such as that of Germany's. Foreign investors' assessments of economic policy, therefore, have to be taken into account by economic policymakers, especially by the central bank. This holds true of all countries whose currencies are widely used for investment by non-residents, but particularly true of countries whose currencies have developed into a significant reserve currency.

The high dependence of economic policy on the assessments of non-resident investors could be a strong incentive for policymakers —especially in the reserve currency countries—to resist a policy that produces inflation, erodes the confidence of market participants, and causes serious economic problems through capital outflows to currencies of countries that are behaving better.

High volatility in the exchange markets and fundamentally changing exchange rates were part of the process that led to the multi-currency system we have today. Now that the multi-currency standard is firmly in place, I believe that we can perhaps rely more than before on the self-interest of all the main players involved to prevent major divergences in inflationary behavior and to encourage the pursuit of stability-oriented domestic economic and monetary policies. If this occurs—as I hope it will—a multi-currency system, too, could again produce—also under a regime of flexible exchange rates—a more stable economic environment throughout the world, an environment similar to that provided by the Bretton Woods system, with the United States playing a hegemonic role, until the mid-1960s.

Let me now turn to the subject of currency zones and the view that the world economy is moving toward a tripolar monetary system. This would imply an increase in monetary coherence within both Europe and eastern Asia, the dollar being already a strong pillar in such a system, an increase based on the continuation of the process of growing economic interdependence among countries in these respective areas. Monetary coherence could be supported strongly if one or more countries of sufficient size were to pursue a policy aimed at forming a core of monetary stability, thus providing the whole area with an anchor that would result in exchange rate stability within that area.

Europe seems to be well on the way toward developing into such a clearly defined monetary zone. The process of monetary integration there is based on age-old trade relationships between countries with a high degree of economic homogeneity and with a common social, historical, and political heritage. And it rests on the political will to create a single market and ultimately to move toward a political union.

Developments in eastern Asia will take a different line. I doubt whether monetary coherence will become strong enough in the foreseeable future to form a homogeneous currency block. The yen will, of course, continue to gain importance as an international currency, mainly as a means of payment and a reserve currency for countries in eastern Asia. But will this be enough to convince Japan's trading partners to tie their currencies to the yen and to establish a regional system of fixed exchange rates with the yen as the dominant currency? The pattern of trade in eastern Asia differs markedly from that in Europe. More than 60 percent of the international trade transactions of EC member countries is accounted for by intra-Community trade; despite a rapid growth of intraregional trade in the last few years, this can certainly not be said of eastern Asia. The degree to which goods markets there are integrated is thus significantly lower than in Europe, and the exchange rates vis-à-vis trading partners outside this area are correspondingly more important. But there are also other reasons for doubt. Without analyzing them in detail, let me merely quote Mr. Gyohten, Japan's former vice minister of finance, who said that—as opposed to North America and Europe—"East Asia is still more divergent and less convergent. In terms of its stage of development, the structure of trade and industry, the social and political constitution, the region of East Asia is full of diversity. East Asia has not yet reached the stage where we can seriously consider it as a homogeneous and convergent economic group."

In my final remarks, I would like to say a few words about the monetary policy and financial implications of the trend toward currency zones. In doing so, I will concentrate on Europe.

One consequence of integrating the European economies into a large single market, and its culmination in a monetary union, will be a substantial reduction of the foreign trade sector. The share of foreign trade and capital transactions in the EC's combined GDP and financial markets will be considerably smaller than the sometimes extremely high proportion in individual member economies. At present, total exports to third countries account for about 10 percent of the EC's aggregate GDP. This share roughly equals the corresponding U.S. ratio.

This means that fluctuations in the foreign exchange rates will have a smaller impact than hitherto on the EC's real economy. These effects have already been mitigated noticeably since the creation of the exchange rate mechanism and the gradual stabilization of exchange relationships within the European Monetary System (EMS). Even under the recently more stable intra-European exchange rate conditions, however, the various EC currencies were still affected to differing degrees by moves into and out of the dollar, in most cases of which the deutsche mark was the main counterpart. This movement has been a constraint on the individual member countries' monetary and interest rate policies. Such pressures on internal monetary cohesion will disappear once the EC has irrevocably fixed the intra-Community exchange rates or has gone even further by establishing a single currency and, as a logical consequence, pursued a uniform monetary policy. And while major dollar fluctuations will continue to influence the overall situation in the EC, their immediate adverse effects will—if they occur—become more tolerable than under present conditions. This does not mean pleading for a policy of "benign neglect" with respect to the exchange rate. But as is proved by the United States with its repeated pursuit of a policy of "benign neglect" in the past, a large domestic market is able— at least to some degree and for a certain period of time—to absorb the impact of exchange rate movements better than economies with large foreign trade sectors. International cooperation would nevertheless remain necessary, and should be based on the primary goal of keeping prices stable.

The draft statutes of the future common monetary authority of the EC, which is now under discussion in the intergovernmental conference on the European Monetary Union (EMU), include a strong commitment to price stability as the primary objective. By pursuing such a policy, monetary authorities in an economically unified Europe will be less likely to be confronted with the well-known dilemma of domestic versus exchange rate stability, as has often been faced by the smaller member economies. This does not necessarily mean that the EC will become a hesitant participant in international monetary cooperation. The scope for influencing exchange rates through intervention in the foreign exchange markets may become even larger, their impact on liquidity and the financial markets being relatively smaller than hitherto in smaller economies. But even close cooperation will not always exclude the possibility that an attempt to stabilize exchange rates via intervention and interst rate policy could impair the conduct of monetary policy geared to domestic stability. There remains a need for some elasticity of exchange rates between these currency areas in order to cope with remaining differences in inflation behavior, interest rate movements, and the impact of political events.

But on account of their size, these currency zones would, as I have already mentioned, be better able than smaller economies to cope with such exchange rate movements, and this even more so, if they succeed in keeping their currencies stable in terms of domestic price levels.

Commentary: Global Implications of Trade and Currency Zones

Kumiharu Shigehara

The paper that Professor Meltzer has prepared for this symposium addresses many important issues concerning the regionalization of the world economy. There is little that I can add by way of criticism. My remarks will basically focus on a few related broad policy issues as Mr. Guffey has asked me to give my own views on them, in addition to comments on Professor Meltzer's paper.

Professor Meltzer has argued that the remarkable rise of living standards in the democratic market economies for more than forty years after World War II owes much to the political, trade, and monetary stability achieved under U.S. leadership. The rules for political, trade, and monetary stability imposed by the United States as "hegemon" of the postwar, market economies were not ideal, nor was the implementation ideal. But the rules worked so well that the relative positions of the United States and other countries have changed markedly. Professor Meltzer then notes that the United States is now less willing to enforce rules for trade and political stability and less able to impose the rules of the trade and monetary system on others. He also observes that fortunately, Japan and Germany have been more committed to monetary stability than the United States, but unfortunately they seem less committed to extending, strengthening, and enforcing rules for trade and political stability when such actions would impose costs on them. He concludes by noting that new rules for trade, defense, or police, and price stability are required to ensure a sustained rise in living standards for the market economies in the future at the rates of the past four (or even two) decades.

In a statement before the Committee on Ways and Means of the U.S. House of Representatives in March this year, Fred Bergsten discussed how collective leadership should be exercised beyond the Cold War and the Gulf War. He first observed that the sharing of the economic and financial burden of the coalition effort in the Gulf was handled as effectively as the military effort. He then argued:

> "The United States and other members of the military coalition would almost certainly have pursued their military strategy even without external financing so there was a great temptation for other countries to 'free ride'. No compelling formula for sharing the costs was even put forward, let alone debated and agreed by the payers. After the broad policy guidelines were set by the Security Council, the United States (with a few close allies) made all the crucial tactical decisions and the largest non-regional contributors, Japan and Germany, were not even represented in the Security Council. Taxation occurred without full representation."

Our experience in burdensharing for the coalition effort in the Gulf was probably unique. One might wonder if the burdensharing would have been handled in the same way as it was, if the military intervention had continued longer and entailed greater costs both militarily and economically. Bergsten argued that, in order to develop an effective system of collective security to deal with future crises both political and economic, decisionmaking must be more closely aligned with burdensharing than at the time of the Gulf crisis.

In a more multipolar world, with a more even distribution of power, it will be more difficult to secure and implement international consensus for the management of conflicts. The challenge of formulating and working out a set of rules for dividing up responsibilities is daunting. This process will be painful for countries losing their relative positions in decisionmaking. This was clearly evidenced, for example, by difficulties in the negotiations for increasing the quota shares of Japan and Germany in the International Monetary

Fund (IMF) which had continued for quite a number of years before both of them obtained the second largest shares to the United States.

The expanding number of participants in international trade negotiations, and the growing diversity of their interests, points of view, and technical capabilities, have tended to reduce the efficacy of multilateral fora. Bilateralism and regionalism appear as an increasingly attractive alternative to multilateralism.

The issue of regional trade cooperation has been accentuated with the European Community's (EC) program for internal market integration by the end of 1992, and the start of negotiations for a proposed free trade zone for the United States, Canada, and Mexico, building on the U.S.-Canada Free Trade Agreement which went into effect in January 1989. Some approaches to strengthening cooperation both within East Asia and in the Pacific Rim are being pursued, although there are thus far no trade or currency arrangements in place for further regional integration in this area.

After a review of the broad evolution of intraregional and interregional trade patterns which suggests the importance of interregional trade, Professor Meltzer argues that it would not be in the interest of either Japan or the United States to develop intraregional trade as a substitute for open, multilateral trade. Europe is more highly integrated than the other regions in terms of intraregional trade, and has been so for a long time. One can probably argue that the EC typically represents the case of "natural integration." But, it is noteworthy that for the original EC group, intratrade has tended to stagnate in relative terms since 1970. While the apparent loss of momentum in integration within the EC has been cited by the European Commission as a reason for initiating the program for completing internal market integration by the end of 1992, removing trade barriers with the rest of the world should be a top priority of the EC, if the main competitive pressure—a source of greater economic efficiency—should come from the rest of the world rather than from within the EC, as suggested in a recent study by European economists.

Trade diversion will be an unavoidable consequence of a free trade

zone. It will take place even if the average level of external protection
for the trade zone remains unchanged. A key question for producers
outside the zone is the extent to which this trade-diverting effect will
be offset by an expansion of extra-zone trade resulting from faster
income growth within the zone through its internal integration. The
net result for producers in the rest of the world may be influenced
not only by the "static" trade effects but also by the long-run
"dynamic" effect which a larger, integrated regional market can
have on investment and growth. It is because of this that countries
outside the trade zone should be concerned about the process of
internal industrial reorganization in the enlarged regional market, as
well as the course of the external trade policy to be adopted under
the regional trade arrangement.

An important question in this respect is how industrial reorganization will proceed within the EC. Greater scale economies will be an
essential source of increased efficiency and competitiveness for the
industrial sector, but this means that the number of firms must be
reduced. There is the risk that long-run efficiency considerations will
be subordinated to short-run sociopolitical pressures to reduce conflicts of interest within member countries where losers are likely to
be many. Political pressure may mount to offset the competitive
threat to domestic losers by protectionist measures against producers
outside the region, especially if macroeconomic conditions
deteriorate within the region. This points to the importance of good
macroeconomic policy management in the process of industrial
reorganization.

Adoption of a common currency within a trade zone could foster
regional economic integration. It could increase wage and price
flexibility if the central body for monetary policy decisionmaking
gains the credibility of its commitment to price stability, as the
experience of a "hard currency" option in smaller countries neighboring Germany has typically shown. But, we must recall that during
the gold standard period, resort to trade policy was frequently made
as an adjustment mechanism alternative to exchange rate changes.
Too early attempts to introduce a common currency in a trade zone
may lead to increased use of trade restrictions as an alternative
adjustment mechanism, if such a zone covers a wide range of

countries including those where institutional factors are such that wage and price flexibility is likely to remain more limited than in the other member countries.

In East Asia, diversity in the stage of economic and financial development as well as historical and cultural background in individual countries, and the absence of institutional arrangements for economic integration, will limit the development of an EC-type of monetary integration. Currencies of most of East Asian economies other than Japan are not completely convertible for capital transactions, and the Japanese capital market is not used as actively by private economic agents in these Asian economies as by those in the Organization for Economic Cooperation and Development (OECD) area. While the absolute value of Japan's direct investment that goes to Asian countries tripled between 1983 and 1989, and accounts for a substantial portion of total direct investment inflows into these countries, the share of Japan's total direct investment that Asian countries account for declined by half during the same period from about 28 percent to 14 percent. A recent IMF study reveals that the yen's share in the official reserve holdings of Asian countries rose to about 18 percent in the late 1980s, but a far greater share (56 percent) was held in U.S. dollars, and a significant portion (15 percent) in deutsche marks.

The economic gains from the free movement of capital will be greater when it is achieved on a global basis than when it is limited to regional transactions. The possibility of lowering the real cost of capital to firms in deficit countries will be greater when they have access to borrowing opportunities in surplus countries outside a trade zone as well as those within it. My own view is that it would be wrong for the surplus countries to take deliberate policy action to reduce their presently high national savings. Japan is undergoing the process of population aging at the fastest pace among OECD nations. A number of studies suggest that the projected demographic changes will reduce Japan's savings rate substantially from around the start of the next century. A policy implication of this projection would be that Japan should aim at a higher national savings ratio during the present decade, mainly by higher government savings through an increase in consumption tax, and it should devote most of incremental savings to higher domestic investment in social infrastructure and housing for use by the present and future generations. But a portion of such savings might better be channelled to developing countries in the forms of direct investment and lending to them directly or through multilateral institutions. Repayment of such lending should start after the lapse of a long grace period of, say, 15 years or more. A recent study based on a multicountry model at the IMF concludes that a projected sharp decline in Japan's saving rate due largely to demographic changes will bring about a substantial change in its external position in the first decades of the next century. It can be hoped that presently developing countries will, by that time, have grown into mature economies and will be in a better position for starting the repayment of external debt. The working of this mechanism for *international*, and at the same time *intergenerational*, transfers of savings with technological assistance would be beneficial both to Japan and other industrialized countries with rapidly aging populations and to the developing countries which will continue to have a relatively larger share of younger people in their populations.

Japan should also strengthen efforts to make its capital market more efficient and more readily accessible to foreign investors and borrowers on an *erga omnes* principle, by further financial liberalization and increasing the transparency of its market. While maintenance of noninflationary growth generated basically by domestic demand and further opening of the remaining restricted areas to the outside world constitute Japan's major international responsibilities, the projected trends in its saving rate and external position imply that Japan's continued current account surplus over this decade should not be viewed as a problem in itself in a world of efficient international capital flows. It would be very unfortunate for Japan and for the rest of the world, if Japan's current external payments position were used as an excuse for increasing trade barriers against Japanese products. In passing, I would add a comment on Professor Meltzer's argument that creditor nations such as Japan and Germany cannot be paid, unless the debtor nations such as the United States have current account surpluses through their net exports to the creditors over time. I would say that global resource allocation will improve, if the U.S. current account turns into surplus through budget deficit cuts while Japan and Germany continue to run some reasonable amounts of surpluses over this decade, and if their surplus funds are channelled, in the way I explained earlier, mainly to developing countries and Central and Eastern European countries moving toward market economies.

At the same time, major trading partners should strengthen collective efforts to measure and reduce the *effective* degree of trade protection. It is well known that data on average tariffs alone do not measure the effective degree of trade protection, because of growing resort to nontariff measures, such as voluntary export restraints, import quotas, local content requirements, and subsidies to domestic industries. Such collective efforts should include a thorough and objective assessment of the view expressed in the United States and Europe that administrative impediments and restricted business practice in Japan make its domestic market practically inaccessible to foreign firms—the view often used as justification for erecting and maintaining barriers against Japanese products. Over the past years, the OECD has made a major contribution to the quantification of the degree of agricultural protection. Beginning this fiscal year, EC member states are asked to provide the European Commission with fuller information on industrial subsidies in various forms, and the OECD has been attempting to collect data on such subsidies from all member countries. More generally, the G-7 leaders who met at the Houston Summit last year encouraged the OECD to strengthen its surveillance of structural reforms in individual member countries, to review procedures, and to find ways of making its work more effective.

As structural reform proceeds, trade conflicts arising from greater multipolarity and interdependence should weaken. In the context of noninflationary growth, it should be easier to absorb changes in competitive advantage which characterize a dynamic economy. Nevertheless, powerful pressure groups will continue to seek protection from international competition. The future of the multilateral trading system will depend on the resistance of trade policy to such sectional interests. In any democratic society, policymaking will be influenced by the reaction of the electorate. Consumer organizations must be mobilized in opposing protectionist measures which would reduce their welfare. Economists must play an important role in this regard by offering a thorough and objective assessment of the costs and benefits of protection.

References

Bergsten, C. Fred. "Burdensharing in the Gulf and Beyond." A statement before the Committee on Ways and Means, U.S. House of Representatives, March 13, 1991.

Bhagwati, Jagdish. *The World Trading System at Risk.* Princeton University Press, 1991.

Destler, I. M. "The United States and Japan: What is New?" A paper presented at the 32nd Annual Convention of the International Studies Association, Vancouver, B.C., Canada, March 21, 1991. (mimeo)

Gordon, Bernard K. "The Asian-Pacific Rim: Success at a Price," *Foreign Affairs 1990/91,* Vol. 70, No. 1.

Jacquemin, Alexies and Andre Sapir. "Europe Post-1992: Internal and External Liberalization," *The American Economic Review,* May 1991.

Kasper, Wolfgang. "Globalization, Locational Investment and East Asian Development." Pacific Basin Working Paper Series No. RB91-02, Federal Reserve Bank of San Francisco, January 1991.

Marston, Paul R. and Ralph W. Tryon. "Macroeconomic Effects of Projected Population Aging in Industrial Countries." IMF *Staff Papers* Vol. 37, No. 3 (September 1990).

Montgomery, David B. "Understanding the Japanese as Customers, Competitors, and Collaborators," *Japan and World Economy,* 3 (1991) pp. 61-91.

Neven, Damien J. and Lars-Hendrik Poller. "European Integration and Trade Flows," Centre for Economic Policy Research Discussion Paper Series No. 367, (February 1990).

Shigehara, Kumiharu. "The External Dimension of Europe 1992: Its Effects on Relations Between Europe, the United States, and Japan," in Padoa-Schioppa, Tommaso ed., *Europe After 1992: Three Essays,* Essays in International Finance No. 182, Princeton University, May 1991.

Tarnoff, Peter. "America's New Special Relationships," *Foreign Affairs,* Vol. 69, No. 3, Summer 1990.

Tavlas, George S. and Yuzuru Ozeki. "The Japanese Yen as an International Currency," IMF Working Paper, January 1991.

Tobin, James. "On Living and Trading with Japan—United States Commercial and Macroeconomic Policies." Adam Smith Lecture, National Association of Business Economists, Washington D.C., September 24, 1990.

General Remarks on Trade Zones and the Uruguay Round

Charles R. Carlisle

I very much regret that I cannot be with you to discuss matters personally with so many distinguished economists and officials. I am sure that I would have left the symposium with a number of fresh ideas and insights.

I do want to make some observations about trade zones, but before doing that, perhaps I should say something about the Uruguay Round trade negotiations.

The Uruguay Round

You know, of course, about the very serious setback we suffered at Brussels last December and that since then we have managed to revive the Uruguay Round and keep it going, mainly on the basis of technical discussions plus a small amount of serious negotiation.

A consensus has emerged that we should complete our negotiations around the end of this year, and I strongly hope that governments will resolutely stick to that "target period." I refrain from using the word, " deadline."

To let the Uruguay Round drift on into 1992 would give too many hostages to fortune. The Presidential elections in the United States are not the only political developments that could affect the Round. And as each month passes it will become more difficult to maintain a strong sense of purpose and to prevent the unraveling of matters already agreed.

This autumn is the time to make the deals that will put the Uruguay Round over the top, the time when if we cannot end it, we must put the end clearly in sight. And although a vast amount of work remains to be done, the elements are at hand to carry the Uruguay Round to a successful conclusion.

In short, what we need are political decisions—the right political decisions. With the right political decisions we will finish the Uruguay Round in a very credible way. Without them, technical work and endless meetings of negotiators will be to no avail.

Clearly, there is a political consensus that the Uruguay Round must be concluded successfully. And clearly, one government after another in the developing world, in Central and Eastern Europe, and in Australia and New Zealand has been moving autonomously to liberalize its economy and its trade regime. This autonomous liberalization creates a propitious atmosphere for the Uruguay Round; indeed, failure of the Round would be doubly bitter if it were to occur in such an atmosphere.

So, the elements are in place; there is a consensus that the Round must be finished successfully, and soon; and many governments are acting independently to meet key objectives of the Round. But we all know that some major problems remain, and if they are to be resolved, great and politically powerful lobbies—especially in the European Community (EC), the United States, and Japan—must be told that things have to change, gradually to be sure, but change must occur.

Only the people at the very pinnacles of government—presidents and prime ministers—have the authority and, let us hope, the political courage and vision to make the very difficult decisions on these matters. If they do, we shall have a successful Uruguay Round.

Financial services negotiations

The organizers of this symposium have asked me to comment on the financial services negotiations. Before I do, I wish to say just a few words about the overall services negotiations, which embrace, of course, much more than just financial services.

On the basis of all that I know at this time, I can give you a relatively optimistic report. We are actually negotiating in services, and we are making progress. Progress is not as fast as many of us would like, but in our July meetings we were able to move forward.

There are some very difficult problems to be worked out, especially in the areas of maritime transport, telecommunications, and television programming and films, areas where governments may seek to apply trade restrictions in a discriminatory manner; that means not fully in accordance with the General Agreement on Tariffs and Trade's (GATT) cornerstone, the most-favored-nation principle which requires that trade restrictions be applied equally to all nations. But I see no insuperable obstacles to a successful negotiation.

The "north-south" gap that bedeviled earlier efforts to launch a successful services negotiation has largely disappeared. Developing countries are negotiating constructively, partly because they realize that there must be a successful outcome in services if there are to be successful outcomes in areas of prime interest to them, such as textiles and agriculture. But I think that is only part of the reason. They also have begun to see clearly that a modern economy requires, for example, efficient banking and telecommunications services, best provided perhaps by foreign companies. Moreover, and possibly most important, they are beginning to identify service sectors where they can be quite competitive—construction, other labor-intensive services, software, and all sorts of back-office financial work, for instance.

Just as I believe that a successful negotiation in services is within grasp, I also believe that we can resolve the problems in financial services. First, there is now a consensus that financial services must be a part of a general agreement on trade in services, not apart from a *"GATS"* as was earlier suggested. Institutional questions do remain, however: the relationship of *GATS* itself to *GATT* and whether there should be an independent, or relatively independent, financial services body, staffed by experts, to handle problems in this area.

Two major substantive problems concern a proposed "dual track" approach to financial services and what the negotiators call a "prudential carve out." The dual track proposed by Canada, Japan, Sweden, and Switzerland envisages a first track setting out an ambitious level of liberalization to which governments would commit themselves, although reservations from this level could be negotiated.

These developed countries also envisage a second track that will allow participants to negotiate and inscribe commitments through the provisions contained in the agreement. Although a similar level of commitments could be obtained under either approach, a number of countries, especially developing countries, are concerned about the dual-track approach.

The "prudential carve out" issue simply is about the degree of discretion which regulatory authorities should have under the GATS in regulating banks, insurance companies, and other financial institutions. All governments agree on the need for a carve out and that regulators must continue to regulate. The question, again, is about how much discretion they should have. The Asian nations and Korea argue that they should have complete discretion. Others fear that complete discretion could be used to frustrate liberalization.

These are difficult questions, of course. Moreover, there is the further issue of initial liberalization commitments, not just in financial services but in other service sectors too. At this time we have initial commitments from more than 35 countries but many of these commitments would simply maintain the status quo. Some governments—for example, the United States—want significant initial liberalization, so this is another issue to be pursued this autumn.

You can see from this brief, nontechnical discussion that we have much work to do and that "nothing is in the bag" either in general services negotiations or in those on financial services. Assuming, however, that we can move forward in other major areas of the Round, we are likely to reach a successful outcome on services.

Trade zones

We are keenly aware in Geneva that the world is not standing still, patiently waiting for us to finish our job. The international press has articles almost every day—some of them a trifle apocalyptic—about the emergence of trade and currency zones, or as they are frequently called, " blocs."

There is such a great array of high-powered banking and financial talent at this symposium that I am diffident about commenting on currency zones. I will venture a few observations, however, about trade zones.

First, contrary to popular opinion, GATT's statistics do not support the view that trade is becoming more regionalized. The following table shows the importance of intraregional trade for North America, Western Europe, and Asia for the years 1979 and 1989. It excludes their trade with the Middle East and Africa in order to prevent skewing of the statistics by declining petroleum prices. (As world oil prices dropped, the dollar value of the three regions' petroleum imports from Africa and the Middle East also declined, automatically increasing the relative size of their *intra*regional trade.)

Table 1
Share of Intraregional Trade in Exports and Imports Excluding the Middle East and Africa

	1979	1989
North America	34	32
Western Europe	76	76
Asia	48	48

Second, political considerations make it unlikely that the world will be divided any time soon into three or four great trading zones or free trade areas. How many new members will the EC or the North American free trade area have in the next few years? A few in each case, perhaps, but one has only to witness the struggle in the U.S. Congress over entering into negotiations with Mexico, and the European Community's hesitancy, particularly about Central and Eastern Europe, to realize that the process is unlikely to be swift.

The former U.S. deputy secretary of state, Kenneth Dam, argued in a recent article that "the political basis has not been laid for *major* new free trade areas" (my emphasis). Mr. Dam was speaking about the United States, but his argument can be applied to other parts of the world as well.

How likely is a Pacific free trade zone with Japan, either with or without the United States? Again, the political obstacles seem formidable.

None of this is intended to argue that there will not be any expansion of existing zones or that no new zones will be created. Indeed, I believe that the march will continue but both trade statistics and political considerations suggest that it is likely to be slow and undramatic.

Third, regional zones are not necessarily incompatible with multilateral trade liberalization. The GATT itself explicitly recognizes the right to form free trade areas and customs unions provided (1) that all the trade barriers (there are some exceptions) among members are eliminated and (2) that trade barriers to nonmembers are not increased.

As my colleague, Richard Blackhurst, director of GATT's economic research unit, has written:

> "Certain types of agreements were expressly foreseen by the inclusion of GATT's Article XXIV, permitting the formation of free trade areas and customs unions as exceptions to most-favored-nation treatment under Article I. As a result, regional

arrangements have coexisted with multilateralism throughout most of GATT's history. Nor was it simply a matter of tolerating such regional trading arrangements.

"Generally speaking, the motivation behind integration has not been the negative one of wanting to discriminate against third countries, but rather the positive one of wanting to increase efficiency by creating larger markets and stimulating competition (the resulting faster economic growth, in turn, expanding the demand for imports). They were seen as an optional route to the broader goal of an increasingly open and liberal world trade system.

"The role which the newly formed European Communities played in the 1960s is often cited as an example for the positive interaction which is possible between the two approaches to lowering trade barriers. Multilateral trade liberalization contributed to the regional integration process by helping to keep it on a liberal track, and the regional integration helped the multilateral trade negotiations in the 1960s by boosting the optimism and confidence in the future of the participating countries. Another way in which regional trade agreements have complemented the multilateral process is by extending trade liberalization and rule making to areas not covered by the GATT at the time.

"Current efforts to achieve closer integration in Western Europe are a logical continuation of a process of integration that began more than 30 years ago. Plans to dissolve customs frontiers between most Western European nations are no more protectionist than the constitutional ban on trade barriers between states in the United States. In other words, if France and Germany want to make their mutual trade more like trade between New York and New Jersey, that is hardly a threat or challenge to the multilateral trading system. In Canada there are internal barriers to trade between the provinces and the same is true of trade between states in Australia. If either of these countries began removing their internal trade barriers, would we accuse them of creating a trade bloc?

"The principal risk to third countries is trade diversion (that is, that efficient third country suppliers will lose markets to inefficient insiders). The likelihood of trade diversion will be minimized, however, if the process of regional integration is embedded in a parallel process of multilateral trade liberalization. As was noted above, this was the case in the 1950s and 1960s when the process of European integration was accompanied by the Dillon and Kennedy Rounds under the auspices of the GATT. Indeed, empirical analyses of European integration show that trade diversion was negligible, except for those areas in which the multilateral liberalization process stalled, notably agriculture, textiles and clothing."

I agree with Mr. Blackhurst's analysis, and I think that much of the press commentary has missed the real question. This takes me to my fourth observation.

The real question is whether regional trade zones will be an adjunct to, or a substitute for, a vigorously liberalizing multilateral trading system. Whatever happens in the Uruguay Round we will have trade zones. But a truly successful Uruguay Round will minimize trade diversion and, it follows logically, maximize the opportunities for the global connections that modern business requires.

Further, by bringing sectors, such as textiles, clothing, and agriculture that are scarcely covered by the GATT's rules effectively under the GATT and by agreeing on rules for the new subjects, such as services, intellectual property, and investment, a successful Round will diminish serious trade disputes. And I need hardly point out that success would have beneficial political, as well as economic, consequences.

Finally, if multilateral liberalization stalls and we must rely on trade zones, who gets hurt? The short answer is, "everyone." A system of trade zones, with many outsiders, cannot be as efficient as a truly liberal multilateral system.

The long-term trend in world merchandise trade growth is *down* from an average of 8.1 percent in the 1950s and 1960s, to 4.7 percent a year from 1970 to 1990, and a further drop to 4.1 percent in the 1980s.

Trade growth, along with investment, is one of the great engines of economic growth. Empirical evidence shows that for every 1 percent drop in trade growth, world economic growth drops by 0.7 percent. In other words, if world trade were to grow just 1 percent a year faster over the next decade as the result of a successful Uruguay Round, we might reasonably expect world economic growth to average 0.7 percent higher.

That is not an inconsequential number when applied to a $25 trillion ($25,000 billion) a year world economy. A quick calculation shows that if the world economy were to grow 0.7 percent a year faster over the next ten years, then total world output—the increments cumulated over the entire ten-year period—would be about $10 trillion ($10,000 billion) greater. (And do not forget the political consequences.)

Well, if everyone would be hurt, who would be hurt the most? The answer, I fear, is ages old: the weak, the small, the poor. Let us ask, which small, *developed* countries are fairly certain by, say, the year 2000, of being members of a free trade zone that includes either the United States, the European Community, or Japan? Perhaps two or three members of the European free trade area, but who else?

Now ask the same question about *developing* countries. Mexico, yes, perhaps several more in Latin America, but what about the others? No one can be certain, of course, but many developing countries are likely to be on the outside looking in, as are, perhaps, some developed nations. It is, however, the developing nations that could be especially hurt, perhaps rather badly. Table 2 helps make this point.

Table 2

Export Dependence of Developing Countries on
Developed Country Markets, 1980-1988 (percentage)

	1980	1988
Food	62	66
Fuels	77	65
Machinery and Transport Equipment	55	69
Textiles and Clothing	68	70
Total Manufacturing	60.5	68.5
Total Exports	71.5	67

It is doubtful that any developing country would be left completely out in the cold. Some regional integration, not involving the great industrial countries, already is taking place and more could occur. Moreover, the developed nations probably would "do something" for the exports of developing nations, but recent developments demonstrate again that "import sensitive" products are likely to be dropped from a liberalizing process.

It would surely be one of the great paradoxes of this century if the Uruguay Round could not be completed successfully precisely at the time when many governments are showing real political courage and adopting—because it is in their interest to do so—the trade and economic policies so long urged on them by the World Bank, the International Monetary Fund, and the major industrial nations.

But neither fine rhetoric nor clinging to the belief that "the Round is too important to fail" will, by themselves, pull us through. It will take lots of work—and we shall be hard at it in Geneva this autumn—and a strong push or two right from the very top.

———————
Editor's Note: Charles R. Carlisle prepared this paper for delivery at the Federal Reserve Bank of Kansas City's Symposium on "Policy Implications of Trade and Currency Zones," Jackson Hole, Wyoming, August 1991. Though Mr. Carlisle was unable to be present, his paper is being published with the proceedings.

European Integration
and the World Economy

Jacques de Larosière

This symposium covers a vast topic—the implications of the development of trade and monetary zones—and many timely subjects.

As the only European on the overview panel, I shall try to present my general remarks from a European point of view. My intervention shall be based on the three following ideas:

(1) The Common Market has stimulated its member states' economic growth and trade;

(2) from a trade zone, the European Community (EC) has evolved into a zone of exchange rate stability and will soon become a single market. It is moving toward monetary union;

(3) increased integration does not mean that the EC will close itself off from the rest of the world.

The Common Market has stimulated crossborder trade as well as growth both in Europe and abroad.

Since 1958, the primary and fundamental goal of the European Community has been to create a common market between member countries in which people, services, capital, and merchandise could circulate freely. It was in the area of merchandise that significant

285

progress was the most quickly obtained, thanks to the creation of a customs union; quantitative restrictions on intracommunity trade were lifted in 1961, and by 1968, all customs duties between members had been gradually abolished.

The liberalization of merchandise trade prompted a sharp rise in intracommunity trade.

The EC has progressively acquired a dominant position in the international community. With the considerable liberalization of trade, the EC has become the world's leading trading power, accounting for 36 percent of international trade today. Even if we exclude intracommunity flows (which now represent 22.3 percent of world trade compared with only 11.8 percent in 1957), the EC, as a whole, is still the world leader, accounting for around 18 percent of all world trade, intracommunity trade excluded.

Most of the European Community's trade is, indeed, carried out between member states. Since the creation of the EC, intracommunity trade has grown more quickly than world trade. Between 1958 and 1987, trade between EC members increased in volume terms by a factor of eight while world trade grew only by a factor of five. The proportion of intracommunity trade in the twelve members' foreign trade represented 43 percent in 1961 and 61 percent in 1990.

The liberalization of trade, which had as its main consequences intensified competition and a better use of economies of scale, undoubtedly played a major role in developing the EC's economic potential. As a result, the combined GDP of the twelve member states, which in 1960 represented only 57.7 percent of the American GDP, now accounts for 91.6 percent of the U.S. figure.

Economic integration has spread from the twelve nations of the European Community to the entire Western European area. Since the signature of free trade agreements between the EC and the European Free Trade Area (EFTA) in the 1970s in particular, trade between the two areas has increased noticeably. Today, EFTA is both the EC's leading importer and leading supplier, ahead of the

United States. Today, 70 percent of Western European nations' foreign trade is made within the EC-EFTA zone.

The EC's trade relations with the rest of the world have strengthened markedly.

First of all, the Common Market has not isolated the EC from the rest of the world; as it developed, the EC progressively reduced the common external tariff, which represented the only form of EC protection on industrial products, even if a few national quantitative restrictions remain.

While EC trade with non-EC countries (which increased in volume terms by a factor of 3.5 between 1958 and 1987) grew more slowly than intracommunity and world trade (respectively multiplied by 8 and by 5), it rose substantially nonetheless. Since the beginning of the 1970s, the lower level of growth can mainly be explained by the leveling-off, and even the slide, in the volume of exports to non-EC countries, and especially to areas in recession, such as Africa and Latin America. On the other hand, the volume of EC imports from non-EC countries has soared. The deficit in the EC's trade balance (CIF/FOB) with the rest of the world that appeared in 1987 has increased since, rocketing from 0.7 billion ECU (0.02 percent of EC GDP) to 42.9 billion ECU (1 percent of EC GDP) in 1990. European economic integration did not, therefore, penalize imports from non-EC countries but rather, actively furthered the development of trade and world economic growth.

It should also be noted that trade between Europe and other developed nations grew at about the same pace as trade between other areas. Trade between Europe and Asia increased in value by 10.5 percent each year from 1980 to 1989; during the same period, trade between North America and Asia rose by 11 percent per year. Similarly, North America's trade with Western Europe grew more quickly (+ 6.5 percent) than world trade in general (+ 5 percent).

From a trade zone, the EC has evolved into a zone of exchange rate stability and will soon become a single market. It is already moving toward monetary union.

The European experience shows that economic integration, the will to strive for exchange rate stability, and the implementation of converging economic and monetary policies are three complementary processes.

The European Monetary System: a zone of stability and convergence

Whereas monetary cooperation, in the form of the "snake," was a relative failure in the 1970s, substantial progress was made in the 1980s. In a world where floating exchange rates prevailed, the EMS helped provide significant stability to the participating countries throughout the 1980s, and contributed to a higher degree of convergence in economic policies and performances. The most striking success in this area was the general reduction in inflation rates and in their dispersion. Indeed, the member countries consider that disinflation is a requirement for healthy and lasting growth.

This emphasis on internal and external monetary stability progressively attracted the attention of certain other EC countries whose currencies were either fluctuating within wider margins or were not participating in the Exchange Rate Mechanism at all. In the last two years, the Spanish peseta and the British pound have joined the Exchange Rate Mechanism (in June 1989 and October 1990, respectively), and the Italian lira has entered the narrow fluctuation band (January 1990). In addition, three European countries that are not members of the EC (Norway, Sweden, Finland) have decided in the last few months to peg their currencies to the ECU as well.

The completion of the single market

Until the middle of the 1980s, European economic integration moved ahead in a rather uneven way. As we have already seen, merchandise trade was liberalized. Nontariff barriers continued to be used, however, and tended to become even tougher after the first oil shock. The free movement of people and services lagged behind, and above all, progress on financial integration (the right to establish and provide financial services in any member country, the freedom of capital movements) remained very limited.

All of these imperfections led political leaders in the EC countries to give a new impetus to the EC's development in 1986, with a far more encompassing and ambitious project than ever before: the completion of the single market. It was in 1986 that the EC set as its goal the creation, by the end of 1992, of "a unified economic area in which people, goods, services and capital would be able to move freely." In essence, this meant completing economic integration by removing all administrative, tax, or technical barriers to free exchange, as well as competition between member states.

I would like to remind you that if the EC has managed over time to become a major power, it is because of the constant increase in competition between its members and because of each country's individual dynamism. By gradually eliminating trade barriers, it is the European Community's role to reveal each member state's true competitiveness (or its lack of competitiveness) and encourage efficiency and streamlined production methods. The approach adopted for completing the single market is in keeping with this thinking. Indeed, with the principle of mutual recognition, any product, service, or establishment of one member country will be able to circulate freely in the other member countries as long as it fulfills its home country's regulations. This is a very flexible principle that gives companies more initiative. It also encourages competition and even more liberalization when it comes to the conditions for exercising production activities in the different member countries.

The most important change, however, may lie in the prospect of creating—for the first time—an integrated financial area by 1993 including the right to establish and provide financial services in any other EC country, and complete freedom of capital movements. Most EC countries, in fact, have allowed the free movement of capital since July 1, 1990.

The completion of the single market will stimulate member states' growth. According to the Cecchini report, with an unchanged macroeconomic policy, the single market's cumulative impact in terms of GDP should be an increase of 4.5 percent after five or six years (2.1 percent of which will stem from supply-side effects involved by the strengthening of both competition and market effects, and 1.4 percent of which will result from the liberalization of financial services).

The single market has led to the idea of monetary union

The crucial decision to aim for a single market led the twelve countries' leaders to take a new and decisive step between 1988 and 1990 toward Economic and Monetary Union. In the long run, EMU entails setting irrevocably locked parities and moving toward a single currency. In an environment where capital movements are free, this implies formulating and implementing a single and indivisible monetary policy to be carried out by a single and independent body. This body will have a federative structure and its primary objective shall be to maintain price stability. Monetary union will also bring about tighter economic and budget policy coordination.

EMU is truly the natural and logical outcome of the single market. While the single market means that free competition will lead to unified price formation, it is also clear that a single currency is likely to amplify the single market's effects from the moment it is introduced by eliminating costs linked to exchange rate variability and uncertainty, as well as noticeable transaction costs (administrative costs, bank fees) which, according to the European Commission, now account for 0.5 percent of the EC's GDP.

Three stages have been set for the path to Economic and Monetary Union. The first stage, which began in July 1990 (at the same time as the last restrictions on the movement of capital were lifted), is mainly devoted to strengthening economic and monetary policy coordination within the existing institutional framework. In the second, transitional stage, which should get under way at the beginning of 1994, and which I believe should be as short as possible, the common monetary authority should be set up but would not yet exercise all of its prerogatives. The EC would move onto the final stage—the single monetary policy—once sufficient convergence has been reached and transitional measures have been taken for countries which still have significant progress to achieve.

Increased integration does not mean closed doors.

The European Community has always affirmed that it does not want to remain an "exclusive club." The expansion of the European Community toward Northern Europe in the 1970s and toward Southern Europe in the 1980s attests to this. But even stronger proof can be found in the multitude of trade and cooperation agreements that have been signed between the EC and non-EC countries or groups of countries—agreements that have successively become more and more wide-ranging. The constant reinforcement of agreements with EFTA over the last twenty years is about to lead to this creation of a "European Economic Area."

Recent developments in Eastern Europe naturally open perspectives for closer ties, but this can be done only gradually, given these countries' numerous structural difficulties. Outside Europe, the EC has for several years affirmed its desire to promote a better integration of the Third World in world trade, in particular through the various Lomé conventions.

The European Community's increased economic integration and the added growth it will create will continue to benefit non-EC countries.

The European Community has already made a large contribution to its major partners' trade and growth. The single market will give them an additional boost. With the system of mutual recognition, non-EC countries which want to export to or establish in Europe will no longer have to abide by twelve different sets of regulations, but just one. With more than 340 million consumers, the European single market will be the largest integrated market in the Western world. A recent United Nations study said that the single market would bring about an increase of 15 percent in imports from non-EC countries over five to six years.

The perspective of the single market has led to a rise in direct investment toward the European Community, but this is, in fact, a worldwide phenomenon that is not specific to Europe.

Since the second half of the 1980s, the members of the European Community have become more and more attractive to foreign investors. Foreign direct investment in the EC doubled between 1984 and 1988 to reach 14.2 billion ECU ($16.2 billion). During the same period, the flow of investment between EC countries themselves grew even more noticeably—by a factor of 4.5—to reach 19.1 billion ECU in 1988 ($22.5 billion).

However, this development was not made at the expense of other countries as it was due to a worldwide, rather than European phenomenon mainly attributable to the growing internationalization of companies. More and more European companies have become international in size, strengthening their ties with foreign markets and adopting a global attitude in their forecasts, strategies, and operations. In particular, mergers, acquisitions, and strategic alliances have become important methods of investment as companies try to boost their sales as quickly as possible at the lowest cost. This is the reason why the United States remains the leading beneficiary of foreign direct investment, according to the Organization for Economic Cooperation and Development (OECD); the flow of foreign direct investment grew more rapidly in the United States than in any other OECD country, and the EC has remained a net exporter of direct investment capital. The EC's direct investments outside the EC have increased noticeably ($36.2 billion in 1988), and exceed, by far, those received by the EC from non-EC nations, as well as intracommunity investments. According to estimates from the EC's statistical office, each time an EC company invests 2 ECU in another member state, it also invests 3 ECU outside the EC.

Europe: a major financial power?

Already a major economic and trading power, Europe has every chance of becoming a major financial power given its considerable assets: a sound financial system, a universal bank system that has allowed Europe to spread its risks and deal in most financial sectors, the generalized freedom of capital movements, smooth coordination among supervisory authorities, and a harmonization of prudential rules. The progress made in harmonizing regulations in the banking and financial sectors will also be an additional advantage for the EC's foreign partners.

I would like to note that both the creation of an integrated financial area and monetary union in the EC are being carried out in a regulatory framework characterized by a great deal of economic liberalism. As of January 1, 1994, banks will be able to open branches and provide services outside their home countries according to the second banking directive of December 1989. This directive sets the principle of mutual recognition of national regulations by which the authorization granted to an institution in its home country is recognized throughout the entire European Community. With this system, which is just like that for goods trade and direct investments, banks from outside the EC that want to establish in the EC will no longer have to comply with several different national legislations. I would also like to mention that the European solvency ratio was developed in keeping with the international rules set up by the Banking Supervision Committee of the BIS in Basle, both in its contents and in its timetable which calls for gradual implementation by the end of 1992. Europe will thus be a major financial power open to the rest of the world.

The European example demonstrates that while the creation of a free trade zone tends to increase the share of internal trade in the total trade of the area, it does not necessarily lead to a closing of the area to the rest of the world. In any case, the European Community has always spoken out against an excessive compartmentalization of international trade and has rather campaigned for the development of trade between large trading blocks. The increasing concentration of trade around three large zones—Western Europe, North America, and Asia—as well as the temporary failure of the GATT negotiations have raised fears that these blocs-in-formation will close themselves off from external partners. It is, however, in everyone's interest that trade (of goods, services, and in particular, financial services) continues to be organized on a multilateral basis.

Regional organization should, therefore, be thought of more as a means of strengthening free trade and competition between countries with close geographical, economic, political, and cultural ties than as an independent system to replace the web of multilateral relations. This is true for trade and finance, and should also be true for currency. Far from being obstacles to multilateral relations, regional organizations should one day play an important role in spreading the rules of the economic liberalism they practice to the rest of the world. In this process, it will be the most dynamic organizations—those that have been able to create the largest growth potential and that have been the most successful in generating monetary stability and financial market confidence—that will be in the best position to provide the inspiration for the future "world model" that mankind will always dream of creating.

Regionalism and the World Trading System

Lawrence H. Summers

Increasing economic integration has been one of the major forces driving the world economy's impressive growth over the last forty-five years. Today, however, more than at any time since World War II, the future of the world trading system is in doubt. Ironically, just as the Soviet Union, Eastern Europe, and many developing countries rush to join the General Agreement on Tariffs and Trade (GATT), many in the developed world have become disillusioned with the GATT process. The nearing completion of Europe's 1991 process, the North American Free Trade Agreement (NAFTA) apparently on the way, and even the dissolution of Comecon has forced the question of regional trading blocs increasingly to the fore. It is useful at the outset to consider how the world trading system is now faring. World trade grew 3 percent a year faster than GNP in the 1960s, 2 percent a year faster in the 1970s, and 1 percent a year faster in the 1980s. The good news is that integration has continued; the bad news is that it has increased ever more slowly.

Why did integration increase less rapidly in the 1980s? I think there are two important reasons. First, the technological push toward integration has slowed. Transportation and communication costs fell less quickly in the 1980s than in previous decades. Air transport, for example, is usually thought of as a dynamic industry. Yet the last major innovation was the jumbo jet, introduced nearly a generation ago. Moreover, as the total share of transportation and communication costs declines, incremental reductions have ever smaller effects;

a reduction from $5 a minute to $2.50 a minute will have a greater impact on communication than a fall from 50 cents a minute to 25 cents a minute. Progress in this sense reduces the potential for future progress.

Second, the momentum of trade liberalization has slowed as well. While sixty developing nations significantly reduced barriers to imports over the last decade, twenty of twenty-four Organization for Economic Cooperation and Development (OECD) countries, including the United States, raised such barriers. The United States, which on some measures has trebled the protectionist impact of its policies, has a particularly ignominious record.

In the long run, however, it is those sixty liberalizing developing countries and those that emulate them that are ultimately of greatest importance for the future development of the world trading system. Ninety-five percent of the growth in the world's labor force over the next twenty-five years will occur in what are now developing nations. Even assuming only modest productivity performance, these demographic trends imply that these nations will be the most rapidly growing markets in the world over the next two decades. And this is a moment of historic opportunity in the developing world. There is abundant evidence—most obviously in Eastern Europe, but also in large parts of Latin America, in China, where industrial production has grown at a 30 percent annual rate over the last six years, in India, where a new finance minister has pledged radical change, and even in Africa, where twenty nations are undertaking adjustment programs—that the desirability of market systems has become apparent. Our top priority must be to reinforce these trends.

Trade policy not only needs to proceed on all fronts to lock in the gains that have occurred but also to provide examples that will lead to new trade gains, and even to insure viable investment opportunities for OECD companies—GATT yes, but regional arrangements as well. I therefore assert and will defend the following principle: economists should maintain a strong, but rebuttable, presumption in favor of all lateral reductions in trade barriers, whether they be multi, uni, bi, tri, plurilateral. Global liberalization may be best, but regional liberalization is very likely to be good.

This position is based on four propositions: (1) given the existing structure of trade, plausible regional arrangements are likely to have trade creating effects that exceed their trade diverting effects; (2) there is a very good chance that even trade diverting regional arrangements will increase welfare; (3) apart from their impact on trade, regional trading arrangements are likely to have other beneficial effects; (4) reasonable regional arrangements are as likely to accelerate the general liberalization process as to slow it down.

Are trading blocs likely to divert large amounts of trade? In answering this question, the issue of natural trading blocs is crucial because to the extent that blocs are created between countries that already trade disproportionately, the risk of large amounts of trade diversion is reduced. Table 1 sheds some light on the importance of natural trading blocs. It compares the ratio of observed trade for various entities to the trade one would expect if it were equiproportional to GNP. For example, the number in the upper lefthand corner indicates that the United States and Canada engaged in six times as much trade as they would if U.S. trade with Canada were proportional to Canada's share of world, non-U.S., GDP. Looking at the table, I draw three conclusions:

(1) Existing and many contemplated regional arrangements link nations that are already natural trading partners. Note the disproportionate share of U.S. trade with Canada, of trade within the developing Asian countries, and of trade within industrialized Europe. If I included Mexico in the table it would have a ratio of about 7 with the United States, Korea would have a ratio of nearly 4, and even Israel would have a ratio well in excess of unity.

(2) There is very little sense in which the United States and Canada have a natural affinity with the rest of the Western Hemisphere. American, and to an even greater extent Canadian, trade is disproportionately low, with Europe about equivalent between developing Asia and Latin America. This suggests that America should not be content with an Americas-based approach to trade reduction.

(3) What is striking about the numbers in Table 1 is the isolation of industrial Europe, which trades disproportionately with itself.

This is not an artifact of the fact that Europe is broken up into many countries; this rationalization would fail to explain why it occupies so small a fraction of both Asian and Western Hemisphere trade.

Table 1
Trading Neighbors: Ratio of Share of Trade to Partner's Share of World Output, 1989

Trader   **with:**

	U.S.	Canada	Other Americas	Japan	Developing Asia	EC
United States	—	6.06	2.38	0.87	2.34	0.61
Canada	2.63	—	0.66	0.47	0.97	0.39
Other Americas	1.13	0.63	3.16	0.31	0.57	0.67
Japan	0.95	1.15	0.75	—	4.33	0.53
Developing Asia	0.73	0.62	0.43	1.26	4.83	0.54
EC	0.22	0.30	0.42	0.17	0.63	1.75

I conclude from this exercise that most seriously contemplated efforts at regional integration involving industrialized countries cement what are already large and disproportionately strong trading relationships. To this extent they are likely to be trade creating rather than trade diverting. The one idea that looks bad from this perspective is that of a North Atlantic trading bloc which would be building on

Table 2
Trading Neighbors: Ratio of Share of Trade to Partner's Share of World Output, 1975

Trader   **with:**

	U.S.	Canada	Other Americas	Japan	Developing Asia	EC
United States	—	6.42	2.68	0.60	1.56	0.51
Canada	2.32	—	0.90	0.37	0.58	0.36
Other Americas	1.19	0.74	2.81	0.55	0.23	0.72
Japan	0.65	1.17	1.12	—	4.70	0.26
Developing Asia	0.71	0.65	0.19	1.53	3.68	0.56
EC	0.18	0.37	0.46	0.09	0.44	1.25

a weak trading relationship. Amongst regional groups of smaller developing countries, even trade disproportionate to GDP may constitute a small fraction of total trade and hence the argument carries less force.

It is sometimes suggested that whatever may have been true in the past, today's market is worldwide and regional arrangements are therefore more likely to be damaging than would once have been the case. Table 2 provides a fragment of evidence on this issue by redoing the exercise reported in Table 1 for 1975. It is striking how similar the pattern of trade is. Perhaps this should not be too surprising; it is well known that intra-European trade has risen much faster than Europe's external trade.

Let me come now to my second point: trade diverting regional arrangements may be desirable despite their trade diverting effects. I find it surprising that this issue is taken so seriously—in most other situations, economists laugh off second best considerations and focus on direct impacts. Further, it is a consequential error to think that just because a regional trading agreement's trade diverting effects exceed trade creating effects it is undesirable. Suppose that Korea and Taiwan were identical—a free trade area between the United States and Korea would divert Taiwanese trade to Korea but would have no welfare costs. Only where trade diversion involves replacing efficient producers with inefficient producers is it a problem.

I think this point has considerable force. We too often forget that more than half of U.S. imports are either from U.S. firms operating abroad or to foreign firms operating within the United States. And the fraction is rising rapidly. Under these circumstances, trade and investment decisions are inseparable. With many similar sites for investment by U.S. firms producing for the U.S. market, it is far from clear that trade diversion would have important welfare impacts.

While trade diversion is unlikely to involve large efficiency costs, trade creation is much more likely to involve real efficiency gains. First, it will help realize economies of scale which can be gained through creation, but are unlikely to be lost due to trade diversion. Second, especially where agreements link developed and developing countries, or developing countries that are heavily specialized, the trade they create is likely to be substantially welfare enhancing.

My third reason for eclectically favoring integration schemes is a reading of where the real benefits are. To the chagrin of economists, the real gains from trade policies of any kind cannot, with the possible exception of agriculture, lie in the triangles and welfare measures we are so good at calculating. Instead, they can be found in the salutary effects of competition and openness on domestic policy more generally. Pedro Aspe in his speech yesterday clearly thought more of NAFTA as a device for locking in good domestic policies and attracting investment than as a mechanism for gaining market access. To the extent that the benefits of trade integration lie in these areas, it may not be important how geographically general it is, or whether it is trade diverting. Take the case of Enterprise for the Americas. If the rest of Latin America desires to follow in Mexico's footsteps, a standstill on future U.S. protection for reassurance, and the political and symbolic benefit that it can bring in promoting domestic reform, it seems almost absurd to resist them on the grounds that some trade might be diverted from some part of Asia that would produce a little more efficiently.

It is instructive to consider the breadth of the European Community (EC) 1992 and GATT agendas. No small part of what is good about 1992 is the downward pressure on regulation created by mutual recognition policies. Similarly, competition for investment within the EC will have salutary effects on tax and regulatory policies. But there are diminishing returns to increasing numbers of policy competitors. A significant part of the benefits of trade liberalization in improving domestic policy may be realizable within small groups of countries.

The fourth and final part of the case for supporting regional arrangements is their impact on the multilateral system. I do not share the view held by some that GATT is to trade policy what the League of Nations became to security policy. I believe that a successful completion of the Uruguay Round and its successors would be highly beneficial to the world economy and that the developed nations especially must work to bring one about.

But I am far from persuaded that over time regional arrangements make multilateral trade reduction impossible. The essential reason for concern is that large blocs will have more monopoly power than small ones—and will then use it. The argument is that the resulting reduced cross bloc trade would do more harm than increased within bloc trade would do good. This is a legitimate concern. But it is also true that three parties with a lot to gain from a successful negotiation are more likely to complete it than are seventy-one parties, each with only a small amount to gain. It may be well that a smaller number of trade blocs are more likely to be able to reach agreement than a larger number of separate countries.

This is not just a theoretical proposition. I doubt that the existence of the EC has complicated the process of reaching multilateral trade agreements. Instead, I suspect that the ability of Europe to speak with a more common voice would have helped, not hurt, over time.

Furthermore, there is the beneficial effect of successful arrangements in attracting imitation and in providing a vehicle for keeping up the momentum of liberalization. Those concerned that the U.S.-Mexico or possible follow-on agreements will divert attention from the Uruguay Round ought to consider whether they will also divert Congress' attention from the Super 301 process, or that of the business community from negotiating further import restrictions.

Even strong presumptions remain rebuttable. Obviously some past and current proposals for regional integration would fail to satisfy the conditions. Agreements within groups of small, highly distorted, and protectionist countries that diminish momentum for greater overall liberality are clear candidates for welfare worsening regional agreements.

But the crux of the argument is this: regional arrangements will necessarily speed up the GATT, and moving the GATT along is important if it is possible. But, holding the degree of multilateral progress constant, the world will be better off with more regional liberalization. And the case that regional integration will slow multilateral progress is highly speculative at best. The Uruguay Round may well be the best hope for the world trading system, but it is surely not the last best hope.

Overview

Paul Volcker

Let me say at the outset that I recognize that I am at the end of this parade of excellent speakers and discussants. The chairman has quite firmly and politely indicated that we have a time limit. I don't want to use up too much of that time. In that context, therefore, and after listening to so much of the conversation and reading so much of the material over the last few days, I would like to report on a few impressions that I have from both reading and listening to the material.

To orient you in terms of my reactions, I count myself as one of those who worry about regional trading areas. Presumably, they are justified as a move toward trade liberalization, but there is also a possibility for drifting into what could end up as restrictive blocks. In other words, I am much closer to Fred Bergsten, than to Paul Krugman and Larry Summers. Moreover, my gut feeling is that the danger will be increased by exchange rate volatility between regional areas. Now I said my gut instinct and that's something to be embarrassed about reporting. However, I noticed at this conference—more so than at others I have attended—that a lot of professional economists were reporting their gut instincts. Or sometimes they put it more politely, saying their hypotheses could not be empirically tested. I will not apologize for this in my case, because so many others have said the same thing. Moreover, as my own analytical capacities have declined over the years, my gut has increased.

I will not spend a lot of time on my first point, because Jacques de Larosière and many others have made the same point. Many of these regional arrangements are driven by considerations other than static economic analysis of the gains from trade and the dynamics of competition. Many of the papers, and some of the discussion, are rather peripheral because they have focused on the interesting and absorbing analytical and economic problems posed by trading arrangements.

The Common Market is the big example of a regional trading area. Obviously, what drove the Common Market initially was concern about a cycle of warfare in Europe, concern about Franco-German rivalries, and concern about how to deal with it. Later, as monetary unity assumed more importance, I don't think that Giscard d'Estaing and Helmut Schmidt had long discussions about the nature of economic shocks—whether they were external or internal, real or nominal—when they sat down and put the European Community (EC) on the road toward monetary unity. I think it's a safe bet that they had a larger vision of Europe and how to hold it together. That was what loomed so large in their discussion about how to proceed, and in the urgings and the impetus they gave that process.

Even in saying that, and emphasizing the importance of the political, I do think economists have the responsibility to subject the dreams of statesmen and the politics of politicians to the test of economic consistency and sustainability. And that's what a lot of this discussion has been about. Moreover, I think there is good reason to think that in some cases, the economic argument might reasonably overcome the political argument.

My second point is more economic. It seems to me that the extent to which the Common Market countries have moved toward a closer economic relationship reflects their concern about the disintegrating effects of flexible exchange rates. Much of the discussion at this symposium seem to me to reflect a naive view of the practical efficiency of flexible exchange rates in dealing with economic shocks of any kind. The most important economic consideration in the vision of European monetary union was the perception that the potential exchange rate volatility within Europe, and the the certain volatility between the European currencies and the dollar, would undermine prospects for coherent and freer trade relationships within Europe. Perhaps they were unduly concerned, or perhaps they exaggerated the problem.

But from my viewpoint, it's hard to take great satisfaction in the operation of the floating rate system since the 1970s. We have seen increased volatility over time. Moreover, exchange rate fluctuations often seem unrelated to any discernible real or nominal shocks to the economy. And indeed, as I suggested earlier, I think there is some reality to the fear that volatility in exchange rates gives justification, politically or economically, to those who want to move toward protectionism.

It seems to me that it is very hard for governments, or for markets, to know in real time which shocks are real and lasting, which are nominal and passing, and which are reversible by macroeconomic policy and which are not. Much of the effort in textbooks to make these distinctions reminds me of the other distinction that a central banker always reads about in textbooks, namely that a lender of last resort lends freely when there is a liquidity problem, but does not lend when there is a solvency problem. However, I have never found a central banker that could distinguish between a solvency problem and a liquidity problem in real time. I think we have a similar question here.

I think it's quite legitimate for the EC to fear the introduction of exchange rate flexibility into the European Monetary System (EMS). Such fear in the end might, based upon the actual operation of the floating system, shake the internal dynamics of the Common Market to the point that trading relationships themselves might break. Therefore, the choice of a common currency seems to me entirely rational; it's certainly a choice that I would make.

We could say that the EC is a special case. I was interested that those from Canada, Mexico, and elsewhere were very forceful about saying that monetary union in a North American free trade area is quite different. The political dimension is lacking. And if I were in their position, I would say what the Mexicans and Canadians are saying: these agreements do not call for a fixed exchange rate. It may be politically suicidal, and economically premature, to say anything else. But I also have the feeling that they doth protest too much.

The peso was, in fact, fixed for decades, before a free trade agreement with the United States. It was a remarkable period of growth and stability and open capital markets in Mexico.

And it has been a long time since the Canadian dollar was fixed against the American dollar. But if I read the Canadian experience correctly, the exchange rate is a matter of some preoccupation from time to time in the conduct of Canadian monetary policy. I understand why it affects monetary policy. But the present system has not been perfect. There's been a chronic tendency toward higher interest rates, lower growth, higher unemployment, and higher inflation in Canada. I will make a prediction that if we come back here in five years, you will find a fixed exchange rate among the peso, the U.S. dollar, and the Canadian dollar.

Turning to my third point, I agree with much of what Fred Bergsten had to say. Europe is a special case and there's no point in crying about a regional trading arrangement in Europe. But I think one can question the extension to Eastern Europe and elsewhere. And one can certainly question whether the North America free trade area is inevitable, and what its implications are. I think that if we see large exchange rate volatility between the European bloc and the North American bloc, there will be a tendency to push toward more protectionism, not less.

I think we would be blind if we did not see the potential here. I hope it doesn't develop, but there is a potential for a kind of ganging up on Japan. Japan will certainly worry about that. But I think they will find it hard to react politically or economically because there isn't a natural economic region in the Far East. They don't have the political or economic background. However, the attempt to form such a region may add to the difficulties, the temptations, and the antagonisms that might develop. While this may be a potential problem, I think the risks are low, assuming that the general tenor of trade and the general progress in the General Agreement on

Tariffs and Trade (GATT) proceed.

Let me now make one very simple point about the GATT negotiations. However, since I never seem able to convince anybody of this point, I'm not too hopeful today. The GATT negotiations have an enormously ambitious agenda. They are breaking new grounds in services, intellectual property, and agriculture. There is some risk—perhaps substantial—that there may be a breakdown. Amid all of this, why don't we reinforce the meaning of Article XXIV, the article that restricts trading areas from taking protectionist actions? When I say this to GATT experts, they say the words are already there, and indeed they are. I think there are two sentences—or maybe there is one long sentence—saying, "Thou shall not increase tariffs if you have a free trade agreeement," and then it says something vague about other barriers.

But, in fact, we see the article violated, not so much with tariffs, but certainly with nontariff barriers. Have we had any remedial action from the GATT? Not that I'm aware of. Is the GATT really prepared to deal effectively with this issue if there are more movements in that direction by regional trading areas? I doubt it. Why don't we have negotiations to reinforce that provision? How could anybody object to it with all the nice words that everybody uses about regional trading areas? Why don't we figure out a dispute settlement procedure to go with that article? Why don't we figure out some way to have arbitration or some other system for dealing with practical cases of, for instance, automobile agreements, which happen to be a rather live case at the moment in the EC.

Finally, let me say I think U.S. policy remains pivotal for several reasons. Partly because we have indirect control in the development of the North American free trade area, we can insure that it is outward looking, not inward looking. And I agree with Mr. Summers, we should keep it open-ended, and not look just to Latin America. Let's look toward a Pacific Basin initiative. Under the circumstances, this would be the most constructive way to make regional agreements outward looking instead of inward looking. It would not take a full-blown free trade agreement, but couldn't we improve dispute settlement procedures with Japan? Couldn't we develop better investment rules? In effect, couldn't we multilateral-ize the often antagonist Japanese-U.S. trading relationship?

However, I would disagree in one respect with Fred Bergsten. To me, he seems naive on the prospects for a tripolar world moving together in happy harmony with G-3 meetings, instead of G-7 meetings. Maybe I have been to too many G-5 meetings and G-7 meetings. But I do not think we will resolve really difficult political and economic problems among the major nations in such a setting.

For the next 10 or 20 years, a lot is going to depend upon the American ability to continue doing a good deal of what Allan Meltzer was taking about this morning. And with respect to U.S. leadership, I really am a bit pessimistic. If the United States is going to lead, it will have obvious implications for domestic policy, for domestic saving, for the budget, and for domestic investment; we could also go into the educational system, how much we pay for health care, and all the rest. I don't minimize the agenda. But I have a very uneasy feeling that if the United States backs out of its historic role too precipitously, if we end up in the position where we have to pass the hat—or feel we have to pass the hat—financially to pay for our defense or economic initiatives, then it will not be a policy that will last. It will not protect us against the dangers that I see in unconfined regionalism in the world.

Closing Remarks

John W. Crow

In concluding this symposium, I would like to leave you with my impressions on some of the issues addressed in the symposium. Let me warn you, though, these are only impressions—not a comprehensive summary of the discussion. Since they are my impressions, I will keep them brief.

There was a lot of discussion about the merits and demerits of regional trading arrangements versus multilateral trading arrangements. The score is 2 to 2. As chairman, let me put in my two cents on the side of Fred Bergsten and Paul Volcker. We have to work very hard to preserve the global, and I emphasize global, framework. In this regard, Michael Mussa made a very important point. There is Eastern Europe, there is Russia, there are the developing countries. They all want to join a framework; they want to join the General Agreement on Tariffs and Trade (GATT), imperfect as it is. We should do absolutely nothing to discourage them from joining GATT.

Canada's entry into the U.S.-Canadian Free Trade Agreement did have a defensive aspect to it. Namely, we wanted to get in under the wire of emerging protectionism. But it also had the outward looking aspect of bringing Canadian industry up to scratch in a world market environment.

While there are important policy issues arising from currency unions, they are not as important as the issues arising from trading relationships. We are certainly not headed toward a Mundellian world with a single currency. I agree with Allan Meltzer that by maintaining domestic price stability, central banks can provide the surest foundation to the world trading arrangements and world payments arrangements.

Many people have noted that there is more than economics involved in European integration. However, Jacques de Larosière emphasized a lot of the economics discussed by Martin Feldstein and Michael Mussa. And David Laidler had wise words to say on the North American Free Trade Agreement in this regard.

I just note that Pedro Aspe, in a carefully crafted phrase, referred to Mexico's ambitions and policies as "lower inflation and a sustainable real exchange rate appreciation." That seems to me to imply that the exchange rate is a dragging anchor.

In Canada, monetary policy's anchor is domestic price stability. This is what we at the Bank of Canada can deliver through our monetary policy. If others can also deliver price stability, then everyone will be better off. Furthermore, there is no truth in the rumor, not spread by Paul Volcker, that Miguel Mancera and I are here suing for membership to the Tenth Federal Reserve District. That does not mean, of course, that we are not interested in the progress of U.S. monetary policy.

Finally, I would like to extend my appreciation to our host, Roger Guffey. This is your last conference here as host. Once again, you have given us a splendid and imaginative conference, and our appreciation should not be tempered by the fact that the Kansas City Fed does it every year. We appreciate having the opportunity of getting to know you, of getting to know the Kansas City Fed, and of getting the chance to meet together here.

The Participants

AKBAR AKHTAR
Vice President and Assistant
  Director of Research
Federal Reserve Bank
  of New York

WAYNE ANGELL
Governor
Board of Governors of the
  Federal Reserve System

STEPHEN H. AXILROD
Vice Chairman
Nikko Securities International

ANATOL B. BALBACH
Senior Vice President
Federal Reserve Bank
  of St. Louis

RACHEL BALBACH
Vice President
Boatmen's Bank

RICHARD BERNER
Director
Salomon Brothers

JOHN BERRY
Washington Post

ROBERT P. BLACK
President
Federal Reserve Bank
  of Richmond

G.H. BOARD
Assistant Governor
  for Financial Markets
Reserve Bank of Australia

HORST BOCKELMANN
Economic Adviser and Head
  of the Monetary and Economics
  Department
Bank for International Settlements

EDWARD G. BOEHNE
President
Federal Reserve Bank
  of Philadelphia

J. ALFRED BROADDUS, JR.
Senior Vice President
  and Director of Research
Federal Reserve Bank
  of Richmond

ROBERT H. CHANDROSS
Vice President
  and Chief Economist
Lloyds Bank

HANG-SHENG CHENG
Vice President for International
  Studies
Federal Reserve Bank
  of San Francisco

JOSEPH R. COYNE
Assistant to the Board
Board of Governors of the
  Federal Reserve System

J. DEWEY DAANE
Frank K. Houston Professor
  of Finance, Emeritus
Vanderbilt University

MICHAEL R. DARBY
Undersecretary
  for Economic Affairs
U.S. Department of Commerce

JOHN M. DAVIS
Senior Vice President and
  Economist
Federal Reserve Bank
  of Cleveland

THOMAS E. DAVIS
Senior Vice President
  and Director of Research
Federal Reserve Bank
  of Kansas City

TOM DE SWAAN
Executive Director
De Nederlandsche Bank N.V.

RIMMER DE VRIES
Managing Director
Morgan Guaranty Trust Company

BURTON A. DOLE, JR.
Chairman and President
Puritan-Bennett Corporation

MAURICE F. DOYLE
Governor
Bank of Ireland

BILL EMMOTT
The Economist

ROBERT P. FORRESTAL
President
Federal Reserve Bank of Atlanta

HAROLD L. GERHART, JR.
Chairman and CEO
First National Bank
Newman Grove, Nebraska

LYLE E. GRAMLEY
Senior Vice President
  and Chief Economist
Mortgage Bankers Association

ROGER GUFFEY
President
Federal Reserve Bank
  of Kansas City

CRAIG S. HAKKIO
Assistant Vice President
  and Economist
Federal Reserve Bank
  of Kansas City

DAVID D. HALE
First Vice President
  and Chief Economist
Kemper Financial Services, Inc.

SIRKKA HÄMÄLÄINEN
Director, Central Bank Policy and
  Economic Research and Analysis
Bank of Finland

KATHLEEN HAYS
Investor's Daily

HEINZ HERRMANN
Economist
Deutsche Bundesbank

BRYON HIGGINS
Vice President and Associate
  Director of Research
Federal Reserve Bank
  of Kansas City

J. FRENCH HILL
Deputy Assistant Secretary
  for Domestic Finance
U.S. Treasury Department

THOMAS M. HOENIG
Senior Vice President
Federal Reserve Bank
  of Kansas City

RICHARD B. HOEY
Chief Economist
Dreyfus Funds Group

STUART G. HOFFMAN
Chief Economist
PNC Financial Corporation

W. LEE HOSKINS
President
Federal Reserve Bank
  of Cleveland

KAREN H. JOHNSON
Assistant Director
Board of Governors of the
  Federal Reserve System

MANUEL JOHNSON
Director, Center for
  Global Market Studies
George Mason University

JERRY L. JORDAN
Senior Vice President
  and Chief Economist
First Interstate Bancorp

GEORGE KAHN
Senior Economist
Federal Reserve Bank
  of Kansas City

SILAS KEEHN
President
Federal Reserve Bank of Chicago

EDWARD W. KELLEY, JR.
Governor
Board of Governors of the
  Federal Reserve System

MICHAEL KERAN
Vice President
  and Chief Economist
Prudential Insurance Company

ANNE KESTER
Study Director
National Academy of Sciences

LAWRENCE KUDLOW
Senior Managing Director
  and Chief Economist
Bear Stearns

EDWARD H. LADD
Chairman
Standish, Ayer & Wood

MARSHALL LOEB
Fortune Magazine

FRED W. LYONS, JR.
President
Marion Merrell Dow Inc.

LAWRENCE MALKIN
International Herald-Tribune

KENNETH T. MAYLAND
Senior Vice President
 and Chief Economist
Society Bank

ROBERT D. McTEER, JR.
President
Federal Reserve Bank of Dallas

STEPHEN A. MEYER
Vice President and Associate
 Director of Research
Federal Reserve Bank
 of Philadelphia

CLAIRE MILLER
Reuters, Ltd.

KLAUS MÜNDL
Executive Director,
 Banking Department
Austria National Bank

ALAN MURRAY
Wall Street Journal

PETER NICHOLL
Deputy Governor
Reserve Bank of New Zealand

WILLIAM A. NISKANEN
Chairman
Cato Institute

SCOTT E. PARDEE
Chairman
Yamaichi International
 (America), Inc.

ROGER L. REISHER
Co-chairman
First Bank Holding Company
 of Colorado

ROBERT REYNDERS
Director
Bank of Belgium

JAMES RISEN
Los Angeles Times

NORMAN ROBERTSON
Senior Vice President
 and Chief Economist
Mellon Bank

LUIS ANGEL ROJO
Deputy Governor
Bank of Spain

ARTHUR ROLNICK
Senior Vice President and
 Director of Research
Federal Reserve Bank
 of Minneapolis

HARVEY ROSENBLUM
Senior Vice President and
 Director of Research
Federal Reserve Bank of Dallas

SHEE YUL RYOO
Assistant Governor
Bank of Korea

ROBERTO SALINAS
Academic Director
Center for Free Enterprise
 Research

LEONARD SANTOW
Managing Director
Griggs and Santow, Inc.

KARL A. SCHELD
Senior Vice President and
 Director of Research
Federal Reserve Bank of Chicago

HORST SCHULMANN
Managing Director
Institute of International Finance

ENRIQUE SEGUEL
Member of the Board
Bank of Chile

LAWRENCE SLIFMAN
Assistant Director,
Division of Research
Board of Governors of the
  Federal Reserve System

ERICH SPÖRNDLI
Assistant Director and
  Head of the Research Unit
Swiss National Bank

GARY STERN
President
Federal Reserve Bank
  of Minneapolis

KJELL STORVIK
Deputy Governor
Bank of Norway

MASAHIRO SUGITA
General Manager in the Americas
Bank of Japan

YOSHIO SUZUKI
Vice Chairman of the
  Board of Councilors
Nomura Research Institute, Ltd.

RICHARD F. SYRON
President
Federal Reserve Bank of Boston

LOUIS UCHITELLE
The New York Times

STUART E. WEINER
Assistant Vice President
  and Economist
Federal Reserve Bank
  of Kansas City

LIAN SIM YEO
Director
International Department
The Monetary Authority
  of Singapore

SEYMOUR ZUCKER
Business Week

Federal Reserve Bank of Kansas City
Symposium Series

For a free copy of the proceedings of this symposium, or any of the Bank's previous symposiums listed below, write the Public Affairs Department, Federal Reserve Bank of Kansas City, 925 Grand Avenue, Kansas City, Missouri 64198-0001.

☐ Policy Implications of Trade and Currency Zones *(1991)*

☐ Central Banking Issues in Emerging Market-Oriented Economies *(1990)*

☐ Monetary Policy Issues in the 1990s *(1989)*

☐ Financial Market Volatility *(1988)*

☐ Restructuring The Financial System *(1987)*

☐ Debt, Financial Stability, and Public Policy *(1986)*

☐ Competing in the World Marketplace: The Challenge for American Agriculture *(1985)*

☐ The U.S. Dollar—Recent Developments, Outlook, and Policy Options *(1985)*

☐ Price Stability and Public Policy *(1984)*

☐ Industrial Change and Public Policy *(1983)*

☐ Monetary Policy Issues in the 1980s *(1982)*

☐ Modeling Agriculture for Policy Analysis in the 1980s *(1981)*

☐ Future Sources of Loanable Funds for Agricultural Banks *(1980)*

☐ Western Water Resources: Coming Problems and the Policy Alternatives *(1979)*

☐ World Agricultural Trade: The Potential for Growth *(1978)*